WITHDRAWN BY THE
UNIVERSITY OF MICHIGAN

This is the first book in the English language to explore the vital but neglected issue of elections in the French Revolution. Based on extensive research in different regions of France, it is the only general survey to examine the full range of local and national contests, from the Estates General of 1789 to the advent of Napoleon a decade later. Focusing on electoral behaviour, it reveals a fascinating experiment with a quasi-universal suffrage, which established some enduring features of French elections, from the multiple ballot to the use of referenda. The retention of the traditional practice of voting in assemblies, together with a dogged refusal to acknowledge candidates, canvassing and competing political parties, inhibited the emergence of a pluralistic electoral culture. None the less, frequent polling offered an unprecedented political opportunity to the millions who took part. This revolutionary apprenticeship in democracy left a lasting imprint upon the development of modern citizenship in France.

Elections in the French Revolution

Elections in the French Revolution

An apprenticeship in democracy, 1789–1799

Malcolm Crook
Keele University

Published by the Press Syndicate of the University of Cambridge
The Pitt Building, Trumpington Street, Cambridge CB2 1RP
40 West 20th Street, New York, NY 10011-4211, USA
10 Stamford Road, Oakleigh, Melbourne 3166, Australia

© Cambridge University Press 1996

First published 1996

Printed in Great Britain at the University Press, Cambridge

A catalogue record for this book is available from the British Library

Library of Congress cataloguing in publication data

Crook, Malcolm, 1948–
   Elections in the French Revolution: An apprenticeship in democracy, 1789–1799/Malcolm Crook
      p. cm.
   Includes bibliographical references
   ISBN 0 521 45191 4 (hb)
   1. Elections – France – History – 18th century   2. France – Politics and government – 1789–1799   I. Title
JN2959.C76   1996
324.944′04–dc20   95–17894   CIP

ISBN 0 521 45191 4 hardback

SE

For Jo

Contents

List of maps	*page* x
List of tables	xi
Acknowledgements	xii
List of abbreviations	xiii
Introduction	1
1 Subjects to citizens? The elections to the Estates General and the Revolution	8
2 Limits of citizenship: The franchise question, 1789–1791	30
3 Biting on the ballot: From enthusiasm to abstention, 1790–1791	54
4 One man one vote? The experiment with electoral democracy in 1792	79
5 Voting the Constitution: The referenda of 1793 and 1795	102
6 Parties, schisms and purges: Elections under the Directory, 1795–1799	131
7 An invisible aristocracy? The departmental assemblies and the emergence of a new political class	158
Conclusion	190
Bibliography	197
Index	217

Maps

1 The Departments of France in 1790 (excluding Corsica) *page* 2
2 The percentage of the population with the right to vote in 1791 40
3 Participation in the vote on the Constitution of 1793 107
4 Participation in the vote on the Constitution of 1795 123
5 The Departments of France under the Directory, 1795–1799 (excluding Corsica) 132

Tables

1	Active and eligible citizens in 1790	page 45
2	Turnout in primary elections, June 1791	58
3	Turnout in primary elections, June 1790	60
4	Urban and rural turnout, 1790–1791	61
5	Municipal elections in the villages, January–February 1790	63
6	Municipal elections in major towns, January–February 1790	64
7	Voting by size of community, February 1790	65
8	Municipal elections, 1790–1791	66
9	Turnout in primary elections, August 1792	85
10	Turnout in municipal elections, November 1791 and December 1792–January 1793	89
11	The right to vote in 1791 and the Year V (1797)	119
12	Urban and rural turnout in the referenda of 1793 and 1795	122
13	The vote on the Constitution and the primary elections of the Year III (1795)	134
14	Urban and rural turnout in primary elections under the Directory, Year III to Year VII (1795–1799)	135
15	Turnout in municipal elections under the Directory, Year IV to Year VII (1795–1799)	137
16	Turnout in primary elections under the Directory, Year III to Year VII (1795–1799)	139
17	Turnout in primary elections of the Year VII (1799)	156
18	The occupational composition of second-degree electors from Paris, 1790–1792	168
19	The occupational composition of second-degree electors from Toulon, 1790–1799	171
20	The occupational composition of second-degree electors from the Seine, Year IV to Year VII (1795–1799)	175

Acknowledgements

In the course of this study I have incurred a large number of debts and it is a pleasure to acknowledge just a few of them here. I am grateful to the British Academy, the ESRC and Keele University for their financial assistance, which enabled me to spend lengthy periods conducting research in Paris and the French provinces. My *tour de France* encompassed some two dozen archives where the staff were unfailingly courteous in supplying the many dossiers I ordered during some brief visits. Jacqueline Ryles and Ann Seaton provided invaluable help with the typing, especially when I began to struggle with a word processor myself. Andy Lawrence, of the Geography Department at Keele, advised me on the cartography and then drew the maps. My family patiently endured my absences from home and supported me as I shirked domestic responsibilities in order to write up the material. Shan Amusan and her family have provided endless hospitality and excellent company on my frequent trips to Paris; sadly her husband Guy is no longer with us.

Thankfully the practice of history is a collaborative and cooperative enterprise; my ideas have been elaborated through the media of seminars, upon which I inflicted my ill-formed thoughts, correspondence that generated so many helpful replies and contacts nurtured by the various *colloques* of the *bicentenaire*. Whatever else the anniversary achieved, it certainly succeeded in bringing together the great revolutionary fraternity in an unprecedented fashion. I have relied heavily upon the published work of countless historians, whose efforts I have ruthlessly exploited though always, I trust, with adequate recognition. Colleagues and friends like Howard Brown, Alan Forrest, Peter Jones and Frank O'Gorman have provided enormous encouragement. Most of all I wish to salute the generosity with which Mel Edelstein, Patrice Gueniffey, Ran Halévi, Georges Fournier, Claude Petitfrère, Yvon Le Gall, Isser Woloch, Jean-Charles Benzaken, Stephen Clay, Bernard Gainot and Serge Aberdam have offered their hospitality and shared their wisdom regarding elections; this is their book as well as mine.

Abbreviations

Actes con. nat.	*Actes du congrès national des sociétés savantes*
AD	Archives départementales
AhRf	*Annales historiques de la Révolution française*
AM	Archives municipales
AN	Archives nationales
Annales ESC	*Annales: Economies, Sociétés, Civilisations*
Ann. Midi	*Annales du Midi*
AP	*Archives parlementaires*
BL	British Library
BN	Bibliothèque nationale
Comm. hist. éc. soc.	*Commission d'histoire économique et sociale de la Révolution française*
FHS	*French Historical Studies*
Moniteur	*Réimpression de l'ancien Moniteur*
Pv.	Procès-verbal
Rf	*La Révolution française*
Rhmc	*Revue d'histoire moderne et contemporaine*

Introduction

When I began work on this project several years ago the study of elections was, to borrow the words of François Furet, 'a poor relation of revolutionary historiography'.[1] Despite the vast amount of time and ingenuity devoted to the franchise and voting during the French Revolution, electoral issues were attracting little attention from scholars, who were otherwise engaged with ideological and cultural matters. Once the development of citizenship was placed on the historical agenda, however, the revolutionary apprenticeship in democracy began to excite much more interest; elections finally began to receive the consideration they deserve.[2] Patrice Gueniffey, a pupil of Furet, has recently published the first monograph on the electoral history of the Revolution and a research group devoted to pursuing the subject further has started to meet on a regular basis in Paris.[3] I may have set out as something of a lone researcher in this area, but I soon encountered a host of fellow-travellers along the way, to whom I owe an enormous debt.

At first sight it seems curious that a country which not only pioneered democratic elections in the modern world, but also initiated their scientific study, should have overlooked this vital phase of its own past for so long.[4] Some early soundings were taken under the aegis of Alphonse Aulard, in the wake of the first centenary of the Revolution and the

---

[1] F. Furet, 'La monarchie et le règlement électoral de 1789', in K.M. Baker et al., eds., The French Revolution and the Creation of Modern Political Culture, 4 vols. (Oxford, 1987–94), I, p. 375.
[2] R. Waldinger, P. Dawson and I. Woloch, eds., The French Revolution and the Meaning of Citizenship (Westport, 1993) and D. Heater, Citizenship: The Civic Ideal in World History, Politics and Education (London, 1990).
[3] P. Gueniffey, Le nombre et la raison. La Révolution française et les élections (Paris, 1993); I have also used the doctoral thesis from which this book originated (La Révolution française et les élections. Suffrage, participation et élections pendant la période constitutionnelle (1790–92), Thèse pour le Doctorat, Ecole des Hautes Etudes en Sciences Sociales, Paris, 1989). The study-group, entitled 'Voter et élire pendant la décennie révolutionnaire', is led by S. Aberdam and B. Gainot.
[4] I am thinking of the work of François Goguel and the Cahiers de la fondation nationale des sciences politiques.

1 The Departments of France in 1790 (excluding Corsica)

consolidation of the Third Republic.[5] The elections to the Estates General of 1789 stimulated a good deal of research, as did the creation of the National Convention in 1792 and the constitutional referenda of 1793 and 1795. Several books tackled electoral issues in surveys of *esprit public* (public opinion), while numerous articles on elections filled the pages of that early house-journal for students of the period, *La Révolution française*. Yet what these early investigations revealed was the low turnout and partisan politics that accompanied the advent of the First Republic.

[5] F.-A. Aulard, *Histoire politique de la Révolution française. Origines et développement de la démocratie et de la République (1789–1804)*, first edn (Paris, 1901). The fourth edition, published in 1909, will be used here.

Right-wing critics eagerly seized upon such publications to show how democracy had been hijacked by a small, determined Jacobin minority. Cochin in particular enjoyed highlighting the illberal and anti-pluralist practices that he associated with elections from 1789 onwards.[6]

It was doubtless the ambiguities embedded in the first French apprenticeship in democracy and citizenship that bred disenchantment with electoral studies. The rival attractions of economic and social history also diverted research into other areas during the interwar years. The resurgence of the revolutionary tradition suggested that the popular movement in town and countryside had achieved far more through riot and revolt than via votes and resolutions; historians turned their attention from the ballot box to the barricades. A political dimension never disappeared entirely, but it no longer dominated revolutionary historiography as it had in the heyday of Aulard's great, undervalued *Histoire politique*. It was the study of prices and wages, seigneurial exactions, or demographic and social structures that constituted the cutting edge of research in the 1950s and 1960s.

Criticism of these economic and social perspectives, carelessly lumped together and cavalierly dismissed as a 'Marxist interpretation', did have the merit of drawing attention back to political, ideological and cultural aspects of the Revolution. This was no mere retreat, for these dimensions were explored from novel angles. In the 1980s developments of this sort began to coalesce around the notion of an emergent 'modern political culture' in revolutionary France, yet elections remained conspicuous by their absence, prompting the comment from Furet with which this introduction began. Melvin Edelstein's pioneering article on revolutionary electoral sociology, like Jean-René Suratteau's work on elections under the Directory, failed to elicit the reponse it deserved or the research it demanded, at least in the short term.[7]

The difficult nature of the task involved offers a practical explanation for this continuing neglect. When Georges Dupeux, an authority on the nineteenth century, wrote that 'French sociologists have an advantage over their British colleagues in disposing of a rich documentation on all that has to do with elections', he had obviously not attempted to explore the revolutionary decade.[8] It represents, to put it mildly, a psephologist's nightmare, since electoral records are for the most part located in the

---

[6] A. Cochin, *L'esprit du jacobinisme*, ed., J. Baechler (Paris, 1979).
[7] M. Edelstein, 'Vers une "sociologie électorale" de la Révolution française: la participation des citadins et campagnards (1789–1793)', *Rhmc*, 22 (1975), pp. 508–29 and J.-R. Suratteau, *Les élections de l'an VI et le coup d'état du 22 floréal (11 mai 1798)* (Paris, 1971).
[8] G. Dupeux, 'The Orientations of Electoral Sociology in France', *British Journal of Sociology*, 6 (1955), p. 328.

provinces and the series are seldom complete. Elections were conducted in primary and secondary assemblies via a series of multiple ballots which generated a profusion of voting figures. Dupeux might underline the 'extraordinary complexity' of nineteenth-century French politics and the difficulties that stem from 'the existence of numerous political parties and groups'.[9] Yet in the Revolution the absence of declared candidates and party-political labels poses even greater problems of interpretation for the historian.

The techniques employed to investigate the history of universal (manhood) suffrage in France since 1848 are simply not applicable to the democratic apprenticeship of the French Revolution.[10] The statistical side of this study accordingly diminished as these difficulties grew more apparent. Some readers may still be dismayed by the tables they will encounter in the text and a healthy scepticism in their regard is fully justified. Clearly, all the calculations cited here must be handled with great care; they indicate an order of grandeur rather than any degree of scientific precision, despite the inclusion of decimal places. When the data base is so insecure there are strict limits to what the application of psephological methodology can achieve.

A number of historians have attempted to construct a political geography of revolutionary France and I salute their endeavour to do so, though I remain rather dubious about the results.[11] In the absence of overt party affiliations, most of the national deputies chosen in 1791 and 1792 have been categorised according to the positions they adopted *after* their election, for what they *became* rather than what they *were*. In few cases were attitudes they subsequently espoused a factor in their election, especially where differences of opinion *within* the revolutionary camp are concerned. For example, when Barbaroux was nominated by the electors of the Bouches-du-Rhône in 1792 it was as an advanced Jacobin; only later was he denounced as a 'traitor' when his Girondin sympathies became apparent to his 'constituents'.[12]

Under the Directory political choice became a more conscious process, since those in contention had revealed their colours during preceding years. Yet, because national deputies were always elected in a series of ballots at departmental electoral colleges, their selection reflects the con-

---

[9] *Ibid.*   [10] R. Huard, *Le suffrage universel en France, 1848–1946* (Paris, 1991).
[11] L. Hunt, *Politics, Culture and Class in the French Revolution* (Berkeley, 1984), pp. 123–48 and, more recently, M. Vovelle, *La découverte de la politique. Géopolitique de la Révolution française* (Paris, 1993), pp. 184–218 in particular. Both draw upon the earlier efforts of A. Patrick, *The Men of the First Republic. Political Alignments in the National Convention of 1792* (Baltimore, 1972) and the work of J.-R. Suratteau, cited in the bibliography.
[12] *Journal des départements méridionaux*, 2, p. 600, 12 Feb. 1793.

Introduction

stantly shifting balance of opinion within these secondary assemblies, not that of the electorate as a whole. The relationship between primary and secondary levels of the voting mechanism is an extremely complicated one, since the politics of cantons and communes were frequently fluid and often opaque. Suffice to say here that abstention, boycott and exclusion rendered the departmental college of the Vendée solidly republican after 1792, despite the incipient or endemic state of rebellion that prevailed there.

The real importance of a wonderfully diverse, sometimes bizarre experiment with elections during the French Revolution lies in what it reveals of those who planned it and others who participated. Virtually every official post in France, whether it was legislative, administrative or judicial, became elective after 1789. Even the military veterans at Les Invalides in Paris were obliged to elect a new chief executive officer and only the kingship remained hereditary until the advent of the Republic in 1792.[13] Yet this study is primarily concerned with who could vote and how they did so, with electoral behaviour rather than elected personnel. During the revolutionary decade the suffrage was modified on four occasions and the voting mechanism was amended almost annually. As a consequence of the multiplicity of elective posts, short terms of office and changes of régime, there were no fewer than twenty rounds of elections in the space of a decade. The results of this veritable explosion of electoral activity were rarely what had been intended or hoped, though neither as unsuccessful nor so irrelevant as some commentators have supposed.

The electoral apprenticeship undertaken during the Revolution was certainly a chequered affair, plagued by the contradiction between a quasi-democratic suffrage on the one hand and an antiquated voting mechanism on the other. The resulting amalgam produced some curious results that call into question the current view of the French Revolution as the progenitor of a new political culture.[14] On the contrary, the electoral system encouraged the persistence of archaisms which inhibited the emergence of modernity (construed as a set of twentieth-century norms). Of course, institutional change is no guarentee of altered behaviour and this study will provide some graphic illustrations of enduring old-regime practices in the 1790s. Nor should a flawed machinery be held solely responsible for the eventual demise of elections; neither the social context, nor the circumstances of the 1790s were conducive to the birth of liberal pluralism.

---

[13] I. Woloch, *The New Regime. Transformations of the French Civic Order, 1789–1820s* (New York, 1994), pp. 62–3.

[14] P. Gueniffey, 'Revolutionary Democracy and the Elections', in Waldinger *et al.*, eds., *The French Revolution and the Meaning of Citizenship* (Westport, 1993), pp. 89–103, makes this point very clearly.

None the less, the operation of these poorly understood elections offers an excellent point of entry into revolutionary politics at the interface between elite thinking and popular practice, between central legislation and local behaviour. This is a subject that must be pursued in the provinces as well as in Paris, for documentation on the primary stages of the electoral process is very sparse in the *archives nationales*. The situation in many departmental archives is no better: the political and topographical cross-section of revolutionary France represented by almost twenty departments in this study was heavily influenced by the availablity of material. My original research at Toulon suggested that a rich archival vein was waiting to be tapped, but barren departments like the Vendée were only too common, while happy hunting grounds such as the Côte-d'Or proved all too rare.[15]

Where the electoral *procès-verbaux* are incomplete there is little choice about what to examine but, in order to obtain a broad geographical spread, I usually resorted to sampling more plentiful documentation. This has sometimes distorted my figures compared with the fuller investigations conducted by fellow scholars, though not to an intolerable degree.[16] Parachuting into unknown terrain, to slash and burn a path through the materials, can also be a disorientating experience because, as Peter Jones puts it: 'The electoral process furnished an alternative arena for gladiatorial combat between clienteles, kin-networks and territorial groups', with little relation to national politics.[17] At Berre in the Bouches-du-Rhône, for example, an official explained that violence during polling in the Year VII (1799) stemmed from personal rather than political animosities which went back to the *ancien régime*, though even he was unable to fathom it completely.[18]

The employment of local monographs can only partially compensate for first-hand intelligence, but this was a price worth paying in order to widen the scope of the inquiry beyond a few, detailed and doubtless unrepresentative case-studies. Despite the risk of sacrificing depth for breadth this unique, general study takes account of all types of election from the municipal to the cantonal and departmental, from the Estates General of 1789 to the last polls of the Directory a decade later. The findings have been presented within an essentially chronological framework

---

[15] M. Crook, *Toulon in War and Revolution. From the Ancien Régime to the Restoration, 1750–1820* (Manchester, 1991).

[16] M. Edelstein has conducted an exhaustive examination of the excellent records conserved in the Côte-d'Or and his (largely unpublished) calculations may conflict with my samples, though not where order of grandeur from one election to another is concerned.

[17] P.M. Jones, *Politics and Rural Society. The Southern Massif Central c.1750–1880* (Cambridge, 1985), p. 214.

[18] AD Bouches-du-Rhône L267, Procès-verbal d'élection, 2 germinal VII (22 Mar. 1799).

Introduction 7

to render them more comprehensible, though the approach is thematic rather than narrative. Indeed, separate chapters have been devoted to the suffrage and the departmental electoral colleges. The focus throughout falls upon the origins and operation of the electoral process rather than its outcome: the nature of the personnel who were chosen is a subject which requires separate treatment.[19]

It is always easier to raise issues than to resolve them and this project has proved no exception; this book simply represents the author's latest draft. Many of my conclusions are provisional and will certainly be challenged as more specific information becomes available. I hope to pursue one or two aspects myself, such as the question of candidatures or the attitude of the press towards elections. Moreover, in this respect as in so many others, the experience of the Revolution needs inserting into a wider context so as to assess its particular contribution to the longer-term development of citizenship in France.[20] This was an uneven rather than a linear process, but the apparent reversals of the Napoleonic and Restoration eras had a role to play in the eventual establishment of universal manhood suffrage in the second half of the nineteenth century, though women had to wait another hundred years for the franchise.[21] The democratic apprenticeship in France also invites some interesting comparisons with other countries, such as Britain or the United States, where the transition was equally protracted but evolved in a different fashion.[22] Clearly much remains to be done, but for the moment the focus falls upon the revolutionary decade as France took its first, fateful footsteps towards transforming subjects into citizens.

---

[19] Hunt, *Politics, Culture and Class*, pp. 149–79 and M. Crook, 'Marseille, Aix et Toulon: vicissitudes du personnel municipal de trois grandes villes provençales à l'époque de la Révolution', in B. Benoit, ed., *Ville et Révolution française* (Lyon, 1994), pp. 203–15.

[20] I beg to differ with E. Weber, *Peasants into Frenchmen. The Modernization of Rural France 1870–1914* (Stanford, 1976), who sees this process as a rather later development. See the comments of M. Edelstein, 'La participation électorale des français (1789–1870)', *Rhmc*, 40 (1993), pp. 629–42.

[21] M. Crook, 'French Elections, 1789–1848', *History Today*, 43 (1993), pp. 41–6, for some preliminary comments in this regard.

[22] F. O'Gorman, *Voters, Patrons and Parties: The Unreformed Electorate of Hanoverian England, 1734–1832* (Oxford, 1989) and R.J. Dinkin, *Voting in Revolutionary America. A Study of Elections in the Original Thirteen States, 1776–1789* (Westport, 1982), for example.

1 Subjects to citizens? The elections to the Estates General and the Revolution

The *cahiers de doléances*, or lists of grievances, drafted in the towns and villages of France during the spring of 1789, have attracted a great deal of attention from historians, unlike the elections to the Estates General which accompanied them. Yet these elections were of great moment, not only because they mobilised the French people in an unprecedented fashion and created the first generation of revolutionary leaders, but also on account of their legacy to the electoral practice and procedure of the Revolution itself. This has rarely been recognised, since the last Estates General met for only two months before it was transformed into a National Assembly and consigned to the past. Contemporaries were naturally loath to acknowledge any influence of the old régime upon the new and sedulously cultivated the myth of the Revolution as a fresh start. In fact, there was a strong electoral tradition to draw upon for, even during the age of absolutism, elections had persisted at the local, if not central level. A careful study of the poll of 1789 helps to demonstrate the extent to which, in the words of François Furet, 'the *ancien régime* influenced the Revolution via the Estates General'.[1]

In the first place, the franchise for the final Estates General provoked disagreements which anticipated the famous suffrage debate of succeeding years. The three orders might continue to meet separately, in time-honoured fashion, but all tax-payers were given the vote. Many of them used it, though there were considerable variations in turnout from one community to another. The choice of electoral procedure was also significant for the future: the graduated assemblies and exhaustive ballots employed in 1789 were to survive during the revolutionary decade and well into the nineteenth century. Polling was conducted in the absence of declared candidates or open campaigning, which the new rulers of the 1790s were equally keen to discourage. Moreover, the

---

An earlier version of this chapter appeared as 'The Persistence of the Ancien Régime in France: the Estates General of 1789 and the Origins of the Revolutionary Electoral System', in *Parliaments, Estates and Representation*, 13 (1993), pp. 29–40.
[1] Furet, 'La monarchie et le règlement électoral', p. 375.

customary practice of issuing deputies with instructions, or mandates, was subsequently adopted by radical democrats. Where elections were concerned the Revolution would preserve or borrow a good deal from the past.

The last Estates General emerged from an amalgam of tradition and innovation, which was produced by the contoversy surrounding its convocation. The vast majority of those who called for its resurrection, in the latter part of the eighteenth century, were unclear as to its precise composition and constitution. The Estates General had last met in 1614 and the French monarchy had characteristically failed to codify a full set of procedural regulations.[2] So recourse to the archives was required when opposition demands for a recall were eventually and reluctantly conceded by the government.[3] In any event, on 5 July 1788, Brienne, the minister in charge, announced that he was prepared to consider revising previous arrangements and he invited suggestions to this end. This was partly a delaying tactic and also a means of dividing the crown's opponents.[4] It was for this reason, as much as any long-planned aristocratic reaction, that members of the Parlement of Paris insisted upon observing the conventions of 1614 in their celebrated pronouncement of 25 September 1788; they discerned despotic intentions behind Brienne's willingness to countenance change.[5]

Government proposals for a revival of dormant provincial estates in the peripheral *pays d'états*, as a counterpart to assemblies being established in the French heartland, had already provoked disagreements among members of the regional elites. The case for giving the third estate greater representation and revising long-standing electoral arrangements had been well-rehearsed in Dauphiné and Provence, for example.[6] Of course, the structure and formation of the Estates General inevitably stirred up far greater dispute, all over the kingdom. Yet its last convocation in 1614 offered no infallible guidance, because there was no single ordinance and

---

[2] *Ibid.*, p. 377. See also, J. Cadart, *Le régime électoral des Etats-généraux de 1789 et ses origines (1302–1614)* (Paris, 1952) and R. Halévi, 'Modalités, participation et luttes électorales en France sous l'ancien régime', in D. Gaxie, ed., *L'explication du vote. Un bilan des études électorales en France* (Paris, 1985).
[3] Y. Durand, 'Les Etats généraux de 1614 et de 1789: vie et mort de la monarchie absolue', *XVIIe Siècle*, 41 (1989), pp. 132–6.
[4] W. Doyle, *Origins of the French Revolution* (Oxford, 1980), pp. 139–41 and J. Egret, *La prérévolution française (1787– 1788)* (Paris, 1962), pp. 325 ff.
[5] B. Stone, *The Parlement of Paris, 1774–1789* (Chapel Hill, 1981), pp. 166–80.
[6] M. Cubells, *Les horizons de la liberté. Naissance de la Révolution en Provence (1787–1789)* (Aix-en-Provence, 1987), pp. 8 ff. and V. Chomel, ed., *Les débuts de la Révolution française en Dauphiné* (Grenoble, 1988).

a good deal had been left to local discretion.⁷ Clarification, if not modification, was urgently required in 1789, though the compromise which emerged was explosive: too innovatory for traditionalists and too cautious for more radical critics.

What was pieced together in *ad hoc* fashion under the guidance of Necker, who succeeded Brienne in August 1788 and recalled the Assembly of Notables to advise him, was a *mélange* of old and new elements, shot through with contradictions. On 27 December 1788 Necker announced a doubling of deputies for the *tiers état* at the Estates General, yet voting by order was to be retained.⁸ The latter decision effectively cancelled out the former and it is difficult to tell whether the minister was acting in a disingenuous fashion, or simply out of confusion under the weight of conflicting pressures. A similar ambiguity had characterised arrangements for the provincial assemblies that had been proposed and, in some cases established, over the past decade.⁹ Eligibility on the basis of property-ownership was juxtaposed against a traditional division into orders, without resolution.

An uneven attempt to reconcile 'respect for customary practice' with 'current circumstances' was equally evident in the electoral statute issued on 24 January 1789.¹⁰ It began with a reassertion of the advisory function traditionally fulfilled by the Estates General: the king was inviting his faithful subjects to meet together and inform him of their 'demands and desires'. Yet the statute broke new ground with the claim that it represented a 'single regulation', universally applicable. The *pays d'états*, which had hitherto elected deputies at their provincial estates were, in 1789, subjected to the system of *bailliages* (or *sénéchaussées*), the judicial divisions employed as 'constituencies' for the *pays d'élection* in 1614. Nonetheless, some exceptions had to be made. Dauphiné was allowed to go its own way, conducting elections at a reformed provincial estates, Brittany's clergy and nobility were given special consideration, while Arles in Provence petitioned successfully for a separate urban deputation and Paris was inevitably treated as a case apart.¹¹

Tradition was most obviously upheld in so far as deputies were to be chosen from corporate bodies. Directly elected clergy and nobility were distinguished from the huge *tiers état*, which was broken down into a series of preliminary assemblies so that rural communities and artisan

---

⁷ R. Chartier and D. Richet, eds., *Représentation et vouloir politique. Autour des Etats-généraux de 1614* (Paris, 1982), and J.R. Major, *The Estates General of 1560* (Princeton, 1951).
⁸ Furet, 'La monarchie et le règlement électoral', pp. 378–81 and Egret, *La pré-révolution*, pp. 338–51.
⁹ M. Bordes, *L'administration provinciale et municipale en France au XVIIIe siècle* (Paris, 1972), pp. 163–72.
¹⁰ A. Brette, ed., *Recueil de documents relatifs à la convocation des Etats-généraux de 1789*, 4 vols. (Paris, 1894–1915), I, pp. 66–87 for the text.   ¹¹ *Ibid.*, I, pp. 259–62.

Subjects to citizens 11

guilds could participate. In this sense the consultation was organic rather than democratic; as one historian puts it, 'the electoral system was intended to represent groups rather than individuals'.[12] On the other hand, in the interests of 'reason and equity', it was decided to award deputies to the *bailliages* and *sénéchaussées* 'according to their population and resources'. This was to introduce a numerical basis for representation at odds with the claims of the past.

In practice, the principle of 'proportional representation' proved difficult to implement. Diminutive rural communities were massively overrepresented at the secondary, or *bailliage/sénéchaussée* level of the elections because they received two deputies for up to 200 electors.[13] As a consequence the tiny hamlet of Ramejan, in Languedoc, obtained a couple of delegates from a meeting attended by just three of its eight householders![14] In comparison the larger bourgs were treated extremely unfairly, since a maximum of four deputies was imposed regardless of how many voters there were. Bigger towns were given additional deputies in 1789, a recognition of their rising status yet, to judge by the case of Provence, the allocation was rather erratic. The metropole of Marseille had one deputy per 1,000 electors, while smaller towns like Sisteron were granted one for every 400 participants.[15]

The Second Assembly of Notables supported the idea of more 'proportional' representation between the *bailliages* and *sénéchaussées*. Indeed, this aristocratic body proposed other innovations, such as the right of parish priests to attend clerical elections in person and unenfeoffed nobles to participate in assemblies of their estate.[16] Having secured their own position by preserving separate orders, the Notables were able to sponsor the subsequent decree that, in rural areas and towns alike, 'all inhabitants from the third estate, born in France or naturalised, aged twenty-five years old and listed on the tax rolls' would be given the opportunity both to vote and to be elected. Necker defended this generous franchise on the grounds that there was no precedent for imposing a higher fiscal threshold. In fact the electorate of 1614 had been significantly smaller, in towns in general and in the Midi in particular.[17]

---

[12] Cadart, *Le régime électoral*, p. 128.
[13] A. Onou, 'La comparution des paroisses en 1789', *R.f.*, XXXII (1897).
[14] J.-P. Donnadieu, ed., *Etats généraux de 1789. Sénéchaussées de Béziers et Montpellier (Procès-verbaux et cahiers de doléances)* (Montpellier, 1989), p. 307.
[15] Cubells, *Les horizons de la liberté*, pp. 122–3.
[16] J. Mavidal and E. Laurent, eds., *Archives parlementaires de 1787 à 1860. Première série (1787–1799)* (Paris, 1867–), I, pp. 389–489 and V. Gruder, 'The Society of Orders at its Demise: the Vision of the Elite at the end of the Ancien Régime', *French History*, 1 (1987), pp. 231–5.
[17] J.R. Major, *The Deputies to the Estates General in Renaissance France* (Madison, 1960), pp. 122–3.

In 1789 it seems that subjects were being transformed into citizens, members of the body politic with full access to public life. François Furet has accordingly hailed the new arrangements as 'a modern and democratic type of procedure'.[18] Necker's biographer, Robert Harris, suggests it was 'a complicated yet truly representative system, beyond reproach from the liberal or even democratic stand point'.[19] Yet this is to exaggerate; gross inequalities prevailed, especially among third-estate voters in the preliminary stages of these elections. A clear bias towards the bourgeoisie and against the popular classes was written into the text of regulations for urban areas. The middle-class professional associations, or *corporations d'arts libéraux* of barristers and doctors, together with 'merchants, shipowners and all other unincorporated persons' were granted two deputies for every 100 members in attendance. By contrast the *corporations d'arts et métiers*, or artisan guilds, received just one deputy for every 100 members who were actually present at the assembly.

Journeymen were usually excluded, because only master artisans were entitled to attend the general assembly of the guild. At Marseille, however, in the wake of popular disturbances which accompanied the elections on 23–24 March 1789, the city magistrates were obliged to announce that 'in order to prevent the outbreak of further disturbances we have arranged a special meeting for journeymen, which will convene tomorrow and send delegates to the general assembly of the *tiers état*'.[20] At nearby Toulon a similar protest by dockyard workers and sailors (who, as naval employees, lacked a corporation) produced an equally dramatic result: over 1,000 additional participants were allowed to meet and elect twenty-two deputies to the urban assembly.[21] Yet in most cases the so-called *quatrième état* of wage-earners was unable to take part in the towns, justifying the complaint that 'the poor have no say at all'.[22]

Village assemblies were in principle more democratic than their urban counterparts (this would remain the case under the Revolution, for the poor and rootless were concentrated in the towns), but not always in practice. Access was equal for all taxpayers, but their numbers and definition depended upon the local system of taxation and the structure of land ownership. In Provence, where small-holders predominated, the franchise was a relatively broad one. Even so, beggars, transients and adult sons without a separate entry on the tax rolls were all ruled out; the tradi-

---

[18] F. Furet, *Penser la Révolution française* (Paris, 1978), p. 62.
[19] R.D. Harris, *Necker and the Revolution of 1789* (Lanham, 1986), p. 344.
[20] Cubells, *Les horizons de la liberté*, pp. 126–7.
[21] AM Toulon L39, Procès-verbaux des élections, Mar. 1789.
[22] Cubells, *Les horizons de la liberté*, p. 127.

Subjects to citizens 13

tion of only assembling male heads of household (*chefs de famille*) died hard. The landless met a similar fate because they paid no *taille* (land tax) and the *capitation*, or poll tax, was either paid as a lump sum by the community (to be recovered via indirect impositions), or calculated on the basis of the local land survey. Some electoral proceedings actually spelled out the exclusion of wage-labourers by referring to 'the general assembly of inhabitants and *property-holders* of this community'. Those left on the sidelines occasionally protested, as they did at Peynier in the *sénéchaussée* of Aix-en-Provence, where a fresh village assembly had to be held after riots had erupted on 26 March 1789. On the second occasion twenty-five soap-boilers took part, despite 'the fact that they held absolutely no property, neither at Peynier itself, nor in the surrounding countryside'.[23]

Finally, attention must be drawn to the city of Paris (*intramuros*) which was, as always, a case apart. There was general agreement that Paris required special treatment, but a bitter dispute erupted between *hôtel de ville* and Châtelet (municipal and judicial authorities) over which body was to convene the assemblies. A royal decree, published tardily on 28 March, awarded each a role in the proceedings, but voting instructions were not issued until 13 April, little more than a fortnight before the Estates General was due to open.[24] These regulations contained a typical *mélange* of old and new conditions. The clergy were to meet in a single assembly while nobles were, extraordinarily, invited to attend twenty 'primary' assemblies organised on a neighbourhood basis. The much more numerous *tiers état* was convoked in a similar fashion, but in sixty electoral districts, while the franchise was offered to 'university graduates, government office-holders, master craftsmen and all those individuals who paid six *livres* in *capitation*'.

The *cens*, or fiscal requirement demanded from members of the *tiers* at Paris was considerably in excess of the simple tax payment which operated elsewhere. Yet it accurately reflected current intellectual opinion on the franchise. As eleven Parisian barristers, the Estates-General deputy Target among them, emphasised in a memorandum published in December 1788: 'Whatever respect one might wish to show for the rights of humanity in general, there is no denying the existence of a class of men who, by virtue of their education and the type of work to which their poverty has condemned them, is . . . incapable at the moment of participating fully in public affairs.'[25] The accompanying proposal for a stringent

---

[23] *Ibid.*, pp. 128–31.
[24] C.-L. Chassin, ed., *Les élections et les cahiers de Paris en 1789*, 4 vols. (Paris, 1888–9) and F. Furet, 'Les élections de 1789 à Paris, le Tiers Etat et la naissance d'une classe dirigeante', in E. Hinrichs, E. Schmitt and R. Vierhaus, eds., *Vom Ancien Régime zur Französischen Revolution. Forschungen und Perspektiven* (Göttingen, 1978), pp. 188–206.
[25] Chassin, ed., *Les élections*, I, p. 94.

tax threshold was generally accepted, founded on physiocratic rather than democratic criteria for citizenship. Provincial elites concurred. The committee of patriots at Nantes, for instance, backed the third-estate cause, but it was equally demanding in its requirements for 'a fixed income, possession of a certain amount of land, or payment of twelve *livres* in *capitation*'.[26]

A year earlier, when Brienne established rural municipal administrations in several provinces, he had imposed a *cens* of ten *livres* in taxation for the vote and thirty *livres* for eligibility to office.[27] Such practice was as deeply rooted in the soil of the *ancien régime* as it was in contemporary thought. Elections of some description had often survived at the local level, though systems varied from region to region and cooption had replaced election altogether in some large towns.[28] In Burgundy, for example, many communities had retained the tradition of general assemblies of *chefs de famille*, though at Dijon mass involvement in choosing the mayor had disappeared in the seventeenth century, at the behest of the city fathers.[29] In the Midi, relatively free municipal elections had also survived, yet restrictions on the franchise were commonplace.[30] In some smaller villages the great mass of adult male inhabitants continued to participate, but on the whole access was narrowing. As Jacques Godechot has remarked: 'There is no doubt that in the eighteenth century local government in Languedoc, Provence and most of Gascony was based on a heavily restricted franchise.'[31] After the Revolution, Sieyès, who originally emanated from Lower Provence, had no need to invent his infamous distinction between 'active' citizens who could vote and 'passive' citizens who did not; he was already conversant with an electoral system that separated voters from non-voters on the basis of taxation.

---

[26] Y. Le Gall, Les consultations générales en Loire-Inférieure, 1789–an VII, Thèse pour le Doctorat en Droit, 2 vols., Université de Nantes, 1976, I, p. 17.

[27] Bordes, *L'administration provinciale*, pp. 334–42.

[28] N. Temple, 'Municipal Elections and Municipal Oligarchies in Eighteenth-Century France', in J.F. Bosher, ed., *French Government and Society 1500–1850* (London, 1973), pp. 70–91.

[29] M.P. Holt, 'Popular Political Culture and Mayoral Elections in Sixteenth-Century Dijon', in M.P. Holt, ed., *Society and Institutions in Early-Modern France* (Athens, Georgia, 1991), pp. 99–110.

[30] G. Fournier, 'Sur l'administration municipale de quelques communautés languedociennes de 1750 à 1789', *Ann. Midi*, 84 (1972), pp. 459–82 and M. Derlange, 'En Provence au XVIIIᵉ siècle: la représentation des habitants aux conseils généraux des communautés', *Ann. Midi*, 86 (1974), pp. 45–67.

[31] J. Godechot, 'Aux origines du régime représentatif en France: des conseils politiques languedociens aux conseils municipaux de l'époque révolutionnaire', in Hinrichs *et al.*, eds., *Vom ancien régime*, p. 15.

Outside of Paris the elections to the Estates General were conducted on an extremely broad basis, but it is difficult to calculate how many people availed themselves of the opportunity to vote in 'primary' elections for the *tiers état* (not to mention the other two orders). No electoral registers were compiled in 1789, because assemblies employed tax rolls and guild membership lists to determine admissibility. For historians the most convenient yardstick is the number of *feux*, or households, which can be roughly equated with the number of taxpayers.[32] The total of *feux* is usually cited in the electoral proceedings (*procès-verbal*), since village deputies were allocated on this basis, rather than according to attendance.

Unfortunately the amount of detail which can be derived from surviving *procès-verbaux* is rather limited; there was rarely any effort to record the number of votes cast. In his splendid study of the elections of 1789 in part of the *bailliage* of Rouen, Bouloiseau refers to seven villages which only listed as present those who signed their names on the document. In other cases the total of signatories outweighed the named participants while, in one exceptional instance where the number of votes was recorded, it exceeded the list of attenders! As Bouloiseau concludes:

> In the minds of those taking part it was not necessary to provide an exact number of votes, but simply to collect a list of names and especially signatures, which would indicate the consent of the community. Those who attended did so essentially to act as witnesses, to guarantee the authenticity of the document that was being drawn up and to accept responsibility for it.[33]

Needless to say this mentality persisted into the 1790s, though after 1789 the *procès-verbaux* do usually record the votes cast. Calculations for turnout from the *procès-verbaux* of 1789 are perforce approximate: in the vicinity of Montlhéry in the Ile-de-France, for example, the numbers signing the document represent only 20 per cent of those entitled to do so, while there is good reason to believe that over 30 per cent actually took part.[34] Yet, *faute de mieux*, estimates emanating from 1789 offer an order of grandeur, besides permitting comparisons with other places and periods.

Such as they are, the figures suggest extremely uneven involvement in 1789, in both rural and urban areas. In the *sergenterie* of Pavilly, in Upper Normandy, which Bouloiseau has subjected to detailed analysis,

---

[32] M. Bouloiseau, 'Elections de 1789 et communautés rurales en Haute-Normandie', *AhRf*, XXVIII (1956), pp. 35–6. [33] *Ibid.*, pp. 33–4.

[34] J. Médard, *La région de Montlhéry dans la Révolution* (Le Mée-sur-Seine, 1989), pp. 110–1.

the level of village attendance ranged from 10 to 88 per cent with an average of 36 per cent.[35] Likewise, in the *sénéchaussée* of Béziers, rural turnout was as low as 4.8 and as high as 82.5 per cent of the total of households, averaging out at 23.7 per cent.[36] It was the same in Provence where, among sixty-seven small communities for which calculations can be made, participation ranged from 21 to 98 per cent.[37] In the vicinity of Vitré, in Brittany, eighteen rural parishes ran the gamut from 6 to 96 per cent, with a mean of 21.7 per cent.[38] In Artois the spectrum was equally broad: from a minimum of 13.6 to a maximum of 97.2 per cent.[39] Only in the *bailliage* of Semur-en-Auxois, in Burgundy, was greater consistency apparent. There, turnouts of 100 per cent were recorded and low figures were rare; even the *chef-lieu*, Semur, managed to attract an attendance of 46.1 per cent at a general assembly for 770 households.[40]

Regional characteristics can be discerned behind this array of statistics. Languedoc, Provence and Brittany generally recorded lower rates of participation in 1789 and they all continued to do so in 1790, whereas Burgundy represented an area of high turnout, in 1790 as in 1789. The explanation for such distinctions may reside in traditions of local government under the *ancien régime*, as well as contrasting rates of literacy or systems of communication. In the Midi the general assembly of inhabitants had often dwindled to meetings of notables, while in Burgundy such assemblies remained in vigour and were even receiving encouragement from the *intendant*, who wished to use them as a counterweight to the *seigneur*.[41] The municipal reform of 1787 had also begun to encourage greater participation in local affairs, in rural areas of Normandy or the Rouergue, where it was applied on the eve of the Revolution.[42]

In 1789 villagers met to deliberate and vote on a Sunday after mass, during the first two weeks of March. Smaller communities were usually more assiduous at the polls than larger ones. This was true of Normandy where, discrepancies notwithstanding, parishes with less than fifty *feux* recorded an average turnout of 58 per cent, those of fifty to 150 *feux* returned 45 per cent and bourgs with over 150 *feux* came last with 22 per

[35] Bouloiseau, 'Elections de 1789', p. 39.
[36] Donnadieu, ed., *Etats généraux de 1789*, pp. 205–319.
[37] Cubells, *Les horizons de la liberté*, pp. 131–2.
[38] R. Crossouard, *La Révolution dans le District de Vitré, 1789–1795* (Rennes, 1989), pp. 19–21.
[39] J.-P. Jessenne, *Pouvoir au village et Révolution, Artois, 1760–1848* (Lille, 1987), Annexe II. 3.
[40] R. Robin, *La société française en 1789: Semur-en-Auxois* (Paris, 1970), pp. 353–459.
[41] H. Root, *Peasants and King in Burgundy. Agrarian Foundations of French Absolutism* (Berkeley, 1987), pp. 66 *ff*.   [42] Jones, *Politics and Rural Society*, pp. 185–6.

cent.[43] The phenomenon was repeated at Béziers and in the neighbouring *sénéchaussée* of Carcassonne, where the highest participation occurred at Nizas, one of the smallest communities, while the large parish of Boussagnes attracted the lowest percentage.[44]

Differentiation of this sort was apparent during the early years of the Revolution too. The first municipal elections were held in the countryside early in 1790, in the same context as those of 1789 and, once again, smaller rural communities polled more heavily than their larger counterparts. The contrast may be explained both by the greater likelihood of a tradition of general assemblies in less populous villages and their greater degree of social solidarity. Bouloiseau has suggested that in Upper Normandy small, wholly agrarian communities voted more enthusiastically than *bourgs* which housed substantial contingents of weavers as well as peasants.[45]

Turnout in towns, in 1789, was often lower than in the surrounding countryside and, once again, this was true during the early years of the Revolution.[46] Yet the level of participation recorded in many towns was rarely bettered during the following decade. Strasbourg and Colmar, in eastern France, did witness a higher turnout in municipal polls held at the beginning of 1790, but at Montpellier, Troyes, Montauban and Toulon the respective figures were all rather lower than a year earlier. A fall was equally apparent at Paris, though the capital's 25–30 per cent turnout in the spring of 1789 was already a relatively poor one (especially in view of the restriction of the franchise to those who were wealthy enough to pay six *livres* in taxation).[47] Levels of electoral participation in Paris would in fact remain conspicuously low throughout the Revolution: despite intense political activity, attendance at the Parisian assemblies rarely exceeded 15 per cent of potential voters.

In Paris polling for the third estate was conducted by *quartier*, or neighbourhood, in a manner adopted for all towns after 1790. Elsewhere, in 1789, preliminary or primary assemblies were held by artisan guilds, professional bodies and at meetings of 'unincorporated' citizens. This renders the business of calculating turnout even more hazardous, although the register of electors, or 'active' citizens, for 1790 may be pressed into service as a rough guide. In some cases it is possible to

[43] Bouloiseau 'Elections de 1789', p. 40. Le Gall, Les consultations générales, I, pp. 56–61, comes to a similar conclusion for the *sénéchaussée* of Nantes and adds that poorer inhabitants were least assiduous in their attendance.
[44] Donnadieu, ed., *Etats généraux de 1789*, pp. 205–319 and G. Larguier, *Cahiers de doléances audois* (Carcassonne, 1989), p. 17.   [45] Bouloiseau, 'Elections de 1789', pp. 46–7.
[46] Edelstein, 'Vers une "sociologie électorale" ', p. 515.
[47] R.B. Rose, *The Making of the Sans-Culottes. Democratic Ideas and Institutions in Paris, 1789–1792* (Manchester, 1983), p. 33.

compare the number of guild-masters who took part in elections to the Estates General with totals on the tax records or membership lists. Naudin has conducted an analysis of this sort at Nîmes, where he reckons that 86 per cent of a sample of master-craftsmen took part. He has carried out similar research at Moulins, where he calculates a 78 per cent turnout.[48]

In the case of Moulins, Naudin suggests that artisans were better attenders than the liberal professions (62 per cent), the associated parish of Yzeure (49 per cent) and those who belonged to no occupational association at all (1.5 per cent). The *lieutenant-général*, or returning officer, in charge of electoral procedure in the *sénéchaussée* of Marseille reported that only 539 'unincorporated' Marseillais merchants turned out in the great sea-port, from a total of some 1,500 potential voters in this category. Rural workers who resided in the city's faubourgs were equally reluctant attenders: an initial assembly attracted only 274 peasants, though 677 of them appeared when the meeting was reconvened a week later.[49] Nonetheless, the urban assemblies of 1789 had been conducted in a familiar professional context, which drew upon occupational loyalties and encouraged a high turnout, especially among the smaller guilds; it would take time for new patterns of electoral sociability to establish themselves instead.

In 1789 all elections, both urban and rural, had proceeded in a traditional fashion at public assemblies. Individual voting was scarcely considered at this juncture, because there was a *cahier* to discuss as well as deputies to choose. Only one scheme for individuals to record their votes, without attending a meeting to do so, has been unearthed from 1789 itself.[50] Such was the weight of custom that assemblies were employed for elections throughout the revolutionary period too. This continuity offers an excellent example of an archaic practice from the *ancien régime* contaminating the supposedly 'modern' political culture of the French Revolution. Assemblies exerted a profound effect upon electoral behaviour, by preserving a corporate rather than individualistic attitude towards voting and maintaining a lively tradition of debate on these occasions.

The deputies of the National Assembly drew heavily upon regulations for the Estates General when they established their uniform electoral system the following year. The detailed guidance for voting at *bailliage* and

---

[48] M. Naudin, 'Les élections aux Etats-généraux pour la ville de Nîmes', *AhRf*, LVI (1984), pp. 499–500 and *ibid.*, *Structures et doléances du tiers état de Moulins en 1789* (Paris, 1987), pp. 203–12.   [49] Cubells, *Les horizons de la liberté*, p. 125.
[50] BL F292, Trois mots aux parisiens . . . sur l'élection de leurs députés, Paris, 1789.

sénéchaussée level was adopted virtually lock, stock and barrel by legislators, who were products of elections conducted on this very basis. Three scrutineers, or tellers, were elected by the assembly to supervise balloting, which was repeated up to three times for each post in contention, in an effort to ensure that the winner achieved an absolute majority. This preoccupation with securing a clear majority, and thus an apparent degree of unanimity, was a terribly time-consuming business, which deterred many voters from taking a fuller part in the elections of the revolutionary period.

Other provisions from 1789 stubbornly persisted during the following decade, despite rather than because of new legislation. The statute on elections to the Estates General prescribed oral voting (*à haute voix*) at the preliminary stages of the electoral process and only introduced written balloting at *bailliage* or *sénéchaussée* level, where deputies for Versailles were chosen. This distinction between the voting mechanism employed at primary and secondary assemblies was presumably made on the assumption that secondary electors were more likely to be literate than those participating at the lower level. The Instructions of July 1787, introducing municipal elections in some provinces, had stipulated a written ballot, unless the majority in attendance was illiterate.[51]

Voting out loud was abolished by the National Assembly, yet the traditional practice of oral voting did not completely disappear after 1789; it was revived by radicals in the summer of 1792 as a guarantee of openness and authenticity. As these revolutionaries strove for unanimity at the polls they also recommended the vote *par acclamation*. This was another echo of the elections of 1789, when the actual number of votes was rarely recorded in the *procès-verbaux*, but it was frequently stated that deputies had been 'chosen by common acclaim'.[52] The attendance of non-voters at the assemblies of 1789 may equally have inspired later demands for such meetings to be held in public, to prevent second-degree electors 'abusing their powers'.[53]

Another means to this particular end was the attempt to circumscribe a deputy's choice at the secondary level by issuing him with a specific set of instructions. Historians such as Soboul and Rose have explained these radical politics by reference to Rousseau and, above all, to his *Contrat social*.[54] Yet they have obvious affinities with the mandating principle

---

[51] Bordes, *L'administration provinciale*, p. 336.
[52] Le Gall, *Les consultations générales*, I, pp. 68–9. See also Cubells, *Les horizons de la liberté*, p. 141.
[53] A. Soboul, *The Parisian Sans-Culottes and the French Revolution, 1793–4*, trans. (Oxford, 1964), p. 138.   [54] *Ibid.*, p. 109.

enshrined in the *cahiers de doléances*, which were an integral aspect of the electoral process in 1789. In this regard the electoral statute of 1789 followed tradition by inviting voters to:

> collectively communicate all the various demands, complaints and grievances, suggestions and advice which they wish to place before the Estates General. Having done this they should choose, elect and name as deputy any person who is worthy of this great mark of esteem, either as a result of their integrity or the good will with which they are imbued ...

Furet has recently stressed that, in these final elections to the Estates General, as in the past:

> The process of 'representation' was not intended to fashion a single will out of the various interests and wishes of the individuals involved, but rather to express and transmit, from below to above, indeed to the highest level, the demands of the different corporate bodies in the kingdom, which were by definition homogeneous. This explains the imperative mandate, by means of which all communities despatched to the next stage of the proceedings delegates who were not to represent them in the modern sense of the word, but simply entrusted with relaying their resolutions.[55]

In other words representation was equated with transmission. The deputy was elected *after* the compilation of grievances, empowered to act as a messenger rather than to exercise his own volition. Thus the deputies of Montpellier elected in 1789 promised to 'faithfully fulfil the mandate' they had been given.[56]

Election was essentially a recognition that an individual was qualified to act on the community's behalf. Writing of earlier Estates General, Russell Major confirms that:

> The deputies . . . were more proctors holding the power of attorney for the community . . . than they were representatives in the modern sense. They were given . . . specific powers and instructions . . . from which they could neither deviate nor depart. If a new situation arose while they were at the national assembly, they were to refer back to their constituents. If they did not, and instead acted on their own initiative, they were subject to recall and perhaps severe punishment.[57]

This language is Rousseauesque and, in drawing up a constitution for Poland, a large country where some form of representation was

---

[55] F. Furet, *La Révolution française. De Turgot à Jules Ferry, 1770–1880* (Paris, 1988), p. 66.
[56] Donnadieu, ed., *Etats généraux de 1789*, p. 58.
[57] Major, *The Estates General of 1560*, p. 73. In the case of Nantes, a second series of primary assemblies was held in September 1789, to decide whether deputies at the Estates General should be 'given' unlimited authority. In the event, a majority voted in favour of rescinding the *mandats impératifs*; Le Gall, Les consultations générales, I, pp. 106–12.

inevitable, Rousseau had actually devised a system of binding mandates for deputies.[58]

In France, in 1789, the mandating principle was repudiated by revolutionary leaders who insisted that deputies represented the nation as a whole, rather than separate corporate bodies. The monarchy had itself pointed in this direction, in the electoral statute of 24 January, which stated that 'the powers with which a deputy is endowed are general ones'. Yves Durand has suggested that Louis XVI created a representative régime in France as a consequence.[59] Whether this was intentional or not is a matter for debate. As always the issue was not pursued with any great urgency and, by the time the king absolved delegates to the Estates General from their binding mandates on 23 June, he had once again surrendered the political initiative. His declaration, a few days later, that 'contrary to the spirit and terms of my letter of convocation, several deputies have been entrusted with imperative mandates, which deprives them of the freedom to vote that they should enjoy as members of the Estates General', coincided exactly with the position of a National Assembly that was anxious to end the distinction between the three orders.[60]

Traditional concepts of the representative's role inhibited any real contest in elections to the Estates General, especially at the preliminary level. Voting *à haute voix* was already a great deterrent to open competition, while the expenses which a deputy was obliged to bear to attend another assembly, in a different location, ruled out many possible contenders. Nonetheless, at Villiers-les-Hauts in Burgundy, landless labourers acted in concert to elect deputies from their own ranks to the *bailliage* assembly, leaving village notables to rage impotently at their betrayal.[61] Not far away, at Flavigny, the bourgeois mayor was initially chosen as a representative, only to be 'de-selected' at another meeting four days later and replaced by a peasant farmer.[62] At Pont-l'Abbé, in Brittany, bourgeoisie and popular classes split into separate assemblies and both elected deputies to the *bailliage* assembly at

---

[58] K.M. Baker, 'Representation', in Baker, ed., *The French Revolution*, I, p. 479. In this excellent article Baker suggests that Rousseau brought his theory of the general will 'into convergence with the traditional constitutional practice of representation under the Old Regime', by employing the mandating principle. A slightly revised version of the essay appears in Baker's, *Inventing the French Revolution* (Cambridge, 1990).
[59] Durand, 'Les Etats généraux', p. 136. [60] Cadart, *Le régime électoral*, pp. 153–5.
[61] Robin, *La société française*, p. 379. At Vertou, in the *sénéchaussée* of Nantes, a similar dispute arose, but in this case it was the labourers who came off worse: Le Gall, Les consultations générales, I, p. 39.
[62] P.M. Jones, *The Peasantry in the French Revolution* (Cambridge, 1988), pp. 63–4.

Quimper (thereby heralding the electoral schisms of the revolutionary period).[63]

At Lyon, Jaurès was excited to find an example of what he considered to be the class struggle in primary elections for the silk industry.[64] Merchants and weavers were part of a single corporation (*la grande fabrique*), but the numerically dominant weavers ensured that all thirty-four deputies to the city's general assembly were drawn from their colleagues rather than among merchants. There had long been friction between the two groups and the weavers' deputies included militants who had participated in the bitter strike of 1786. Yet this dispute at Lyon retained an essentially corporative character. Jaurès was disappointed to discover, as he pursued his research, that the Lyonnais weavers made little impact upon the urban electoral assembly and were prepared to be represented by others at *bailliage* level.

Ran Halévi concludes that bourgeois domination of the secondary stages of the electoral process was a consequence of consent from below, as much as manipulation from above.[65] He concurs with Bouloiseau's verdict that: 'The rural community . . . had no wish to be represented other than by its most influential persons: that is to say syndics or secretaries serving on the municipalities, wealthy landowners and prosperous farmers'.[66] With the interests of the community at stake competence was clearly required. Often the obvious choice was made, well in advance of the meeting, which simply ratified a *fait accompli*. After all, the government had stated in January 1789 that it was seeking the election of 'distinguished persons' and the *lieutenant-général* presiding in the *sénéchaussée* of Aix-en-Provence simply reiterated that 'deputies are to be selected among the most noteworthy inhabitants'.[67]

In many cases existing officials were chosen to continue 'representing' the community in their capacity as mayors or councillors. In the *sénéchaussée* of Béziers, for example, ten rural communities out of seventeen chose a municipal consul as a member of their delegation.[68] It was the same in Lorraine: forty out of fifty-one communities composing the *bailliage* of Mirecourt chose their mayors.[69] At Amboise, in Touraine, where the municipal reform of 1787 was in operation, no less than thirty-two syndics were elected among fifty-two deputies from seventeen vil-

[63] A. Signor, *La Révolution à Pont-l'Abbé* (Paris, 1969), pp. 85–6.
[64] J. Jaurès, *Histoire socialiste de la Révolution française*, 7 vols., Editions sociales (Paris, 1968–73), I, pp. 177–81.
[65] R. Halévi, 'La monarchie et les élections: position des problèmes', in Baker *et al.*, eds., *The French Revolution*, I, p. 396.   [66] Bouloiseau, ' Elections de 1789', pp. 43–4.
[67] Cubells, *Les horizons de la liberté*, p. 144.
[68] Donnadieu, ed., *Etats généraux de 1789*, pp. 205–319.
[69] Jones, *The Peasantry in the French Revolution*, p. 63.

lages.[70] The same phenomenon was repeated in the urban setting of Moulins, where half of the artisan guilds returned existing officials as delegates to the town assembly.[71] In Artois 65 per cent of deputies to the *bailliage* assemblies were seigneurial officials (*fermiers*) who played a decisive role in local government at the end of the *ancien régime*.[72] On the other hand, in the Auvergnat *bailliage* of Salers only seven municipal officials appeared among eighty deputies, while local officials were equally unpopular in the Burgundian *bailliage* of Semur.[73]

What villagers often sought in their delegations was a combination of property and talent, of 'local prestige' and 'a way with words'. As Halévi suggests: 'It was the better-off and the best-educated who were sent to the *bailliage* assembly. The wealthy farmers who constituted the "political" class in rural society, plus those well versed in the law and administration, were inevitably chosen as representatives . . .'[74] Certainly in the Norman *sergenterie* of Pavilly, a school-teacher, a tax-collector or a court usher usually appeared alongside prosperous peasant farmers, although Bouloiseau emphasises that all of them were local men, not outsiders.[75] In Provence, by contrast, it was bourgeois residing in the urbanised villages who tended to represent the rural community rather than peasants.[76] In the *bailliages* of Troyes and Orléans judges appointed to preside over preliminary assemblies (often over a series of assemblies, rather than just a single one) were well-placed to influence the drafting of the *cahier* and then to be elected deputy.[77]

As the authors of the electoral regulations doubtless intended, the progressive stages through which the process passed served as a filter to separate out the more prestigious members of rural and urban communities alike. In the secondary *bailliage* of Semur-en-Auxois, for example, deputies from the primary assemblies comprised: fifty-two barristers, doctors, rentiers and administrators; seventy-three merchants; sixty-

---

[70] M. Bouloiseau and A. Buchoux, 'Les municipalités tourangelles de 1787', *Comm. hist. éc. soc. Mémoires et documents*, 23 (1969), p. 81 and G. Lemarchand, *La fin du féodalisme dans le pays de Caux* (Paris, 1989), p. 429.
[71] Naudin, *Structures et doléances*, pp. 211–12.
[72] Jessenne, *Pouvoir au village*, pp. 60–1.
[73] A. Poitrineau 'Les assemblées primaires du bailliage de Salers en 1789', *Rhmc*, 25 (1978), pp. 424–5 and Robin, *La société française*, pp. 348–459.
[74] Halévi, 'La monarchie et les élections', p. 397.
[75] Bouloiseau, 'Elections de 1789', pp. 44–5.   [76] Cubells, *Les horizons de la liberté*, p.136.
[77] F. Furet, 'Les Etats-généraux de 1789. Deux bailliages élisent leurs députés', in *Conjoncture économique, structures sociales. Hommage à Ernest Labrousse* (Paris-The Hague, 1974), pp. 443–4. Likewise in the *sénéchaussées* of Nantes and Guérande, only forty-four different presidents were elected at 191 primary assemblies: Le Gall, Les consultations générales, I, p. 72.

three wealthy peasant proprietors; twenty-seven winegrowers; twenty-three artisans; twelve rural labourers and two school-teachers.[78] The peasant element was in the numerical ascendancy because many of the merchants were also peasant landowners engaged in commerce. Yet all these deputies paid above-average amounts of tax and many could be described as *coqs du village*. However, the bias against peasants grew more pronounced, when Semur had to reduce its deputation and engage in a further round of voting with delegates from adjacent *bailliages*, before deputies to Versailles could be chosen. When this was done forty-three barristers and administrators survived, but only nineteen merchants and just two artisans. A bourgeois minority at the original *bailliage* assembly had been transformed into a two-thirds majority among those deputies who continued to participate in the final round of voting.

Furet concludes that in the *bailliages* of Troyes and Orléans, 'it was only to be expected that the primary assemblies would turn to men well-versed in administrative matters and already initiated into the mysteries of state',[79] Yet, in larger *bailliages* like these, it was the stipulation that no more than 200 delegates should participate in choosing whom to send to Versailles that really reduced the peasants' ranks; at Chaumont-en-Bassigny rural representatives were bitterly disappointed when this procedure operated to their disadvantage and they returned to their parishes in an angry mood.[80]

The case of Toulon may be cited as an example of the same process at work in an urban context, where elections passed through two stages before reaching *sénéchaussée* level, not to mention a further meeting with neighbouring divisions for the choice of deputies to Versailles.[81] At the town assembly, when the proceedings began, over half of the delegates from guilds and other professional groups may be described as bourgeois, in the sense that their occupational status gave them access to municipal office. The artisan minority was subsequently turned into a majority by the addition of another delegate from the wigmakers' guild and twenty-two dockyard workers. Yet, when forty of the ninety-one deputies were chosen for the *sénéchaussée* assembly, only seventeen of them were drawn from the popular classes. Finally, when these survivors, together with deputies from the surrounding communities of the *sénéchaussée* were further reduced, to meet with deputies from the adjacent divisions of Brignoles and Hyères, just three lower-class Toulonnais survived: a bosun

[78] Robin, *La société française*, pp. 349–51.
[79] Furet, 'Les Etats-généraux de 1789', pp. 447–8.
[80] Jones, *The Peasantry in the French Revolution*, p. 65.
[81] AM Toulon L39, Procès-verbaux, Mar. 1789.

(*maître d'équipage*) and a sail-maker from the dockyards, together with a peasant proprietor.

At Paris, where a relatively high fiscal threshold restricted access to the initial round of voting, it is no surprise to discover a mere thirty artisans and shopkeepers among 407 second-degree electors. Merchants and large retailers were also thin on the ground at this stage of the proceedings, with just seventy-seven deputies between them. By contrast, there were 172 legal types, plus other members of the professional and intellectual bourgeoisie who, *in toto*, comprised well over half of the electoral college. Equally striking in the case of Paris is the way in which no less than a quarter of these electors were chosen again, as members of the departmental college of Paris, in 1790 and 1791.[82]

The elections of 1789 effectively served as a seed bed for the early revolutionary elite, in personal as well as social terms, all over the country. In the District of Chartres, for example, an area roughly congruent with the former *bailliage*, many villages chose the same wealthy peasant proprietors (*laboureurs*) to represent them in 1790 as they had the year before.[83] Similar continuity was apparent in the southern half of the country, though in the Midi rural deputies to the secondary assemblies were bourgeois rather than peasants.[84] In the case of Toulon, an especially close examination can be made of the forty *sénéchaussée* deputies of 1789 and fifty-seven delegates to the departmental electoral college in 1790.[85] This time there was a sharp fall in the contribution of the lower classes: seventeen deputies from the popular classes in 1789 were reduced to just three a year later. This reflected a change in the electoral divisions (from guilds to voting wards, or *sections*) and a significant decline in popular turnout. By contrast, bourgeois representatives achieved a high level of personal continuity, since a dozen elected in 1789 reappeared as electors a year later.

The total number of third-estate electors at *bailliage* and *sénéchaussée* level in 1789 was in fact remarkably similar to the number of departmental electors in France in 1790: roughly 45,000 in both instances.[86] Now, it was at this level of the electoral process, in 1789 and thereafter, that the real electoral contest tended to occur. Furet's suggestion that 'instead of being a foregone conclusion, as in 1614 ... (the elections of 1789) gave

---

[82] Chassin, ed., *Les élections*, II, pp. 325–32.
[83] AN BIII 45, Procès-verbal du tiers état du bailliage de Chartres, Mar. 1789 and F¹cIII Eure-et-Loir 1, Procès-verbal de l'assemblée départementale, 1790.
[84] AN F¹cIII Bouches-du-Rhône 1, Procès-verbal de l'assemblée départementale, 1790.
[85] AM Toulon L39, Procès-verbaux and *ibid*. L109, Procès-verbaux des assemblées primaires, June 1790.   [86] Halévi, 'La monarchie et les élections', p. 394.

rise to some real political competition; an indication that whatever the "unanimity" expressed in the *cahiers* power was up for grabs and people were prepared to fight for it', applies to the *bailliage* or *sénéchaussée* assemblies rather than the earlier stages.[87]

Disputes most frequently erupted over the issue of local representation. At Toulon, for example, when the three secondary *sénéchaussées* gathered at the beginning of April to elect four deputies to Versailles, great care was taken to ensure that at least one was chosen from each of the three divisions.[88] This rule was followed all over Provence, to the extent that Digne and Barcelonnette, two alpine *sénéchaussées* bereft of their 'own' deputy, protested bitterly to the government and denounced a deliberate manoeuvre by rivals from Sisteron and Forcalquier.[89]

Ideological conflict is much harder to tease out, since modern political parties, declared candidatures and open canvassing for votes were not part of the electoral tradition; nor did they become established during the following decade. In theory each elector was left to weigh up the situation in his own mind without being subjected to external pressure (which intellectuals like Condorcet felt would inhibit a free and rational choice) and vote for the individuals best suited to the task in hand.[90] Besides stemming from philosophical considerations this concept was also a product of the small gatherings of past centuries, at which deputies would enjoy a good knowledge of each other, though it was no longer viable in the larger, more impersonal assemblies of 1789.

For Cochin, the turn-of-the-century historian whose work has attracted renewed interest of late, this combination of elections in corporate bodies, by means of an individual vote, constituted a fatal blunder by the monarchy: 'The electoral statute of 24 January 1789 left voters not so much at liberty as in a vacuum.'[91] In 1789, a run-off between two named contenders was only held when the two previous ballots failed to produce an absolute majority in anyone's favour. Yet it was relatively rare for a third ballot to be required in the *sénéchaussée* or *bailliage* assemblies. Votes were generally concentrated rather than widely dispersed, despite the absence of restrictions on eligibility. This points to a degree of local organisation, or collusion for which the evidence is usually second-hand but nonetheless overwhelming.

[87] Furet, *Penser la Révolution*, p. 65.
[88] AN BIII 146, Procès-verbaux du tiers état de la sénéchaussée de Toulon, Mar. 1789.
[89] Cubells, *Les horizons de la liberté*, pp. 147–8.
[90] K.M. Baker, *Condorcet. From Natural Philosophy to Social Mathematics* (Chicago, 1975), p. 259.
[91] Cochin, 'Comment furent élus les députés aux Etats Généraux', in *L'esprit du jacobinisme*, p.83.

Cochin himself has described the process in both Brittany and Burgundy, where campaigning in the *tiers état* is especially well documented.[92] It was, for example, an electoral committee, dominated by youthful barristers from Dijon, which drew up a radical, model *cahier* in March 1789 (a so-called 'draft mandate'). The campaign organised around this document was opposed by reactionary members of the Parlement of Dijon, who succeeded in mobilising support for their opinions among municipal officials in the villages. At Semur, in particular, the strength of the two 'parties' was finely balanced and the 'patriotic' barristers were obliged to redouble their efforts to win over deputies at the *bailliage* assembly.

A good deal of this electoral 'propaganda' was directly conveyed by word of mouth. A correspondent of one of the leading conservative lawyers from the Parlement condemned such unseemly behaviour:

All those endowed with knowledge and foresight in our *bailliage* . . . like you, are bemoaning the vulgar and unworthy cabal that all our young lawyers have become involved in . . . they have made some really crude overtures to the electorate which have scandalised all decent folk; they have even gone into the taverns to grab the attention of unfortunate peasant delegates and distribute lists of those whose election they wish to ensure.[93]

Bouloiseau has described a similar process of arm-twisting taking place at Orléans, where *patriotes* strongly advised peasants 'to defy any noblemen who come seeking your votes'.[94] The local aristocracy riposted by urging rural dwellers to ignore the campaign being waged by urban 'capitalists' and 'to work together to ensure that no delegates from the larger towns were elected to the final stage of the proceedings'.

Campaigns like these could be waged for personal as much as political purposes. In the *sénéchaussée* of Le Puy-en-Velay the *lieutenant-général* reported on the extraordinary efforts of one particular individual who was determined to be elected:

Supporters of Mathieu Bernard esquire, a merchant, posted several persons at various vantage points along the roads into town in order to persuade delegates to vote for him; they distributed handbills and then, during the days that followed, they went into the hostelries where deputies were staying to continue their canvassing. All this intrigue was accompanied by a pack of lies concerning those whom the public seemed likely to appoint as deputies.[95]

---

[92] *Ibid.*, 'La campagne électorale de 1789 en Bourgogne', pp. 49–78.
[93] Robin, *La société française*, pp. 249–53.
[94] M. Bouloiseau, 'La campagne électorale pour les Etats-généraux de 1789. L'exemple d'Orléans', *Actes 88ᵉ con. nat.* (1963), pp. 227–9.
[95] M. Rioufol, *La Révolution de 1789 dans le Velay* (Le Puy, 1904), pp. 44–5.

Bernard's partisans deliberately prolonged the electoral proceedings in an attempt to encourage opponents to quit, but the town gates were shut to prevent them leaving! Bernard's heavy-handed manoeuvres obviously rebounded upon their author, who was not even elected as a teller at the assembly. Yet recourse to such devices was inevitable, indeed often essential to supply some direction to potentially rudderless gatherings.

Cochin argued that the absence of any suitable procedures for declaring candidatures only paved the way for adherents of masonry and reading rooms to manipulate the electoral assemblies. On account of their experience of 'democratic sociability' in lodges and clubs these characters were conversant with the sort of tactics required to succeed in 1789. They thrust aside the traditional notables and hoisted themselves into power, though, in the process, they employed practices which were far from conducive to healthy, liberal politics. It is possible to point to some specific examples of masonic activity in the elections to the Estates General. The rather obscure Abbeville merchant, de Lattre, seems to have owed his designation to a campaign conducted in the local lodges.[96] Yet the graduated process of election, not to mention the disputes of the pre-revolutionary period, had provided the opportunity for many of the deputies sent to Versailles to make a name for themselves at the local level. Factors like these counted for much more than access to any 'secret networks' of patronage and intrigue.

Necker was castigated for his failure to intervene on behalf of the monarchy in 1789, but he lacked the means as well as the will to do so.[97] The rigid separation of the orders for electoral purposes actually worked against the government by depriving clergy and nobles of the influence they had exerted over the *tiers état* in the past. In 1614 deputies to the Estates General had usually been elected by the three orders acting in concert, but this rarely occurred in 1789 and, as a consequence, few individuals from outside the *tiers* were chosen to represent it at Versailles.[98] Intervening social and intellectual change doubtless played a part, but the electoral arrangements for 1789 clearly influenced the composition of the third estate and encouraged less deferential attitudes among its members.

Deputies of the *tiers état* have been dubbed 'the perpetuals', since no less than 50 per cent of them succeeded in prolonging their political or administrative careers during the thirty or forty years which followed the Revolution.[99] The durability of this new political class owed a good deal to

[96] Cited in Halévi, 'La monarchie et les élections', p. 400.
[97] Harris, *Necker*, pp. 344–5.
[98] M. Hayden, *France and the Estates General of 1614* (Cambridge, 1974), p. 96.
[99] E. Lemay, 'La composition de l'Assemblée nationale constituante: les hommes de la continuité?', *Rhmc*, 24 (1977), pp. 341–54.

the retention of the electoral mechanism which had brought it to power in the first place. The bourgeois deputies of the National Assembly, which emerged from the Estates General, were understandably anxious to retain many of the essentials of the traditional electoral system in France precisely because it had already worked to their advantage. Yet the contradictions which had characterised procedures for the Estates General bequeathed a good many anachronisms to the new régime, helping to undermine the creation of a 'modern political culture' which many historians regard as the major achievement of the Revolution. Above all, while indirect elections via electoral colleges undoubtedly safeguarded the interests of the elite, restricted access to the secondary assemblies contrasted sharply with the broad, basic franchise that was retained after its dramatic introduction in 1789.

2 Limits of citizenship: The franchise question, 1789–1791

In June 1789 deputies at the Estates General seized power and, in the name of the people, proclaimed a new parliament, the National or Constituent Assembly. This declaration of popular sovereignty placed the issue of who should vote, and how they should do so, at the heart of the political agenda. The prospect of direct democracy had been raised in 1789, but it was generally acknowledged that the size of the country necessitated a representative system of some sort. The sovereignty of the people was accordingly translated into the election of legislators and administrators. The intricacies of the franchise question provoked some acrimonious debate in the Assembly between 1789 and 1791 for, as Montesquieu had remarked, 'the laws which establish the right of suffrage are fundamental to any state'.[1] The conflict over restrictive measures has, however, been misconstrued by many historians, while their impact and application also require a comprehensive reassessment.

In a report which he presented to the newly created *Comité de Constitution*, towards the end of July 1789, the influential *abbé* Sieyès suggested drawing a distinction between 'active citizens', who would vote and 'passive citizens', who would not. To quote the most celebrated passage:

> All the inhabitants of a country must enjoy the rights of passive citizenship: everyone is entitled to the protection of their person, property and freedom etc; but not everyone has the right to take an active part in the election of public officials; not all are active citizens. Women, at least in current circumstances, children, foreigners and those who make no fiscal contribution to the state should not directly influence public affairs. All may enjoy the benefits of living in a particular society, yet only those who pay taxes are real stakeholders in the great social enterprise. They alone are true active citizens, full members of the association.[2]

---

[1] Montesquieu, *The Spirit of the Laws*, ed. F. Neumann (New-York, 1949), Book II, 2, p. 8.

[2] E.-J. Sieyès, *Préliminaire de la constitution: reconnaissance et exposition raisonnée des droits de l'homme et du citoyen* (Versailles, 1789), pp. 13–14. R. Zapperi's edition of Sieyès work, *Ecrits politiques* (Paris, 1985), contains the whole text, pp. 189–206. See M. Forsyth, *Reason and Revolution. The Political Thought of the Abbé Sieyès* (Leicester, 1987), pp. 162–5.

Sieyès was a leading member of the *Comité de Constitution*, which was responsible for resolving the franchise question. His proposals commanded widespread support, both inside and outside the Assembly, because they reflected received wisdom on the subject. There was general agreement that not everyone was ready to participate in political affairs, as debate surrounding the elections to the Estates General had already demonstrated. This prevailing consensus drew heavily upon the Enlightenment and endorsed Holbach's comment on 'Representatives' in the *Encyclopédie*: 'it is the possession of property which makes a man a citizen'.[3] Perhaps only Rousseau would have disagreed, though not to judge by the practical advice he proffered in his *Considérations sur le gouvernement de Pologne*, which envisaged a form of participatory aristocracy.[4]

According to strict Rousseauian logic the very idea of passive citizenship was a contradiction in terms. A famous passage in the *Contrat social* stated that the people 'are called *citizens* when they are able to participate in political affairs and *subjects* when they have no say in the business of law-making' (my emphasis).[5] When Sieyès conjured up the concept of the *citoyen passif*, in 1789, any recourse to the word subject was unthinkable due to its old-regime connotations. As a result of this conjunction the expression 'passive citizen' was studiously avoided in legislative texts, which constantly referred to active citizens but never their converse. The deputy Dubois-Crancé hid his embarrassment by describing those without a vote as 'citoyens *non-actifs*', while others employed the term '*inactifs*'. Historians have in fact utilised the phrase *citoyens passifs* far more freely than contemporaries.

Despite these difficulties, the *Comité de Constitution* came down firmly in favour of a limited franchise. Thouret, whose importance on the committee was second only to that of Sieyès, presented a set of suffrage proposals to the Assembly on 29 September 1789, as part of a package for the administrative reorganisation of the kingdom.[6] In order to qualify as an active citizen it was necessary to be a born Frenchman or to have been naturalised, to have reached the age of majority, to have lived in the canton for at least a year and to pay an annual sum in direct taxation equivalent to the value of three days' local wages.

for a sympathetic interpretation of Sieyès' views on citizenship and W.H. Sewell, 'Le citoyen/la citoyenne: activity, passivity, and the revolutionary concept of citizenship', in Baker *et al.*, eds., *The French Revolution and the Creation of Modern Political Culture*, II, pp. 107–8, for a rather less flattering verdict.

[3] Cited in J. Lough, *The Philosophes and Post-Revolutionary France* (Oxford, 1982), p. 46.
[4] C.E. Vaughan, ed., *The Political Writings of Jean-Jacques Rousseau*, 2 vols. (Cambridge, 1915), II, pp. 369 ff.
[5] J.-J. Rousseau, *Du contrat social* in *Oeuvres complètes*, Bibliothèque de la Pléiade (Paris, 1964), III, pp. 361–2. [6] *AP* IX, pp. 204–5, 29 Sept. 1789.

In 1789, little disagreement was provoked by this basic distinction between voters and non-voters. The point needs underlining because it is often overlooked in general accounts of the Revolution, where specific opposition to the requirements initially imposed upon national deputies have been misrepresented as hostility to the entire principle of franchise restrictions. On the contrary, most deputies concurred with Démeunier, speaking for the committee in October, when he highlighted the danger of allowing the poor to vote. Their presence, he argued, would only serve to subvert popular sovereignty: 'If we demand no tax payment . . . and allow beggars into the primary assemblies . . . do you think they will be immune from corruption?' After all, he concluded, 'the exclusion of the poor . . . is only provisional', the right to participate 'will become a goal for all working people'.[7]

The *Courrier de Provence*, which bore Mirabeau's imprimatur, praised the proposed *cens* (as the fiscal requirement was known) in similar terms, 'because it attaches citizens to the state by means of the contribution which they make to society's well-being and also because it reminds everyone of their duty to earn their living, thus reinforcing the concept of the dignity of labour that our stupid prejudices and bizarre institutions have for so long cast into disrepute.'[8] It was no accident that the taxpaying criterion for the vote was expressed in terms of a day's wages, nor that after abolishing the *cens* in 1792 legislators would continue to insist on voters enjoying an established livelihood. The new regime was dedicated to stamping out poverty and encouraging industry, thereby paving the way for greater political participation, a utilitarian approach that anticipated Guizot's famous retort to objections against the limited franchise of the nineteenth century: 'Get rich!'

Nonetheless, the silence of the radical press on the basic *cens* is rather astonishing. In 1789, only Camille Desmoulins' *Les Révolutions de France et de Brabant* took up the cudgels against suffrage restrictions, castigating the priests who defended them in the Assembly by pointing out that Christ himself would not have been a *citoyen actif*! The truly active citizens, Desmoulins argued, 'are those who stormed the Bastille, they are those who bring the land under cultivation'.[9] Later proponents of universal male suffrage were suprisingly taciturn at this stage of the Revolution too. Condorcet, for example, expressed practical reservations

---

[7] *AP* IX, p. 479, 22 Oct. 1789.
[8] *Courrier de Provence*, no. LVI, 21–2 Oct. 1789, cited in L.G. Wickham-Legg, ed., *Select Documents Illustrative of the History of the French Revolution*, 2 vols. (Oxford, 1905), I, p. 172.
[9] *Les Révolutions de France et de Brabant*, no. III, Nov. 1789, cited in Wickham-Legg, ed., *Select Documents*, I, pp. 173–4.

about using taxation as a basis for active citizenship, but he did not query the principle of limitations upon the franchise. Since the Paris Jacobins demanded an annual subscription of twelve *livres*, few complaints might have been expected from this quarter. Even the more radical Cordeliers were not prepared to go beyond advocating that all male taxpayers should be allowed to vote.[10]

Only a few dissenting voices were raised in the Assembly in October 1789. The *abbé* Grégoire claimed that full citizenship required only 'sound judgement and a patriotic heart', while Dupont de Nemours pointed to the inconsistency between a limited franchise and the principle of equal rights (though he was not an advocate of universal suffrage).[11] Defermon was more concerned that the fiscal criterion would rule out older sons, who still resided in the parental domicile and were not subject to personal taxation.[12] In practice it appears that they could register as voters, provided their fathers paid more than the minimum demanded.

It was left to Robespierre to mount the major assault on the basic *cens*. He subjected the committee's recommendations to a withering attack, which focused upon issues of principle. He opened his onslaught, on 22 October, by asserting that any restrictions were automatically invalid because they ran counter to no less than three articles in the recently adopted Declaration of Rights. He concluded his tirade by demanding that:

> All citizens, no matter who they are, have the right to aspire to every degree of representation. Anything less would be out of keeping with your declaration of rights, to which every privilege, every distinction and every exception must yield. The constitution has established that sovereignty resides in the People, in every member of the populace. Each individual therefore has the right to a say in the laws by which he is governed and in the choice of the administration which belongs to him. Otherwise it is not true to say that all men are equal in rights, that all men are citizens.[13]

The following day Robespierre reaffirmed that 'a man is by definition a citizen; no one can take away this right which is inseparable from his existence here on earth'.[14] Later, during debates on the final version of the Constitution, in 1791, the Incorruptible reiterated his categorical condemnation of all limitations on the male suffrage. On this occasion he added, in Rousseauian fashion, that the term passive citizen was 'an

---

[10] Rose, *The Making of the Sans-Culottes*, pp. 60–1.
[11] *AP* IX, p. 479, 22 Oct. 1789.   [12] *Ibid.*   [13] *Ibid.*
[14] M. Robespierre, *Oeuvres complètes*, eds. M. Bouloiseau, G. Lefebvre and A. Soboul, 10 vols. (Paris, 1910–67), VI, p. 553.

insidious and barbarous expression, which defiles both our laws and our language'.[15]

By the time the new Constitution came into effect the basic *cens* was attracting much more widespread opposition. Yet, even then, few deputies were prepared to endorse Robespierre's contention that voting was a universal right, as the great Declaration of 1789 seemed to imply. Barnave attempted to square this particular circle by arguing that the franchise was in fact a function, bestowed upon certain citizens by society, as part of the more general division of labour. According to Barnave's interpretation, opponents of the *cens* were confusing the current system of representation with an impractical democratic ideal. In any case, as he observed in August 1791, 'it is not enough to have the desire for freedom, it is equally necessary to know how to behave responsibly'.[16] This echoed an idea attributed to Sieyès, articulated in the Assembly by Mirabeau in 1789, that all young men over twenty-one years old should be enrolled on a civic register in order to be educated in their duties as citizens, though they would not be able to vote until they reached the age of twenty-five.[17]

Youth and lack of a livelihood were not the only grounds for exclusion from the franchise. In keeping with the widely held belief that only persons endowed with 'a free, unfettered and independent will' were entitled to vote, Barère wished to debar indentured servants.[18] The main difficulty lay in the precise definition of servile status. Should private tutors be excluded from the electoral process and what of those rural workers in parts of the Midi who were habitually referred to as 'maîtres valets'?[19] It was left to Target to remove these categories from the injunction, together with 'stewards, bailiffs and seigneurial agents'.[20] It was also argued that voters needed a good knowledge of their fellow inhabitants in order to make a sound electoral choice. Members of the Constituent Assembly were therefore unanimous in demanding a full twelve months' residence in the canton; without it unscrupulous politicians might flood the assemblies with footloose supporters.

Religious affiliation and racial origin were equally contentious issues where the franchise was concerned. Protestants were admitted in the absence of any real dissent (a few were already sitting in the Constituent Assembly) and so, after some lengthy debate in the spring of 1791, were 'free men of colour' in the French colonies.[21] The enfranchisement of

---

[15] *Ibid.*, VII, pp. 161–2. [16] *AP* XXIX, p. 365, 11 Aug. 1791.
[17] *Ibid.*, IX, p. 596, 28 Oct. 1789.
[18] *AP* IX, p. 590, 27 Oct. 1789 and see C. Petitfrère, *L'oeil du maître. Maîtres et serviteurs de l'époque classique au romantisme* (Paris, 1986), pp. 190–9.
[19] AN DIV 30, Communauté de Salles (Haute-Garonne) au Comité de Constitution, no date.   [20] *AP* XII, p. 260, 20 Mar. 1790.   [21] *AP* XXVI, p. 97, 16 May 1791.

Jewish inhabitants in France, however, provoked some especially unsavoury exchanges. In December 1789, a proposal that all non-Catholics be allowed to vote and hold office, provided they fulfilled other requirements, had only been passed when Jews were specifically excluded.[22] The Sephardic Jews of Bordeaux and Avignon were subsequently awarded the franchise, but the much larger contingent of Ashkenazic Jews, who lived in eastern France, were only emancipated in the same fashion in September 1791, during the final sessions of the Constituent Assembly.[23]

Condorcet had tirelessly argued that religion and race were inadmissible as barriers to the franchise and he was almost alone in publicly advocating votes for women. In 1790, in a celebrated journal article, he concluded: 'The proposition that women are inherently incapable of exercising the right to political participation is just not intellectually defensible.'[24] Although some women had voted in 1789, in person or by proxy, and Sieyès qualified his exclusion of females with the phrase 'at least for the moment', their case was never even discussed by the National Assembly.[25] An important women's movement grew out of the Revolution, but it made few inroads into masculine prejudice against the female franchise. The influence of the Enlightenment and the classical tradition preempted any serious consideration of the issue. For Rousseau, above all, women remained subjects rather than citizens, frail vessels with no part to play in the body politic. To enfranchise them, it was alleged, would merely deliver a double vote to their husbands.

The role of adult male taxpayers was itself limited, for all elections above the local level were to be conducted by second-degree electors chosen in the cantons. The retention of indirect elections was yet another legacy of the Estates General of 1789. It was precisely this distinction between primary and secondary stages that enabled deputies to agree upon such a broad, basic suffrage. As Barnave candidly admitted, it was only because the more crucial decisions would be taken by members of electoral colleges in the new departments that he was prepared to entrust the mass electorate with any role in the process; reason at this more rarified level

---

[22] G. Kates, 'Jews into Frenchmen: Nationality and Representation in Revolutionary France', in F. Fehér, ed., *The French Revolution and the Birth of Modernity* (Berkeley, 1990), pp. 103–16.   [23] *AP* XXXI, pp. 372–3, 27 Sept. 1791.
[24] B.-J. Buchez and J.-B. Roux, eds., *Histoire parlementaire de la Révolution française*, 40 vols. (Paris, 1834-38), IX, pp. 98–104.
[25] J.B. Landes, *Women and the Public Sphere in the Age of the French Revolution* (Ithaca, 1988), pp. 106 *ff.* and O.H. Hufton, *Women and the Limits of Citizenship in the French Revolution* (Toronto, 1992), pp. 3–5.

would counterbalance the weight of numbers at the earlier stage.[26] An address from Tours, sent to the National Assembly in October 1789, concurred by emphasising that, in view of the people's ignorance, 'the elections must be held in stages', while a journalist from Strasbourg argued that by delegating tasks to electoral colleges ordinary people were spared a good deal of time and effort.[27]

So deeply ingrained was the belief in indirect election that only as the Revolution developed was this aspect of the electoral process seriously questioned. Eligibility to office was also subject to restrictions, but these attracted more immediate criticism. In his draft Declaration of Rights, published in 1789, Sieyès stated that 'competence' on the part of those elected was essential to protect the 'interests' of taxpayers and property-owners who voted for them. Echoing Montesquieu, who had written that 'most citizens have some ability to choose, but they are unqualified to be chosen', the *abbé* introduced a barrier between *citoyens actifs* and *éligibles*: the former could vote, but only the latter would hold office.[28]

The *Comité de Constitution* accordingly subdivided *citoyens actifs* into three categories: those who could vote, on payment of three days' local wages in personal taxation *per annum*; those who would also be eligible for municipal office and membership of the departmental electoral colleges, provided they paid direct tax equivalent to ten days' labour; and, finally, those who could serve as national deputies, if they made an annual tax return which amounted to the value of a silver mark (worth slighty in excess of 50 *livres*). Active citizenship was thus a graduated status and access grew more selective as the public office became more elevated.[29]

When the qualifications required for election were first discussed, on 29 October 1789, Pétion began by conceding the need for a limited franchise. This was unavoidable 'when the people is steeped in tradition and corruption' but, he continued, the new law was going too far: 'restrictions should stop at the level of voting'.[30] Dupont de Nemours, who also favoured a basic *cens*, was equally hostile to requirements for eligibility. Like Pétion, he believed that the 'confidence' of the electorate constituted a sufficient guarantee for election.[31] Yet even this gathering protest was dwarfed by a veritable explosion of wrath over the silver mark qualification, which had been set at the apex of the electoral system.

---

[26] A. Bernave, *De la Révolution et de la Constitution*, ed. P. Gueniffey (Grenoble, 1988), p. 165.
[27] Cited in H. Faye, *La Révolution au jour le jour en Touraine* (Angers, 1903), p. 22 and R. Marx, *Recherches sur la vie politique de l'Alsace prérévolutionnaire et révolutionnaire* (Strasbourg, 1966) p. 75.   [28] Montesquieu, *The Spirit of the Laws*, Book II, 2, p. 10.
[29] O. Le Cour Grandmaison, 'La citoyenneté à l'époque de la Constituante', *AhRf*, LIX (1987), p. 250.   [30] *AP*, IX, p. 598, 29 Oct. 1789.
[31] *Ibid.*, IX, pp. 597–9, 28–9 Oct. 1789.

The *marc d'argent* provided an emblematic focus for fears of an emergent 'aristocracy of wealth', far more potent than denominations of days' labour. It was tailor-made as a target for journalistic protest and an initially reticent press duly took aim with a volley of protest. The *Courrier de Provence*, which had welcomed the limited suffrage, inveighed just as heavily against the silver mark as its more radical counterparts.[32] The *Révolutions de France et de Brabant*, for its part, suggested that, 'where the silver mark is concerned there is a single voice of condemnation in the capital and it will soon be the same in the provinces'. It went on, 'in order to appreciate the absurdity of this decree, it is sufficient to say that Jean-Jacques Rousseau, Corneille and Mably would not have met its requirements'.

Loustalot, in *Les Révolutions de Paris*, referred to the silver mark as 'the greatest scourge of humanity that one can imagine' and he added, 'a real aristocracy of wealth has been shamelessly set up'. He even went so far as to suggest that Louis XVI should employ his veto against it! As Loustalot perceptively concluded: 'What! Our most worthy deputies, who are currently sitting in the assembly, will not be eligible?' Just so; the *marc d'argent* affected members of the Constituent Assembly personally, in a way that other franchise qualifications did not. Jean Jaurès drew attention to this discrepancy when he wrote, in his great *Histoire socialiste*, that 'it was only the question of eligibility to parliament which seems to have briefly preoccupied these legislators'. As he went on to explain, 'the intellectual bourgeoisie wanted to safeguard its place alongside the property-owning middle classes'.[33]

It is difficult to agree with those historians who argue that, from the very outset, the basic distinction between active and passive citizens was 'one of the most politically explosive features' of the new order.[34] Aulard's contrary assertion that 'in general decrees on the limited franchise were meekly accepted ... there was no overwhelming tide of opinion against the *cens*', is much nearer the truth.[35] The districts of Paris did petition the Assembly to abolish *all* restrictions on the franchise, early in 1790, but this was an isolated example of popular dissent. When the suffrage did become a more prominent issue, it was a consequence rather than the cause of growing radicalism, especially in the capital. Yet, even in 1791, the specific thrust of addresses from the provinces remained suppression of the silver mark.[36]

---

[32] Wickham-Legg, ed., *Select Documents*, I, pp. 171–5, for a selection of comments published in the press between 28 Oct. and 5 Dec. 1789.

[33] Jaurès, *Histoire socialiste*, I, pp. 587–8 and 613.

[34] Sewell, 'Le citoyen/la citoyenne', p. 112.   [35] Aulard, *Histoire politique*, p. 78.

[36] AN DIV 66, Correspondance du Comité de Constitution, Adresses du Var, 1791, for example. *Ibid.*, DIV 24, Amis de la Constitution de Dijon, 19 Aug. 1791, demonstrates that even at this point hostility to the *marc d'argent* did not prevent provincial Jacobins supporting a qualification for second-degree electors, in this case the payment of twenty days' wages in taxation and the ownership of property.

There were those in the Assembly, the nobleman Cazalès among them, who wished to add a property qualification to the payment of taxes in order to delimit eligibility as a deputy.[37] Some hostility towards 'capitalists who lacked roots in the soil', had already been aired by the physiocratic Dupont de Nemours. He felt that even basic voting rights should be anchored in property ownership and he opposed Sieyès' more liberal, fiscal definition of the political shareholder. According to Dupont, 'Only the property-holder has a real stake in society, so they alone should be eligible for office. Those who lack property are not yet full members of society.'[38] This earlier objection had passed unnoticed, but the proposal to attach a property requirement to the tax qualification for national deputies served to stoke up further controversy over the *marc d'argent*.

It is not always clear whether subsequent discussion was aimed at this amendment, or directed against the original proposal for the silver mark. In the event the constitutional committee's original recommendation was modified; it was decided that, 'besides making a tax payment equivalent to a silver mark', a deputy must also possess 'immovable wealth of some description'. There is no indication of the number of votes cast in favour of this resolution, but the opposition was strong enough to secure a rapid reconsideration of the issue. On 7 December 1789, the *Comité de Constitution* tried to preempt renewed controversy by proposing that, when a national deputy received 75 per cent of the poll, fiscal and property requirements could be waived. Some lively debate ensued before this further amendment was rejected by just ten votes.[39]

This was by no means the end of the matter, only the beginning. In view of mounting criticism, restrictions on eligibility for office (but not, significantly, limitations on the basic suffrage) underwent a thorough revision before they were finally enshrined in the Constitution of 1791. In the meantime the arrangements that had been made in 1789 were put into operation and local authorities began compiling lists of voters early the following year. What precisely did the legislation mean in practice? A good deal of material is available where the registration of this first generation of voters is concerned and historians have recently begun to exploit it. Relying upon 'respected political arithmeticians', members of the *Comité de Constitution* estimated that their proposals would enfranchise roughly one-sixth of the population, or 4,000,000 adult males.[40] This was a

---

[37] *AP* IX, p. 598, 29 Oct. 1789. [38] *Ibid.*, IX, p. 479, 22 Oct. 1789.
[39] *Ibid.*, X, pp. 414–15, 7 Dec. 1789.
[40] E.-J. Sieyès, *Observations* (Oct. 1789), cited in Forsyth, *Reason and Revolution*, p. 167.

remarkably accurate prediction if a national table, compiled by the *Comité des Contributions Publiques* in May 1791, is anything to go by; when figures for each of the eighty-three departments are combined, they make a total of 4,298,960 active citizens.[41]

Of course, these data, like the population statistics which accompany them, must be treated with extreme caution. They were not all collected at a single moment in time, some emanating from early in 1790, others from the spring of 1791. Many rural communes proved recalcitrant when required to furnish information of this sort and were careless in its compilation. Perusal of the local archives can yield a variety of totals though, on the whole, later lists were drawn up with greater accuracy than earlier ones. The number of active citizens at Saint-Pazanne in the Loire-Inférieure, for example, rose from 620 to 646 and then as high as 768 during the course of 1790![42] Similarly, in the Pas-de-Calais, the total recorded for the canton of Vitry rose by over one-third between the autumn of 1790 and the spring of 1791.[43]

Whatever its deficiencies, the committee's table does facilitate a global estimate of the number of active citizens under the Constitutional Monarchy. Overall, it would appear that some 15 per cent of the population (which has been revised upwards to 27,500,000 for 1791 in the light of recent demographic calculations) were given the vote.[44] Assuming that men aged over twenty-five comprised a quarter of the population, this would suggest that roughly 60 per cent of adult males had been awarded the franchise. The table is not so serviceable, however, where demographic totals for each department are concerned. For example, Le Gall's meticulous study of the Loire-Inférieure reveals a much larger departmental population than the one listed by the *Comité* and the percentage of voters is accordingly lower than it appears.[45] In fact roughly a third of the population totals in the table were calculated on the basis of the average proportion of active citizens recorded in the rest. In order to make effective comparisons between departments (albeit at the price of lowering the proportion of voters, due to generally larger population totals at the later date), the accompanying map has been based on the first reliable, national census taken in 1806. This reveals the highest percentage of active citizens in the Var, where almost 20 per cent of the population were given the vote, while the Basses-Pyrénées takes the lowest place with under 8 per cent.

[41] *AP* XXVI, pp. 532–3, Tableau 4, 15 May 1791. The printed total of 4,298,360 is erroneous. [42] Le Gall, Les consultations générales, I, p. 127.
[43] J.-P. Jessenne, 'De la citoyenneté proclamée à la citoyenneté appliquée: l'exercice du droit de vote dans le district d'Arras en 1790', *Revue du Nord*, LXXII (1990), pp. 822–3.
[44] Y. Blayo and L. Henry, 'La population de la France de 1740 à 1860,' *Population*, 30 (1975), p. 102. [45] Le Gall, Les consultations générales, I, p. 136.

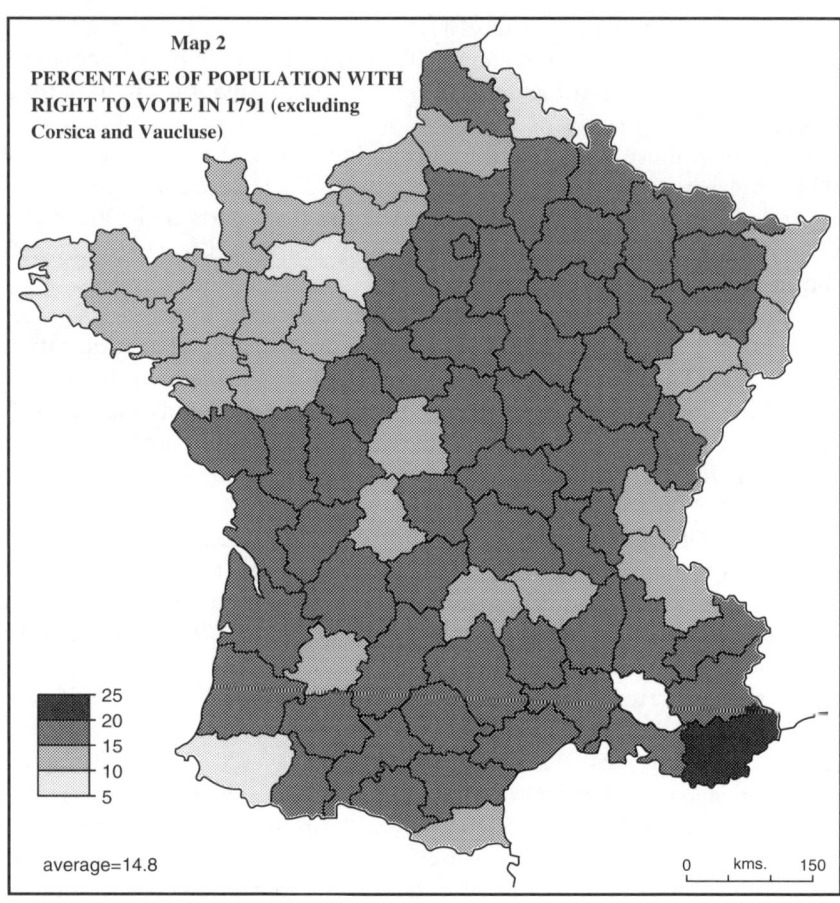

2 The percentage of the population with the right to vote in 1791

Patrice Gueniffey has concluded that 'the peculiarities of the fiscal system in the various regions usually determined the size of the electorate'.[46] Tax rolls from 1789 were employed to operate restrictions on the suffrage in both 1790 and 1791, pending the establishment of a new system of taxation. Since the old system was utterly lacking in uniformity some disparities in enfranchisement undoubtedly arose as a consequence, but the regional distribution of wealth was equally crucial. An *Atlas portatif* published in 1791, which compared tax burden and active citizenship by province, reveals no simple correlation in this regard: in Brittany low taxation and a low percentage of active citizens do go hand-

---

[46] Gueniffey, *Le nombre et la raison*, pp. 83–5.

in-hand; yet the north-east was heavily taxed under the *ancien régime*, only to produce an average proportion of *citoyens actifs*; and the above-average enfranchisement of the south-east was surely a reflection of the prevalence of small property-owners, for the incidence of direct taxation prior to 1789 had been extremely low.[47] Jessenne's work in the Pas-de-Calais also suggests that enfranchisement reflected the social contours of different localities: 'The rate was higher in Upper Artois, where large-scale farming predominated, and lower in zones that were more densely populated, where small-holdings and diminutive parcels of land were more common...'[48]

Still, Robespierre was correct to comment, in his usual, astringent fashion that, as a consequence of fiscal vagaries, the same citizen might receive a vote in one area but not in another. He was especially concerned that the electorate in his native Artois would be unfairly penalised by the pre-revolutionary predominance of indirect taxation.[49] In time the shift to direct taxation would correct this particular anomaly (though, in the longer term, the general reduction of the tax burden promised by the new regime might reduce the overall electorate!). The Constituent Assembly responded, on 2 February 1790, by decreeing that: 'in those localities... where no direct taxation is levied... all those citizens who meet the other requisite conditions... will be deemed both active and eligible... provided that they exercise a profession or hold some property'.[50] This ruling helps explain why the Var recorded such a high percentage of active citizens in 1790 and it was also responsible for allowing Arras, Robespierre's home town, to secure a bigger proportion of voters than its surrounding countryside.

Complications also arose at Marseille, where all taxes were indirect until the crisis of the late *ancien régime* necessitated an extraordinary levy on property in 1789. Members of the popular classes, who had protested against restrictions on voting for the Estates General, indicated their annoyance at the prospect of exclusion from the new franchise because of this exceptional imposition. They had to be reassured by the authorities that in the circumstances only those dependent upon charity would be debarred from the assemblies of 1790.[51] The vagaries of the fiscal system also generated difficulties at Brest, the Atlantic naval port, where dockyard workers claimed to be active citizens on account of 'the four *deniers* per *livre* that was withheld from their pay (to fund sickness benefits and

---

[47] Buchez and Roux, eds., *Histoire parlementaire*, XI, pp. 446–7.
[48] Jessenne, 'De la citoyenneté', pp. 809–10.
[49] *AP* XI, pp. 318–19, 25 Jan. 1790 and see a speech by Robespierre to the Cordeliers, *ibid.*, pp. 320–5.   [50] *Ibid.*, XI, p. 417, 2 Feb. 1790.
[51] AM Marseille 1D2, Délibérations du conseil municipal, 10 Sept. 1790.

pensions) and which amounted to more than three days' wages in taxation over the course of a year . . .'.[52] Having taken advice from the *Comité de Constitution*, the municipal council subsequently announced that all naval employees who paid the levy would enjoy the right to vote regardless of their fiscal contribution.

As a rule, cities housed a relatively smaller electorate than rural areas. Dijon, for instance, set its politically active population at 48 per cent of adult males, compared to 72 per cent in the department of the Côte-d'Or as a whole.[53] Likewise, in the Loire-Inférieure Nantes, with a meagre 30 per cent, fell well below a rather poor departmental average of only 47 per cent.[54] Once again an explanation may be sought in the incidence of taxation under the *ancien régime*, which was generally lighter in the urban context and heavier in rural areas. Yet the concentration of poverty in the towns was also a potent factor in restricting the urban electorate, especially in view of the economic crisis of the preceding years. Lille, Troyes and Bayeux, for instance, all badly hit by a slump in the textile industry, listed less than 40 per cent of adult males as liable for the suffrage.[55]

Urban areas sheltered a more mobile, as well as a poorer population and even wealthier inhabitants might fall foul of the residence or nationality requirement. Some idea of how many persons were excluded on these grounds is furnished by the unusual example of Toulon, the Mediterranean naval port, where no-one was excluded by the *cens* because all taxation had been levied indirectly prior to 1789. As a consequence almost 90 per cent of men aged over twenty-five years old became potential voters.[56] Many of the remaining 10 per cent were ruled out on the grounds of national origin or recent arrival, while others were omitted because they were receiving alms, or on account of domestic service. Towns contained large numbers of *domestiques*. No figures are available for Toulon, but Ligou has calculated that man-servants made up no less than 4 per cent of the population of Dijon in 1790 (some 10 per cent of adult males).[57]

Differences in numbers able to vote are equally apparent from village to village within the same rural area. Since local councils made their

---

[52] AM Brest 1D2 2, Délibérations du conseil général, 1 May 1790.
[53] AD Côte-d'Or, L497, Tableaux des citoyens actifs, Apr.- May 1790.
[54] Le Gall, Les consultations générales, I, pp. 138–40.
[55] G. Bossenga, *The Politics of Privilege. Old Regime and Revolution in Lille* (Cambridge, 1991), p. 109; L. Hunt, *Revolution and Urban Politics in Provincial France: Troyes and Reims, 1786–1790* (Stanford, 1978), p. 115; and O.H. Hufton, *Bayeux in the Late Eighteenth Century. A Social Study* (Oxford, 1967), p. 155. Hufton, however, confuses the number of active and eligible citizens. [56] AM Toulon, L573, Affiche électorale, 1 Feb. 1790.
[57] D. Ligou, 'Population, citoyens actifs et électeurs à Dijon aux débuts de la Révolution française, 1790–1791', *Actes 88ᵉ con. nat.* (1963), p. 253.

own estimates for the value of a day's unskilled labour, it is tempting to attribute such variations to this factor. While better-off inhabitants might be inclined to favour a restricted electorate, it was also the case that the more voters a commune had, the more potential influence it carried at the cantonal assembly (for primary elections to the departmental electoral college). Barnave reported that some totally unrealistic figures were being set, among them a municipality 'where the price of a day's labour has been set as high as 50 *sous*'.[58] The National Assembly quickly intervened to stipulate a maximum of 20 *sous* or 1 *livre* for a day's pay, unless a special case was made to the contrary. In future, acting on advice from the centre, departments and districts were to set norms for their areas and override the municipalities. In 1790 neighbouring *communes* still recorded sums at opposite ends of the scale (effectively from 1½ to 3 *livres* as an overall requirement). Yet it was far from being the case that a low figure invariably produced more active citizens, or vice-versa.[59]

Over the country as a whole, some 2,500,000 adult males, or almost 40 per cent of the age group, were denied the franchise. So Dubois-Crancé was surely wrong to assert in 1791 that: 'The only non-active citizens who exist in the kingdom are beggars and vagabonds, the sort of men whom society must constantly keep under surveillance, for every citizen who possesses a useful skill or who has a roof over his head will always pay 30 or 40 *francs* (30 or 40 *sous* old style) in taxes.'[60] It is true that in regions of substantial peasant holdings the vote was generously distributed. Bois, in his fine study of peasants in the Sarthe, agrees with Dubois-Crancé that only marginal elements were excluded in the countryside: 'The poor were in no way excluded, because the electoral qualification . . . by no means delimited the threshold of poverty.'[61] Yet Le Gall, in a careful analysis of the less well-off Loire-Inférieure, shows that as many as 50 per cent of *citoyens actifs* only just qualified for the vote and enjoyed uncertain status as a consequence.[62] Elsewhere, at Foix, when the *cens* was lowered from 20 to 12 *sous* the electorate rose by two-thirds![63]

Surveys undertaken as part of an investigation into the causes of poverty, in 1790, indicate quite clearly that in many areas numerous, resi-

---

[58] *AP* XI, pp. 187–8, 15 Jan. 1790.
[59] AD Marne 1L286, Listes de citoyens actifs, District d'Epernay, 1790.
[60] *AP* XXV, p. 385, 28 Apr. 1791.
[61] P. Bois, *Paysans de l'Ouest. Des structures économiques et sociales aux options politiques depuis l'époque révolutionnaire dans la Sarthe* (Le Mans, 1960), p. 237.
[62] Le Gall, Les consultations générales, I, pp. 148–51.
[63] G. Arnaud, *Histoire de la Révolution dans le département de l'Ariège (1789–1795)* (Toulouse, 1904), p. 158.

dent wage-earners paid either too little tax to meet the fiscal requirement for the franchise, or none at all. This was especially true of towns. At Epernay in the Champagne, for example, the inclusion of all tax-payers would have raised the total of active citizens by a third. In the surrounding countryside, by contrast, a similar modification would have added only 10 per cent to the electorate.[64] In the Perpignan District of the Pyrénées-Orientales, the inclusion of all taxpayers at Perpignan itself would have raised the electorate by almost 20 per cent, but made a difference of only 12 per cent in rural areas; Gueniffey, meanwhile, has estimated that in the Yonne the same adjustment would have added just 15 per cent to the total.[65]

Compared to eighteenth-century Britain, or even the infant American Republic, the basic suffrage was widely distributed during the early years of the French Revolution.[66] So was eligibility for local office and access to the departmental electoral colleges. The requirement of ten working days in taxation was a significant one, but it was by no means as draconian as many historians have assumed. All too often the number of places available to second-degree electors on the departmental assemblies (one per 100 active citizens, making roughly 45,000 altogether) has been confused with the huge pool of *éligibles* from whom they were chosen. Thus Bill Doyle in his magisterial *Oxford History of the French Revolution* wrongly asserts that: 'All active citizens did was to choose one in a hundred of their number as electors and those eligible for the next level had to be paying taxes to the value of ten days' labour. *Only about 50,000 active citizens met this requirement*' (my emphasis).[67] Contemporaries suggested that only one-fifth of active citizens were also eligible for office, but in fact almost 2,500,000 Frenchmen crossed the eligibility threshold; in other words, over half those who qualified as *citoyens actifs* were also *éligibles*.[68]

In those departments where statistics are available for all or almost every canton, the rate of eligibility runs from over 67 per cent in the Doubs, to an average 60 per cent in the Haute-Saône and the Orne and to

[64] AD Marne 1L313, Municipalité d'Epernay: formation, Jan. 1790.
[65] AD Pyrénées-Orientales L469, Etats de la population, District de Perpignan, 1790 and Gueniffey, *Le nombre et la raison*, pp. 91–2.
[66] R.R. Palmer, *The Age of the Democratic Revolution*, 2 vols. (Princeton, 1959–64), I, pp. 525–7.
[67] W. Doyle, *The Oxford History of the French Revolution* (Oxford, 1989), p. 124. Likewise, A. Soboul, *The French Revolution*, trans., 2 vols. (London, 1974), I, p. 180 and A. Cole and P. Campbell, *French Electoral Systems and Elections*, third edn., (Aldershot, 1989), p. 37.
[68] *AP* XXIX, p. 373, 11 Aug. 1791.

Table 1 *Active and eligible citizens in 1790*

Department	Active Citizens	Eligible Citizens	Percentage Eligible
Doubs	32288	21741	67.3
Vosges	42879	26890	62.7
Haute-Saône	41084	25019	60.9
Orne	57272	34498	60.2
Landes	40034	22956	57.3
Morbihan	43799	23300	53.2
(Paris)	(77590)	(42209)	(54.4)
Total	257356	154404	60.0

Sources: AN DIVbis 37 and 38; AD Landes 11L2; AD Morbihan L234; and M. Genty, *Paris 1789–1795. L'apprentissage de la citoyenneté* (Paris, 1987), pp. 265–6

a low of 53 per cent in the Morbihan.[69] In the Côte-d'Or a substantial sample suggests that over 70 per cent of active citizens were eligible.[70] By contrast in the Loire-Inférieure, where numbers of those able to vote were already small, incomplete evidence indicates a proportion of perhaps only 40 per cent as *éligibles*.[71]

Once again there was considerable variation within, as well as between departments. In the District of Arras, in the Pas-de-Calais, the proportion of *éligibles* in eight cantons ranged from 30 to almost 78 per cent.[72] Differences in the valuation of a day's work obviously exerted a greater influence at this level, since the amount was multiplied by ten rather than by three; in some places it cost 5 *livres* to become a second-degree elector, in others as much as 10 *livres*. There was also a contrast between town and countryside, which doubtless pleased those of physiocratic inclination who believed that landed wealth should secure greater representation. Toulon, in the absence of direct tax records was exceptional, with 100 per cent of its *citoyens actifs* also *éligibles*. At Epernay in the Marne, on the other hand, the figure was less than 60 per cent, while in villages of the surrounding district it might rise as high as 90 per cent.[73] Paris fared even worse, with little more than half its active citizens qualifying as *éligibles*.

Still, the second-degree *cens* did not prevent modest peasants and wealthier artisans from serving as municipal councillors or justices of the peace, nor from becoming members of the departmental electoral

---

[69] AN DIVbis 37 and 38, Listes de citoyens actifs, 1790–91.
[70] AD Côte-d'Or L222, Tableaux des citoyens actifs, 1790.
[71] Le Gall, Les consultations générales, I, pp. 208–13.
[72] Jessenne, 'De la citoyenneté proclamée', p. 815.
[73] AD Marne 1L286, Listes de citoyens actifs.

colleges, even if almost none of them were elected as administrators of department or district before 1792. By contrast, the silver-mark payment demanded of national deputies imposed an elevated hurdle which only a handful of citizens could cross. No statistics have ever been published regarding the impact of the *marc* upon the electorate, though assertions were made in the press that 'nine tenths of the (political) nation' would be precluded from serving as representatives. Other commentators were less optimistic: members of the municipal council at Paris advanced a more modest figure of 6 per cent, while the lawyer Target claimed in the National Assembly that only 5 per cent of active citizens would qualify as deputies.[74]

To judge by surviving documentation, few local authorities attempted any precise calculations, perhaps because the issue was so contentious. At Dijon two sections, or urban electoral wards, did produce lists of those who met the silver-mark criterion: in the Section du Centre they constituted 13 per cent of *citoyens actifs* and in the Section de Saint-Bénigne almost 18 per cent. In both cases nobles, former office-holders and rentiers were heavily represented, but few commercial elements appeared.[75] This coincides closely with Sentou's findings for the quarter of Saint-Etienne in Toulouse, where 13 per cent of active citizens were eligible as national deputies.[76] Perhaps in both cities the *quartiers* in question were not inhabited by the mercantile elites; after all, most merchants did hold significant amounts of real estate.

Nonetheless, the larger towns inscribed a higher percentage of potential deputies than the countryside: the analysis of tax rolls from the District of Versailles suggests that only 10.3 per cent of *citoyens actifs* paid the *marc d'argent*; similar calculations for the District of Epernay in the Marne yields 10.2 per cent; those of Aix-en-Provence (minus Aix itself) 8.4 per cent; and Landerneau in the Finistère only 3.2 per cent.[77] The structure of property-ownership was evidently an important determining factor. Barère and Garat, who were both deputies from the Midi, protested bitterly that the southern regions would be disadvantaged in this regard, because the custom of partible inheritance inhibited the acquisition of large holdings.[78] Their contention cannot be tested here but, at best, no more than one active citizen in ten, in France as a whole, seems to have paid the silver mark and thus qualified to serve as a national deputy.

[74] *AP* IX, p. 599, 29 Oct. 1789 and Gueniffey, *Le nombre et la raison*, pp. 100–1.
[75] AD Côte-d'Or L232, Procès-verbaux des assemblées primaires de Dijon, June 1791.
[76] J. Sentou, 'Impôts et citoyens actifs à Toulouse au début de la Révolution', *Ann. Midi*, 60 (1948), pp. 177–8.
[77] AD Bouches-du-Rhône L567, District d'Aix-en-Provence, listes de citoyens actifs, 1790; AD Marne 1L286, Listes de citoyens actifs; AD Finistère 10L 76, Citoyens éligibles, 1790–91; and Gueniffey, *Le nombre et la raison*, p. 100.
[78] *AP* IX, p. 599, 29 Oct. 1789.

In the light of this calculation, the focus of opposition upon the *marc d'argent*, rather than other aspects of the limited franchise, becomes quite comprehensible. Mounting protests eventually bore fruit and the silver mark was removed from the published text of the 1791 Constitution. When this document was finalised Thouret, still acting as *porte-parole* for the *Comité de Constitution*, proposed instead that every active citizen should be eligible for election as a deputy.[79] Some historians have regarded this as a victory for democracy, yet it came in August 1791 when radicals had been forced on to the defensive. The split at the Jacobin club and the general backlash against anti-monarchical opinion, which followed the king's flight to Varennes and subsequent republican demonstrations in Paris, allowed conservatives to dominate the business of constitutional revision.[80] Many radical deputies resisted Thouret's amendment because, in return for abolishing the *marc d'argent*, he wished to raise the requirement for second-degree electors. Opponents found themselves in the uncomfortable position of defending the *status quo*, though Robespierre robustly seized the opportunity to denounce the entire principle of franchise restrictions.[81]

Finding an alternative to the ten days' wages in taxation, which had recently been employed for the second time, to create new electoral colleges in June 1791, proved to be an extremely divisive issue. It reopened all the old wounds over the criteria for eligibility and provoked another prolonged debate over the merits and demerits of a property qualification at this level. Thouret proposed forty days' wages instead, but he was obliged to offer a graduated tariff after complaints that he was penalising rural areas. On 27 August the matter was finally settled in favour of property rather than taxation, with the adoption of a complex system which varied according to different types of community:

> No one can be chosen as an elector unless, in addition to the qualifications for an active citizen, he fulfils the following requirements: in towns with a population of over 6,000 persons, to own property with a rental value worth 200 days' local wages, or to rent a dwelling with a value equivalent to 150 days; in towns with a population of less than 6,000 inhabitants, to be the owner of property with a rental value estimated at 150 days' local wages, or to rent a dwelling to the value of 100 days; and in the countryside, to own property to the tune of 150 days' local wages in rental value, or to be a tenant or sharecropper of land estimated to be worth 400 days' wages in rent . . .[82]

---

[79] *Ibid.*, XXIX, p. 210, 5 Aug. 1791.
[80] E. Thompson, *Popular Sovereignty and the French Constituent Assembly, 1789–1791* (Manchester, 1952), p. 52, is in error in this regard.
[81] *AP* XXIX, pp. 356–90, 11–12 Aug. 1791.   [82] *Ibid.*, XXIX, p. 748, 27 Aug. 1791.

Thouret, for the committee, reckoned that roughly one-sixth of these values should be paid in taxation (though others put it rather higher, at a quarter).[83] So, in fiscal terms, eligibility for the electoral colleges was now effectively raised from ten, to between at least twenty-five and sixty-six days' work in tax, depending upon size of community and the type of property involved.

This revised machinery was not intended to come into operation until March 1793, when regular legislative elections were due to be held under the new Constitution. In the event, the republican revolution of 10 August 1792 intervened, the Constitution of 1791 was scrapped and a National Convention was elected on a more democratic franchise instead. The only elections to the Legislative Assembly were thus conducted on the old basis, which included the *marc d'argent*. Yet the untried alterations of August 1791 were resurrected during the Thermidorean reaction and incorporated into the Constitution of 1795. Just one minor amendment was made: the requirement for tenants and sharecroppers was reduced to holdings which produced 200, rather than 400 days' wages in revenue. It is, therefore, possible to gauge the effects of the revision of 1791 by examining the situation when the Directory was inaugurated four years later.

The system was extremely complicated and statistics are far from plentiful, so generalisation is a risky business. In the Meuse, in 1797 (the revolutionary Year V), some 18 per cent of (active) citizens were liable to serve as members of the departmental electoral college.[84] In the *chef-lieu* of Bar (le Duc) the figure was 23 per cent, while in adjacent rural areas the proportions were generally lower, descending to a mere 7 per cent at Chardogne. Gueniffey reckons that just over 10 per cent of voters were eligible in the canton of La Maule and at most 15 per cent at Les Essarts (both in the Seine-et-Oise).[85] Meanwhile, in the Midi, *communes* from the hinterland of Toulouse put the incidence of eligibility at almost 12 per cent.[86] Comparable percentages for 1791 would be slightly higher, because after 1795 the number of ordinary voters was raised by giving the vote to all men aged over twenty-one and the award of the franchise to all taxpayers. Yet less than half of those eligible in 1790 would have remained so under the revised arrangements of 1791. No wonder radicals had felt so cheated; in practice the more narrowly recruited departmental colleges were unlikely to choose citizens of modest means as national deputies, even though in theory they were now free to do so. As

[83] Gueniffey, *Le nombre et la raison*, pp. 101–2.
[84] AD Meuse L347–8, Listes de citoyens, an V (1797).
[85] Gueniffey, *Le nombre et la raison*, pp. 101–5.
[86] AD Haute-Garonne L237, Listes de citoyens, canton de Toulouse, an V (1797).

Pétion and Grégoire feared, the *marc d'argent* had effectively been translated into a requirement for eligibility at a lower level of the electoral process.

Qualifications for the franchise were frequently and extensively debated in the Legislature during the Revolution. They provoked a good deal of debate at the time and they have elicited a huge amount of comment ever since. Yet relatively little attention, contemporary or historical, has been given to the mechanics of voter-registration. The lists of active citizens which local authorities compiled from the tax rolls only represented a register of *potential* voters (*ayant droit de voter*), because there were other requirements which had to be fulfilled by these individuals themselves, before they could be admitted to the electoral assemblies. These additional obligations included the up-to-date payment of tax (according to the 1791 Constitution it was necessary to 'produce a receipt'), membership of the National Guard (which one Parisian section suggested was tantamount to a 'tax' because of the expenses involved) and an oath of allegiance (*le serment civique*) to accompany registration. In other words, the right to vote constituted a test of loyalty to the régime, designed to help it function by ensuring that *citoyens actifs* really were active in a variety of ways.

There are regrettably few indications of the extent to which these demanding conditions were applied in practice. Given the veritable flood of decrees and regulations issuing from the Assembly, it is unlikely that the local authorities had either the means or the inclination to enforce every single detail of this complicated legislation. The ambitious, but youthful Saint-Just, for example, was able to vote in 1790 and 1791 thanks to the complaisance of the municipal clerk who registered him as a tax-payer and ignored his real age (twenty-three rather than the requisite twenty-five years).[87] In the Pas-de-Calais one list of voters concluded with the customary comment 'all of them heads of household', another excluded sons over twenty-five years old 'whose father was still alive' and yet another included several widows. In the first municipal elections held at Gouy-sous-Belloune, in the same department, the proceedings (*procès-verbal*) record that 'all non-active citizens were anxious to attend and cast their votes with the other inhabitants and there was no way of stopping them'![88]

It was left to the electoral assemblies themselves to verify the credentials of those who attended. In some cases, as at Brunoy in the Seine-et-

---

[87] N. Hampson, *Saint-Just* (Oxford, 1991), p. 24. Elected to the departmental college of the Aisne, in 1791, Saint-Just was refused admission.
[88] Jessenne, 'De la citoyenneté', pp. 820–1.

Oise, voters' names were read out loud to facilitate objections.[89] Non-payment of tax was rarely used as a reason to exclude would-be voters from assemblies in the Loire-Inférieure: Le Gall's painstaking study reveals that elections continued to be held in *communes* where fiscal returns were hopelessly in arrears. In 1790 there were, conversely, numerous examples of demands that wealthier voters present proof of payment of the *contribution patriotique* (a surtax levied on incomes in excess of 400 livres *per annum*), though whether or not this was a correct interpretation of the law was debatable.[90] Nobles who had not paid direct taxation prior to 1790, like the similarly exempt clergy, were placed in a difficult position. At Dijon they were denied the vote in 1790 as a consequence, but wrote to the local administration asking to make a voluntary contribution so as to be enfranchised.[91] The outcome of such disputes depended as much on the balance of sympathy within the assembly, as myriad complaints to the *Comité de Constitution* demonstrate.

The requirement to serve in the National Guard was easier to impose and it certainly seems to have been enforced at Toulon. Early in 1791 citizens were reminded that, 'according to the law of 12 June 1790 . . . those who wish to remain in possession of their voting rights . . . *must* enter their names . . . on a register which has been opened for those who are liable to serve in the National Guard'.[92] Almost 5,000 Toulonnais did so; any discrepancy between this figure and a total of 5,500 *citoyens actifs* is due to the exemption of men in military service in this naval town. At Paris in 1791, however, primary elections in one section were annulled because several voters were not members of the National Guard.[93] Control of admission to the assemblies was equally lax in rural areas of the Loire-Inférieure, where the election of one village mayor was invalidated because the individual in question had registered himself in the Guard after, rather than before polling![94]

In departments like the Indre-et-Loire a blind eye was often turned towards dubious claims of eligibility for office.[95] This may have been a pragmatic response to the absence of sufficient, properly qualified contenders for posts. Certainly at Sainte-Foi, a village of the Revel district in the Haute-Garonne, ineligible citizens were elected to the municipal

[89] Gueniffey, La Révolution française et les élections, p. 200.
[90] AD Meuse L353, Procès-verbal du canton de Beurey, May 1790, for example.
[91] AN DIV 24, Adresse au Comité de Constitution, 18 Apr. 1790.
[92] AM Toulon L78, Convocation de l'assemblée générale, 5 Feb. 1791 and *ibid*. L392, Inscription pour le service de la garde nationale, 1791.
[93] DIV 49, Section des Enfants-Rouges, 19 June 1791.
[94] Le Gall, Les consultations générales, I, p. 197.
[95] Gueniffey, La Révolution française et les élections, pp. 99–100.

Limits of citizenship 51

council in March 1790, *faute de mieux*.⁹⁶ Le Gall has also shown that *éligibles* were elected to the departmental college of the Loire-Inférieure, despite their palpable failure to fulfil the additional requirement of registration for jury service.⁹⁷ In the Gard, by contrast, a clear warning was issued in November 1791 that all who failed to become jurymen would lose their eligibility rights as a consequence.⁹⁸

Many individuals who were either unable, or unwilling to meet these demanding obligations for the franchise and office-holding simply never bothered to register themselves as voters. In any modern psephological study they would simply cease to count, but in revolutionary France they appear as abstentionists because, generally speaking, only lists of potential voters are available to calculate degrees of participation. This huge drawback has rarely been recognised by historians, yet it has tremendous implications for any analysis of turnout during this period. The percentage of participants will always be reduced by comparing it with an inflated number of putative, as opposed to registered voters.

Some statistical, rather than anecdotal evidence for the phenomenon of under-registration is to be found at Paris. All-told almost 80,000 Parisians were liable for the franchise on the basis of age, residence and taxation. Yet, in the right-bank section (successors to the districts of 1789) of Fontaine-Montmorency a list, probably drawn up in 1790, published the names of only 534 individuals who had actually registered with the administration, out of over 1,000 who were entitled to do so.⁹⁹ It should be noted that 426 of the inscriptions had been made by wealthier citizens, who were eligible for office as well as for the vote; roughly a half of these *éligibles* had enrolled, as opposed to less than a third of those who were merely *citoyens actifs*. The same phenomenon was repeated in the left-bank section of Luxembourg, where an enquiry was conducted into poor turnout for the municipal elections of 1791.¹⁰⁰ This revealed that only 701 voters had actually registered out of a possible total of 1,611 and, again, a preponderance of those enrolled were *éligibles*.

Information from other sections suggests that the general situation might be even worse, with registration as low as 26 per cent of the full contingent in some areas of the city.¹⁰¹ As one disenchanted, would-be voter explained:

---

⁹⁶ AD Haute-Garonne L258, Procès-verbal d'élection, Sainte-Foi, 30 Mar. 1790.
⁹⁷ Le Gall, Les consultations générales, I, p. 216.
⁹⁸ AN F¹cIII Gard 1, Arrêté du directoire du département, 24 Nov. 1791.
⁹⁹ BL F61* (25), Liste des citoyens actifs de la section de Fontaine-Montmorency, no date.
¹⁰⁰ BN Lb⁴⁰ 1932, Procès-verbal de l'assemblée générale de la section du Luxembourg, 21 Nov. 1791 and *ibid.* Lb⁴⁰ 1938, Liste de citoyens, no date.
¹⁰¹ Gueniffey, *Le nombre et la raison*, p. 83.

I had every intention of registering as an active and eligible citizen, yet the law bestowed the right with one hand and then took it away with the other ... because in order to comply with the law I would have consumed a whole day presenting my credentials at the section ... another day enrolling in the National Guard, another to go to the municipal secretariat in order to take the oath of allegiance, and a final day at the tax office to obtain a certificate of payment.[102]

It is perhaps more surprising that anybody bothered to take such pains, rather than that so many failed to do so.

There was a final feature affecting the operation of the franchise which has also received far too little attention, from contemporaries and historians alike: namely the custom of voting in assemblies. The *Comité de Constitution* has not left behind any detailed minutes of its deliberations, but it seems safe to assume that it more or less unhesitatingly adopted the system employed for elections to the Estates General, which rested upon age-old practice with ecclesiastical as well as municipal origins.[103] The committee introduced only two real innovations: the election of presiding officials, who had been nominated or appointed themselves in the past; and the double list, which involved nominating twice as many individuals as there were administrative posts to fill.

Both these measures rendered the process of voting still more time-consuming, but there was a general consensus among members of the National Assembly that 'corruption and illiteracy' could only be combatted by traditional arrangements of this sort. No fundamental objections were raised by deputies, merely points of detail. One commentator thought the system would prove 'longwinded', though he was only criticising the principle of individual election and absolute majorities, proposing lists and relative majorities instead[104] Brissot subsequently took issue with the double list system when he wrote in 1790: 'The recent elections in Paris prove conclusively just how disastrous this method of voting is. The long lists of names prolongs the counting of votes, makes martyrs of the tellers and completely fails in its object of deterring cabals.'[105] A year later, following a disappointing turnout in the primary elections of 1791, Buzot blamed the protracted nature of the business, but once again it was voting methods he had in mind rather than the system of electoral assemblies itself.[106]

The spectacle of the hustings in Britain merely served to confirm the

---

[102] Cited in *ibid.*, p. 82.
[103] L. Moulin, 'Les origines religieuses des techniques électorales et délibératives modernes', *Revue internationale d' histoire politique et constitutionnelle*, Nouvelle série, 3–4 (1953–54), pp. 106–48.   [104] *AP* X, p.254, 25 Nov. 1789.
[105] E. Charavay, ed., *Assemblée électorale de Paris*, 3 vols.(Paris, 1890–1905), I, p. xi.
[106] *AP* XXIX, p. 364, 11 Aug. 1791.

French in their persistent refusal to consider an alternative; the casting of an individual ballot at the voter's convenience was scarcely suggested during the ensuing decade and only introduced briefly under Napoleon.[107] Yet the complicated, collective arrangements for exercising the franchise imposed a burden, rather than conferring a right upon the many Frenchmen who received the vote in 1790. Of course, these were heady days of idealism, when *homo suffragans* appeared as more than an abstract entity, when it was possible to believe in 'the strong enthusiasm for freedom and the noble pride associated with the title and rank of French citizenship'.[108] As Démeunier, a member of the *Comité de Constitution*, optimistically put it, even when peasants are pressed by the demands of the season they will still vote: 'they realise what they owe to the Revolution; they will not regret a few moments of inconvenience ... I have no hesitation in assuring you that they will participate with pleasure!'[109]

Turnout had been high in the elections to the Estates General of 1789, so surely it would be higher still under the new regime, now that subjects had become full-blown citizens. What is astonishing is not the misplaced zeal that marked these initial debates on the franchise question, but rather the fact that intelligent deputies such as Démeunier should retain their confidence and persevere with their original scheme even when its shortcomings were becoming painfully apparent. For in 1791, after a generally encouraging display of electoral enthusiasm in 1790, there was ample opportunity to study the system at work and to ponder the declining interest that the vast electorate was beginning to evince.

[107] Gueniffey, 'Revolutionary Democracy', pp. 100–1, for a rare proposal in this regard, published in 1795.   [108] *Moniteur*, I, p. 322, 29–30 Oct. 1789.
[109] *AP* XXVI, p. 501, 27 May 1791.

3 Biting on the ballot: From enthusiasm to abstention, 1790–1791

The first and last legislative elections to be held under the Constitutional Monarchy, during the summer of 1791, produced a poor turnout; thereafter abstention became endemic. It is tempting to blame the electoral system for this disappointing trend. Yet the local elections of 1790 had often attracted a majority of the electorate, especially in rural areas. In 1791, by contrast, the context of disaffection and discontent in which citizens were asked to vote clearly began to take a toll on the level of attendance. Frustrated in their expectations of change and dismayed by the emergence of religious divisions, voters began to desert the polls *en masse*. Abstention was a product of more than just ignorance or indifference but, before any serious attempt is made to explain why turnout plummeted after 1790, an effort must be made to determine more precisely the degree of participation.

This is far easier said than done, for the historical psephology of the revolutionary period cannot pretend to be an exact science in the same way as contemporary electoral studies. In one respect there are too few statistics: with the exception of the two constitutional referenda (or plebiscites) of 1793 and 1795, no endeavour was made to collect returns at the national level.[1] This is indicative of governmental indifference and ineptitude where the electoral process was concerned, but above all it reflects the practice of indirect elections in which the primary stage was considered a purely local matter. Yet the conservation of relevant *procès-verbaux* in municipal and departmental archives leaves a great deal to be desired. Though fuller documentation is usually available for larger towns, few rural communes have preserved a set of records for the whole decade.[2] Second-degree electors, who attended the departmental elec-

---

[1] AN F¹cIII, Esprit public, a departmental series, contains a good deal of relevant material, but it mostly relates to electoral disputes referred for adjudication and rarely contains any voting statistics.

[2] Towns with their own municipal archives are generally well-served. This is not often the case for smaller communities, which have deposited their records at the *archives départementales*.

toral college, were required to submit copies of the proceedings as their *bona fides*. Even so, few departments possess *procès-verbaux* for all cantons, for every single year.[3]

In any case, the quality of these records is extremely variable, ranging from minutely detailed documents to glib accounts which give little numerical or descriptive information. As subsequent protests show, the *procès-verbaux* often passed over a good deal in silence, though partisan complaints are hardly more reliable. Figures must sometimes be taken with a pinch of salt: at Villedieu in the Loir-et-Cher, in the Year VI (1798) for example, a breakaway assembly (*assemblée scissionnaire*) was held which, according to opponents 'in order to lend greater credibility to its operations did not fail to raise the number of participants to double the real total'.[4] Finally, in the absence of up-to-date or accurate voter-registers (a problem discussed in the preceding chapter), it is not possible to calculate turnout with complete confidence. Indeed, the electoral assemblies were able to admit or deny access to any person provided those present agreed, regardless of existing lists. The basis for the calculations that follow is the *ayant droit de voter* (*ADV*); those who paid the requisite amount of tax, rather than those who had actually registered to vote.

Much has been lost and remains uncertain, yet, in another sense, there are simply too many statistics. The system of electoral assemblies that was retained from the past involved a series of votes, which often took place over more than one day. Inevitably attendance fluctuated, from the initial election of president, secretary and scrutineers (with the oldest citizens present serving as provisional officials at the outset), to the actual election of local personnel or delegates to the departmental assembly.[5] In the case of municipal elections each category of posts, from mayor to councillor, was separately contested and, like second-degree electors, involved three ballots unless an absolute majority was achieved in the first or second round. Contests in the big cities could last for weeks rather than days and, in the process, an extensive series of voting figures would be recorded.

The comings and goings which marked the assemblies are nicely described by one disenchanted Parisian participant: 'Constant movement in and out of the hall, lots of groups of people engaged in conversation . . .

---

[3] AD Basses-Alpes (Alpes de Haute-Provence) possesses a complete set of *procès-verbaux* while, at the other extreme, AD Saône-et-Loire contains virtually nothing.
[4] AD Loir-et-Cher L247, Procès-verbal d'élection, Villedieu, germinal V (Mar. 1798).
[5] Lettres patentes . . . pour la constitution des municipalités, 14 Dec. 1789 and Lettres patentes . . . pour la constitution des assemblées primaires . . ., 22 Dec. 1789, provide a basic guide to electoral procedure, supplemented by specimen *procès-verbaux* and more detailed instructions.

and the resulting hubbub, all rendered the roll-call (to go to the teller's table and vote, individually and in writing) exceedingly difficult . . .'[6] Although it was frequently the first session that was best attended and voters deserted the polls the longer the proceedings went on, this was not always the case. An especially hard-fought contest for the final place as a second-degree elector, for example, could attract unprecedented numbers to the third ballot at the very end; those who had abandoned the polls earlier might be persuaded to return, while there was nothing to prevent a first appearance from absentees.

This unusual pattern of participation was recorded in 1791 in the section, or ward of Saint-Jean at Toulon, where a remarkably detailed set of *procès-verbaux* has survived. The primary election began at 8.00 am on 24 June, in the presence of 150 voters, just 21.5 per cent of those entitled to attend.[7] Only the preliminaries of creating a *bureau* of officials had been completed, when the 129 participants who remained present decided to adjourn the assembly at 9.30 pm. It was the following evening before 153 individuals cast a vote in the first round of balloting for the seven electors (one per hundred registered voters), who were to go forward to the departmental electoral college of the Var. Only two men received an absolute majority and were declared elected; the other five positions remained to be resolved. The next day, Sunday 26 June, 122 voters reconvened and a second ballot took place in the afternoon but only one further individual achieved an absolute majority. The four outstanding places were filled at the third and final ballot on 27 June, with the highest turnout of the session: 181 voters, or 25.9 per cent of those eligible to vote.

In the exceptional case of Toulon it is possible to identify the total of persons who made at least one documented appearance at any of these protracted proceedings. There were 192 different voters in all (27.5 per cent of the register) and 105 of them represented a hard-core who faithfully attended each day. Such precise calculations are rarely feasible elsewhere, so there is no alternative but to choose a particular figure in order to assess the turnout. Specialists like Gueniffey, Fournier, Le Gall and Edelstein, have all opted to retain the largest recorded vote at any point in the polling. I have selected the first round of voting for the personnel to be returned by the assembly instead. In other words, my calculations for turnout relate to a fixed point: the initial votes cast for electors or justices of the peace, in the case of primary polls in the cantons, and mayors or councillors in municipal contests.

---

[6] Cited in Genty, *Paris 1789–1795. L'apprentissage de la citoyenneté* (Paris, 1987), p. 137.
[7] AD Var 1L218, Procès-verbaux d'élection, June 1791.

There is certainly room for disagreement as to what constituted the decisive vote in the assembly system. On the basis of soundings he has taken in the Haute-Garonne, Hérault and Aude, Fournier has demonstrated that most electoral conflicts arose from the creation of the *bureau*.[8] Later in the Revolution, when schisms and rival assemblies became commonplace, separation did usually occur after president, secretary and scrutineers had been elected; it then became clear where the majority lay and seemed to condemn the minority to defeat later. This would suggest that the early votes were the most important ones yet, as the revolutionary decade progressed, those cast for electors and municipal officers were often the only ones to be recorded in increasingly perfunctory *procès-verbaux*.

In these circumstances it is preferable to retain particular votes for comparative purposes, rather than larger, but variable ones. The figures cited in this study are therefore lower than those given by other historians, though the difference after 1790 is usually insignificant.[9] In any case, given the statistical uncertainties surrounding this exercise, it is order of grandeur from one year, or from one place to another that really counts. The golden rule, when employing any electoral data emanating from the Revolution, is to frankly acknowledge their shortcomings and to specify exactly the votes to which they refer.

Once the peculiar, or rather archaic nature of the electoral mechanism has been grasped, statistics can be presented with a little more confidence. Primary assemblies for the first legislative elections of the Revolution took place in 1791, when the proceedings began in the cantons between 12 and 25 June. Sunday was well-established as the usual day to begin polling – another *ancien-régime* tradition – and most departments opted for Sunday 19 June. Table 2, compiled from *procès-verbaux* available in seventeen of the departments that I have studied, does not include figures cited in other secondary sources because of the different, or incomplete bases from which they have been derived. Having said that, a set of twenty departments mustered by Edelstein suggests an average turnout of just under 23 per cent, compared to just over 20 per cent in table 2, a negligible difference.[10]

In June 1791 it would appear that turnout was in the region of 20 per

---

[8] G. Fournier, 'Les incidents électoraux dans la Haute-Garonne, l'Aude, l'Hérault, pendant la Révolution', in *Les pratiques politiques*, p. 64.
[9] G. Fournier, 'La participation électorale en Haute-Garonne pendant la Révolution', *Ann. Midi*, 101 (1989), pp 47–9.
[10] Edelstein has generously shared his unpublished research with me, in this as in other areas.

Table 2 *Turnout in primary elections, June 1791*

Department	Total of *ADV* in sample	Percentage of *ADV* in dept.	Voters at first round for electors	Percentage turnout
Meuse	4473	8.9	1824	40.8
Charente	5651	9.9	2184	38.6
Côte-d'Or	11631	19.5	3373	31.3
Marne	46169	85.0	14346	31.1
Finistère	25750	48.2	6757	26.2
Orne	10313	17.4	2307	22.4
Allier	4289	10.7	904	21.1
Haute-Garonne	23179	28.2	4839	20.9
Var	23095	42.4	4705	20.4
Aveyron	20260	36.4	3975	19.6
Landes	6605	16.5	1268	19.2
Morbihan	41696	95.2	6194	14.9
Aude	18960	48.4	2723	14.4
Basses-Alpes	12011	38.4	1456	12.2
Seine	449929	51.6	5984	12.0
Pyrénées-Orientales	5807	25.8	648	11.3
Bouches-du-Rhône	4828	6.7	426	8.8
Total	314646	7.3*	63913	20.3

Note: * Percentage of 'national' register, 1791
Sources: AD Meuse L355; AD Charente L532/1679; AD Côte-d'Or L232–3; AD Marne 1L297–304 ; AD Finistère 10L81–94; AD Orne L364–8; AD Allier L133; AD Haute-Garonne L240; AD Var 1L218 and AD Alpes-Maritimes L547; AD Aveyron 1L590–6; AD Landes 11L1; AD Morbihan L236; AD Aude L365/370; AD Basses-Alpes L199–203; AN BI 8–9; AD Pyrénées-Orientales L430; and AD Bouches-du-Rhône L569

cent. In other words, some four-fifths of the huge (potential) electorate abstained from the first round of voting for departmental electors. Overall, it is unlikely that more than one active citizen in four participated in any of the proceedings, which were often completed in a single day but sometimes lasted a little longer. In most areas, therefore, the elections were completed before news of the king's flight to Varennes, on 21 June, could exert any influence over the outcome, though the departmental assemblies were postponed as a consequence.

Considerable variation is evident from one department to another. Indeed, great disparities are apparent within departments too and this renders sampling a risky business. For instance, drawing upon a solid monograph for the District of Pontivy, in the Morbihan, Gueniffey has suggested a turnout of 29.8 per cent for the department as a whole.[11] However, exploitation of an exceptionally full set of printed electoral returns, covering almost every canton, reveals a level of participation that was, on average, half that recorded in the relatively high-polling District of Pontivy.

Sampling from a variety of locations throughout a department (often an involuntary choice given the poor conservation of *procès-verbaux*) is perhaps a safeguard against these local distortions. In those departments where only a handful of *procès-verbaux* have survived it is best to ignore them completely, for there were often huge differences in turnout from one neighbouring canton to another. The average for the Marne in 1791 was 31.1 per cent, but the canton of Saint-Thierry scored 79.7 while that of Avize recorded just 15.3.[12] There was also great diversity within cantons, as villages brought together in the same assembly demonstrated very different degrees of enthusiasm: in the Loire-Inférieure, one commune in the canton of Aigrefeuille – not the *chef-lieu* where the assembly was held – managed a turnout of almost 23 per cent, while another recorded less than 2 per cent.[13] There were even significant discrepancies between different sections of the same town: at Toulon, in 1791, turnout ranged from 26 to 47 per cent.[14]

At this level it is impossible to discern the particular reasons behind such variable responses. Yet, inevitable exceptions notwithstanding, a regional pattern did emerge in 1791. Despite a high poll in the Charente and a low one in the Pas-de-Calais, bigger turnouts tended to occur along a northerly and easterly axis. Before any explanations for these trends are offered, however, it is essential to see if they were repeated on other occasions. Such a comparative approach can help offset shortcomings in the statistics, besides revealing the shift in participation from one year, and from one type of election to another.

All commentators agree that turnout for these 'legislative' elections of 1791 was lower than a year earlier, when 'administrative' elections were held to establish councils for newly created districts and departments. Table 3 demonstrates that, in 1790, 39.8 per cent of the electorate in

---

[11] E. Corgne, *Pontivy et son district pendant la Révolution, 1789–germinal an V* (Rennes, 1938), pp. 217 ff., utilisé in Gueniffey, La Révolution française et les élections, p. 220.

[12] AD Marne 1L298, Procès-verbaux d'élection, June 1791.

[13] Le Gall, Les consultations générales, II, pp. 902–3. AD Landes 11L2, Tableau général du résultat des assemblées primaires, 10 Sept. 1790 (a copy of which is also to be found in AN F¹cIII Landes 1), contains a comprehensive set of figures on levels of participation within cantons, though for 1790. In the canton of Parentis one commune, again not the *chef-lieu*, achieved a turnout of 71 per cent, another only 19 per cent. M. Edelstein has conducted an extensive analysis of this remarkable document, which he has passed on to me. [14] AD Var 1L218, Procès-verbaux d'élection, June 1791.

Table 3 *Turnout in primary elections, 1790*

Department	Total of ADV in sample	Percentage of ADV in dept. in sample	Voters at first round for electors	Percentage turnout
Marne	46041	84.8	29442	63.9
Côte-d'Or	9907	17.9	6045	61.0
Meuse	10421	20.7	6044	58.0
Allier	2806	7.0	1612	57.4
Charente	12314	21.5	6831	55.5
Aveyron	22598	40.6	11512	50.9
Aude	19500	48.8	8780	45.0
Finistère	3014	6.8	1283	42.6
Morbihan	41391	95.4	17278	41.7
Haute-Garonne	19492	25.2	7775	39.9
Pyrénées-Orientales	5817	34.3	2013	34.6
Orne	12162	20.5	3781	31.1
Basses-Alpes	14481	46.3	3895	26.9
Seine	60548	66.5	9588	15.8
Var	15516	29.7	1885	12.1
Total	296008	6.9*	117764	39.8

Note: * Percentage of 'national' register 1791
Sources: AD Marne 1L297–304; AD Côte-d'Or L225–7; AD Meuse L353; AD Allier L132; AD Charente L532/1678; AD Aveyron 1L576–8; AD Aude L356/360; AN F¹cIII Finistère 5; AD Morbihan L233; AD Haute-Garonne L238–9; AD Pyrénées-Orientales L428–9; AD Orne L343–6; AD Basses-Alpes L199–203; AN BI 1–2; AD Var 1L218 and AD Alpes-Maritimes L542

fifteen sample departments voted in the first ballot for electors, twice as many as the primaries a year later. The department of the Landes recorded a turnout of 61 per cent (replete with data for each canton) but, since this has not been corroborated by reference to the original *procès-verbaux*, it has not been included in these results.[15] According to Edelstein's somewhat different calculations for a total of over thirty departments, roughly half those listed as active citizens took part in these polls, an outcome not too far removed from mine.[16]

[15] AD Landes 11L2, Tableau général. The original *procès-verbaux* have not been preserved, but a disputed election in the Mugron canton (AD Landes 11L8) does suggest an accurate compilation.
[16] Once again I am indebted to Edelstein for sharing his unpublished findings with me. Turnout of over 70 per cent was recorded in the Aube, see J. Horn, Elections and Elites: The Development of Local Political Power in Southern Champagne, 1765–1812, PhD Thesis, University of Pennsylvania, 1993, p. 220.

Table 4 *Urban and rural turnout, 1790–1791*

Location	Percentage Turnout in Primary Elections	
	1790	1791
Carcassone (Aude)	28.6	25.4
Rural cantons in *district*	35.7	12.2
Châlons-sur-Marne (Marne)	24.6	16.1
Rural cantons in *district*	66.5	27.5
Dijon (Côte-d'Or)	36.3	21.0
Rural cantons in *département*	72.1	40.4
Paris (Seine)	12.1	11.4
Rural cantons in *département*	26.4	12.1
Toulon (Var)	11.7	30.3
Sample of rural cantons in *département*	18.4	29.1
Vannes (Morbihan)	47.0	24.6
Rural cantons in *district*	40.0	9.6

Sources: AD Aude L356/65; AD Marne 1L297; AD Côte-d'Or L225–7/32–3; AN BI 1/2/8; AD Alpes-Maritimes L542/7 and AD Var 1L218; and AD Morbihan L233/6

Only the Var, among the departments listed on the table, witnessed a lower turnout in 1790 than 1791. The highest levels of participation were again to be found in the north and east though, in 1790 as 1791, there were relatively high turnouts in the Charente and the Finistère. Whether or not these regional variations constituted durable trends will only become apparent later, but at the outset of the Revolution there was no clear-cut correlation between high voter turnout and a greater degree of economic and social development, as measured by communications networks or rates of literacy. The fact that a more backward area like the Aveyron, located in the *massif central*, produced a high level of participation in 1790, suggests that electoral practice under the *ancien régime* should also be taken into account.

Rural areas, which had often retained general assemblies prior to 1789, invariably polled more heavily than towns in 1790. On the other hand, as table 4 reveals, the former generally witnessed a sharp decline in participation in the primary elections of 1791, while the latter fared less badly. Bois, one of the first historians to treat electoral data seriously, noted a dramatic fall in turnout in the Sarthe, from roughly 50 per cent in May 1790, to as low as 10 per cent in June 1791.[17] He suggested that this collapse stemmed from the contrast between 'local' or administrative

---

[17] Bois, *Paysans de l'Ouest*, pp. 262–5.

elections in 1790 and 'national', or legislative ones a year later. According to him the peasants, whose participation declined more than townsmen, were prepared to invest time and effort in the creation of district and departmental councils which would impinge directly upon their existence. When it came to electing deputies to a distant assembly, however, their interest evaporated: 'For ignorant and short-sighted rural inhabitants the wider concerns of the kingdom disappeared in a cloud of mist.'[18]

At first sight Bois' supposition of a parochial rural mentality seems a plausible one. It appears to be buttressed by generally high turnout, especially in the countryside, for municipal elections held earlier in 1790. These were the first elections to take place under the new system and, unlike their counterparts in higher echelons of the recently established administrative structure, municipal personnel were directly elected in the towns and villages. Unfortunately, statistics for the initial, municipal polls, which abound in isolation, are not easily gathered in a more concentrated fashion, particularly where smaller communes of less than 2,000 inhabitants are involved.

A sample of ninety rural communes in the Jura reveals a 100 per cent turnout in half of them, over 90 per cent in three-quarters and nowhere less than 65 per cent.[19] Bricaud claims that only a third of the electorate abstained in the Ille-et-Vilaine, while Audevart's survey of the Haute-Vienne shows smaller villages polling at almost 80 per cent on average.[20] Table 5 suggests a more modest, overall average of roughly 60 per cent, with the Côte-d'Or and Marne scoring heavily, while the Var once more brings up the rear.

Data for larger towns are more readily available in serial form. Voting for mayors in these cities was, as table 6 indicates, rather less enthusiastically embraced than in smaller communities. The tendency of the north and east to poll more heavily is again apparent, though with the salient exception of Paris, which comes out last.

Generally speaking, the bigger the commune, the lower the vote and vice-versa. Audevart's detailed research in the Haute-Vienne shows a consistent decline in the rate of participation as the size of the community increases, as does the District of Epernay in the Marne (see table 7). The

---

[18] *Ibid.*, p. 262.
[19] C. Grandadam and H. Hours, 'Les élections municipales du début de l'année 1790 dans le Jura', *Travaux de la Société d'Emulation du Jura* (1990), p. 215.
[20] J. Bricaud, *L'administration du département d'Ille-et-Vilaine au début de la Révolution, 1790–1791* (Rennes, 1965), p.53 and O. Audevart, 'Les élections en Haute-Vienne pendant la Revolution', in J. Boutier, M. Cassan, P. d'Hollander and B. Pommaret, eds., *Limousin en Révolution* (Treignac, 1989), p. 133.

Table 5 *Municipal elections in the villages, January–February 1790*

Department	Number of communes sampled	Total of ADV	Voters at first round for mayor	Percentage turnout
Côte-d'Or	11	1342	1164	86.7
Marne (Epernay district)	24	2866	1820	63.5
Pas-de-Calais (Arras district)	27	2453	1464	59.7
Ille-et-Villaine (Vitré district)	15	1684	976	58.0
Finistère	5	877	477	44.9
Var	4	799	356	44.9
Total	86	10021	6240	62.3

Sources: AD Côte-d'Or L258–65; AD Marne 1L313; Jessenne, 'De la citoyenneté proclamée', p. 826; Crossouard, *La Révolution dans le District de Vitré*, p. 46; AD Finistère 21L44; and AD Alpes-Maritimes L544

same was true of the District of Arras in the Pas-de-Calais and the pattern was repeated, to some extent at least, in the Haute-Garonne (where villages of less than 1,000 inhabitants polled most heavily, but those over 2,000 outvoted communities of 1–2,000 persons).[21]

This conclusion confirms the impression derived from more scattered data available for preliminary elections to the Estates General of 1789. The greater assiduity of peasants in smaller communes may be attributed to *ancien-régime* traditions of meetings of all heads of family: in the District of Arras some proceedings in 1790 still referred to assemblies of inhabitants and parish, even in one case 'meeting according to the usual practice'.[22] In towns, by contrast, the old gatherings by craft, utilised in 1789, were replaced by sections or neighbourhood assemblies, which represented a novelty. Moreover, in small communities the elections were rapidly conducted, while those in big cities must have seemed endless. Above all, rural communes benefited from greater social solidarity. As Jessenne puts it: 'Belonging to a more restricted community, with a greater sense of integration, engendered a stronger urge to participate in

---

[21] Towns also voted less heavily in the Côte-d'Or, as C. Lamarre has demonstrated in 'Les élections de 1790 et la révolution municipale en Côte-d'Or', in B. Benoit, ed., *Ville et Révolution française* (Lyon, 1994), pp. 188–9.

[22] Jessenne, 'De la citoyenneté', p. 820 and Fournier, 'La participation électorale en Haute-Garonne', p. 51.

Table 6 *Municipal elections in major towns, January–February 1790*

Town	Total of ADV	Voters at first round for mayor	Percentage turnout
Colmar	2042	1653	81.0
Strasbourg	7474	5685	76.1
Dijon	2720	1756	64.6
Bar-le-Duc	1980	992	50.1
Brest	4957	1554	31.3
Carcassonne	1255	370	29.5
Montauban	4780	1226	25.6
Châlons-sur-Marne	1672	414	24.8
Toulouse	5555	1239	22.3
Montpellier	5610	1232	22.0
Aix-en-Provence	3962	858	21.7
Toulon	5634	1023	18.2
Paris*	77590	14010	18.1
Total	120174	30458	25.3
(minus Paris	42684	16448	38.5)

Note: * The first municipal elections in Paris were held in August 1790
Sources: R. Marx, *Recherches sur la vie politique de l'Alsace prérévolutionnaire et révolutionnaire* (Strasbourg, 1966), pp. 61–2; AM Strasbourg, Délibérations du Conseil municipal vol. I; AD Côte-d'Or L258; C. Aimond, *Histoire de Bar-le-Duc*, new ed. (Bar-le-Duc, 1982), p. 287; P. Levot, *Histoire de la ville et du port de Brest*, 4 vols. (Brest, 1864–70), III, p. 215; AD Aude L358; D. Ligou, *Montauban à la fin de l'ancien régime et aux débuts de la Révolution, 1787–1794* (Paris, 1958), p. 219; AD Marne E 5872; AM Toulouse 1 K5; AM Montpellier K1/4; C. Derobert-Ratel, *Institutions et vie municipale à Aix-en-Provence sous la Révolution, 1789–an VIII* (Millau, 1981), p.104; AM Toulon L572; and Genty, *Paris 1789–1795*, pp. 74–5

collective activities while, conversely, the slackening of social ties in a larger community tended to produce a higher level of electoral abstention.'[23]

In fact, like most villages, nearly all large towns polled more heavily in their first municipal elections than in either the primary elections of summer 1790, or those of June 1791. Bois' thesis that local elections, especially in the countryside, excited greater interest thus appears to hold true, not just of the department he studied, but for France as a whole. Yet on closer inspection the contrast crumbles, not least because the distinction Bois made between local, 'administrative' elections in 1790 and

[23] Jessenne, 'De la citoyenneté', p. 825.

Table 7 *Voting by size of community, February 1790*

Haute-Vienne	Average Turnout
0–500 Inhabitants	77.8
500–1000	67.4
1000–1500	57.2
1500–2500	51.0
2500+	35.9

Epernay District, Marne	
0–50 Registered Voters	94.0
5–100	70.8
100–200	61.2
200–500	57.6
500+	31.6

Sources: Audevart, 'Les élections en Haute-Vienne', p. 133; and AD Marne 1L313

national, 'legislative' elections a year later is overdrawn. In 1791, primary elections renewed departmental electoral colleges which were given the task of replacing district and departmental personnel, as well as sending deputies to Paris. The elections of June 1791 thus had a local dimension which Bois failed to acknowledge.

Bois also ignored a general decline in turnout of all types of elections after the early summer of 1790, a decrease which badly affected local as well as so-called 'national' polls. In November 1790 a partial renewal of municipal councils was effected, in all towns and villages. Despite the fragmentary nature of the available data it is evident that turnout was falling fast. Indeed, as table 8 indicates, in many cases the comparison with January-February 1790 reveals a decline of more than 50 per cent. In the countryside the downward slide usually continued when the next annual renewal of municipal personnel occurred. By contrast, in several towns participation began to rise in November 1791 and, in the case of Toulon, this particular mayoral election attracted a higher turnout than February 1790. A possible explanation for this revival of interest among urban voters, at variance with their rural counterparts, resides in the increasing politicisation of the urban electorate.

The factors encouraging citizens to vote, to use 'their most precious rights of citizenship', will be explored in the next chapter. Before the

Table 8 *Municipal elections, 1790–1791*

Location	Creation Jan./Feb. 1970 percentage of ADV at first round for mayor	Renewal Nov. 1790 percentage of ADV at first round for councillors	Renewal Nov. 1791 percentage of ADV at first round for mayor
Haute-Vienne:			
0–500 inhabitants	77.8	77.7	59.2
500–1,000	67.4	41.0	49.2
1,00–1,500	57.2	39.9	26.4
1,500–2,500	51.0	35.8	35.8
Vitré district (Ille-et-Vilaine): villages	85.1	55.1	39.7
Côte-d'Or: villages	82.8	55.1	44.9
Grasse district (Var)			
0–2,000 inhabitants	–	18.4	20.2
2,000 +	–	5.1	5.3
Strasbourg	76.1	25.2	66.8
Dijon	64.6	42.1	27.8
Bar-le-Duc	50.1	18.4	15.5
Brest	31.3	19.0	36.9
Châlons-sur-Marne	22.4	9.1	9.3
Toulouse	22.3	12.1	7.1
Montpellier	22.0	10.6	20.9
Aix-en-Provence	20.9	8.0	12.3
Toulon	18.2	5.4	25.2
Paris	18.2 (Oct. 1790)	–	13.7

Sources: Audevart, 'Les élections en Haute-Vienne', p. 133; Crossouard, *La Révolution dans le District de Vitré*, pp. 56–7; E. Fortunet, M. Fossier, N. Kozlowski and S. Vienne, *Pouvoir municipal et communauté rurale à l'époque révolutionnaire en Côte-d'Or, 1789–an IV* (Dijon, 1981), p. 19; AD Alpes-Maritimes L543/4/8; AM Strasbourg, Délibérations, vols. I and II; AD Côte-d'Or L258 and AM Dijon 1D1/2; Aimond, *Histoire de Bar-le-Duc*, pp. 287–304; Levot, *Histoire... de Brest*, III, p. 215 and AM Brest LL311; AD Marne E 5872/3; AM Toulouse 1 K5/8/10; AM Montpellier K1/3 and 4; Derobert-Ratel, *Institutions et vie municipale à Aix-en-Provence*, p. 605; AM Toulon L572/4/9; and Genty, *Paris 1789–1795*, pp. 74–7

reasons for mounting abstention, from 1790 to 1791, are discussed here, one final series of elections deserves a mention: the polls which established justices of the peace in the rural and urban cantons of France. This particular institution has received little attention from historians, despite the importance contemporaries attached to it as 'one of the greatest benefits of the Revolution'.[24] Like all judicial personnel, the newly created *juges de paix* were elected and their direct election by the primary assemblies 'enthused the voters to a much greater extent than purely administrative elections', according to one historian of the Aveyron.[25]

This assertion is sometimes borne out by the figures, but not always. At Toulon, the election of two justices of the peace in 1791 provoked a battle royal, which mobilised the town's reluctant voters to an unprecedented degree. Some 38 per cent of citizens took part in the initial contest in June, which was re-staged on two further occasions following allegations of irregularities at the assemblies.[26] In the Haute-Vienne, in November 1791, turnout in these elections was as high as 65 per cent.[27] Elsewhere, however, the level of participation was less impressive: in the Allier turnout in November-December 1790 was only 37 per cent on average, compared to 57 per cent in the May primaries, while in the District of Grasse, in the Var, only 16 per cent of a poll-shy electorate voted in January 1791.[28]

When these justices of the peace and their assistants, the *assesseurs* (whose election attracted less interest than the *juges* themselves), were replaced a couple of years later, a sharp decline in turnout was apparent.[29] As a rule, the initial enthusiasm for taking part in the creation of a new institution – be it municipal, departmental or judicial – was not repeated when these bodies were subjected to renewal. The novelty quickly wore off and turnout was in free fall; by the end of 1790 a majority of the vast French electorate was already abstaining.

There can be no doubt that complex and protracted voting procedures deterred a good many potential voters. The *procès-verbal* of Montautour

---

[24] AD Orne L407, Placard, 9 ventôse VI (27 Feb. 1789) and see J. Godechot, *Les institutions de la France sous la Révolution et l'Empire*, second edn (Paris, 1968), pp. 146–8.
[25] A. Roquette, *J.-J. Roquette, ou la Révolution à Saint-Amans-des-Cots, 1789–1795* (no place, no date), p. 166.
[26] AD Var 1L1848, Procès-verbaux d'élection, 19–21 June 1791 and Crook, *Toulon*, pp. 107–9. [27] Audevart, 'Les élections en Haute-Vienne', p. 135.
[28] AD Allier L146–7, Procès-verbaux d'élection, Nov.-Dec. 1790 and AD Alpes-Maritimes L543–4 and 548, Procès-verbaux d'élection, Jan. 1791.
[29] AD Allier L146–7, Procès-verbaux d'élection, Nov. 1792 and Audevart, 'Les élections en Haute-Vienne', p. 135.

in the Ille-et-Vilaine specifically blamed the progressive desertion of the polls on this factor: 'numerous participants left on account of the lengthy session'.[30] Large numbers often attended the opening of the assemblies only to disappear shortly afterwards. At Saint-Vallier in the Var, in 1791 for example, 249 citizens were listed at the outset, but only ninety-one of them returned after lunch.[31] The delivery of speeches, consideration of petitions and the discussion of individuals' rights to participate could all delay the proceedings and send the election into a second day, with only the preliminaries completed. The prospect of returning to the fray for yet another session was unattractive to all but the most determined participants, especially those from outlying villages. By the time a third ballot took place for delegates to the departmental college, or to choose remaining municipal councillors, only a small rump would usually remain to vote. The 157 citizens who initially assembled in the canton of Chahaignes in the Sarthe, in June 1791, were reduced to a mere thirty by the finish.[32] The gradual erosion is nicely illustrated by the first municipal elections of the Revolution at Toulon, in February 1790. In the section of Saint-Jean, eighty-six citizens voted for a mayor on 10 February, sixty-two for councillors two days afterwards and just twenty-three for deputy-councillors a fortnight later.[33]

It can only be assumed that one or two assemblies in the Loire-Inférieure which held four, or even five rounds of voting in 1791 were misinformed and rather masochistic, since many citizens found the exhaustive ballot extremely enervating.[34] Voters frequently vented their irritation by breaking the rules that governed balloting and stipulated absolute majorities. A favourite ploy was to accept a relative majority on a first or second vote, rather than the requisite third, 'so that work in the fields would not be subject to any further interruption'.[35] An interesting variation on this short-cut occurred at Flavigny in the Côte-d'Or in 1790: the final departmental delegate was one short of an absolute majority on the second round of voting, so he was unanimously awarded an extra vote in order to avoid a further ballot.[36] Such tactics could backfire, if defeated factions complained or the infringement was spotted by a zealous administrator; invalidation of the original contest would lead to a tiresome re-enactment of the whole time-consuming business. According to one

[30] Crossouard, *La Révolution dans le District de Vitré*, p. 53.
[31] AD Alpes-Maritimes L547, Procès-verbal d'élection, June 1791.
[32] Bois, *Paysans de l'Ouest*, p. 262.
[33] AM Toulon L572, Procès-verbal d'élection, Feb. 1790.
[34] Le Gall, Les consultations générales, II, p. 566.
[35] AD Morbihan L233, Procès-verbal d'élection, Noyal, May 1790 and Grandadam and Hours, 'Les élections municipales', p. 213.
[36] AD Côte-d'Or L225, Procès-verbal, Apr.–May 1790.

historian, many *procès-verbaux* were drawn up in an orderly fashion, despite irregularities, precisely to avoid this fate.[37]

In several cases the traditional, verbal endorsement (*acclamation*) was employed instead of the written ballot.[38] Not only was this much quicker, it also avoided the practical difficulties raised by the prescribed method of voting. Illiterate participants had to ask the scrutineers to write down names for them (in their case the ballot was not secret) and there were frequent disputes over whether their exact instructions had been obeyed. Even literate citizens had sometimes forgotten whom they wished to vote for by the time they reached the tellers' table. To overcome this difficulty, in 1790, the assembly at Saint-Affrique, in the Aveyron, permitted the use of pre-written lists, though these were strictly forbidden in the electoral regulations and a frequent reason for annulment.[39]

It was no easy matter to recall a long list of names for councillors in the larger cities. The double-list system employed in 1790 required voters to advance twice as many names as posts to be filled. In Paris, where the sections were naming as many as thirty-nine deputies to the departmental assembly of the Seine, the requirement had startling consequences. In the section of Quatre-Nations, for example, each voter was to list seventy-eight names. This was bad enough but, with some 300 citizens present, the scrutineers had to process over 20,000 nominations, many of them ill-written and sharing the same surname.[40] In 1791 there was uproar at the electoral college of the Seine over the identity of a certain Monneron, who was designated in several different ways; the following year in the Oise two Bourdons, both from Paris, were hopelessly confused.[41]

Even in rural areas counting was a protracted affair. The tellers at Parizot in the Aveyron apologised for taking a whole day over the task, 'as a result of a huge range of names . . . with different persons appearing on each ballot paper'.[42] This adverse comment highlights a further difficulty confronting the revolutionary electorate: the absence of declared candidates. They had no place in French tradition and the example of England was usually cited as a conclusive argument against the introduction of such candidatures. They would, it was alleged, legitimise cabals, encourage the canvassing of votes, and lead to elections being decided by 'the

---

[37] M. Bruneau, *Les débuts de la Révolution dans les départements du Cher et de l'Indre, 1789–1791* (Paris, 1902), p. 140.
[38] AD Haute-Garonne L238, Procès-verbal d'élection, Cazères, July 1790.
[39] AD Aveyron 1L578, Procès-verbal d'élection, June 1790.
[40] AN BI 1, Procès-verbal d'élection, Oct. 1790.
[41] Charavay, ed., *Assemblée électorale*, II, pp. 528–9 and H. Baumont, 'Les assemblées primaires et électorale de l'Oise en 1792 (août-septembre)', *Rf*, 47 (1904), pp. 164–71.
[42] AD Aveyron 1L582, Procès-verbal, June 1790.

distribution of pints of beer'.[43] Since no overt campaigning was allowed, each citizen was in theory free to choose the persons best suited to a particular task. This ban on soliciting support was frequently ignored in practice but, in the absence of closed lists, nominations ran riot. At Toulon, in the first municipal elections of 1790, no less than thirty individuals were proposed as mayor, while 461 names emerged for deputy-councillor, many of them attracting a single vote (presumably the author of the ballot paper nominating himself).[44]

A rather more serious result of the absence of declared candidates was the immediate resignation of those elected. This happened in the initial mayoral elections of January 1790 at Montpellier, where a second contest had to be held to find a replacement after the former intendant declined to accept the honour.[45] Holders of unsolicited posts sometimes came under strong pressure from their electorates to soldier on and thus avoid a further poll. In the village of Aigre in the Charente, in the autumn of 1791, an elected mayor who wished to resign was prevailed upon to remain in post: 'the whole community descended upon his house and, with a single voice implored him to stay, which he duly did to oblige his fellow citizens'.[46] Such was the magnitude of this problem that Démeunier, for the *Comité de Constitution*, suggested that in future a fine should be paid by those who 'ignored their patriotic obligations' and refused to take up elected office.[47]

Far from selecting the best-qualified individual, voters often chose inappropriate persons. The newly elected mayor of Montgazin, in the Haute-Garonne, complained to the *Comité de Constitution* that he had been 'elected very much against his wishes, in view of his poor state of health, his business interests and the recent loss of his wife [in that order!]'. In some cases a choice was evidently made out of spite, a fate which befell one individual who was made a departmental delegate for the canton of Ploëmerl in the Morbihan, in 1790. He was seventy-eight years old and infirm – and he had not even attended the assembly. He subsequently asked to be released from the unwelcome obligation and to be allowed to 'die quietly at home'.[48]

The election of *suppléants*, or substitutes, was required by law for more important posts like national deputy, to cover death or indisposition, but it was a device that was occasionally adopted at local level as a safeguard

---

[43] *AP* XXIX, p. 367, Barnave, 11 Aug. 1791, for example.
[44] AM Toulon L572, Procès-verbaux d'élection, Feb. 1790.
[45] AM Montpellier K1/4, Procès-verbaux d'élection, Jan.–Feb. 1790.
[46] AD Charente L1681, Procès-verbal d'élection, Oct. 1791.
[47] *AP* XI, p. 422, 3 Feb. 1790.
[48] AD Morbihan L233, Procès-verbal d'élection, May 1790.

against immediate resignations. There were literally hundreds of thousands of positions to be filled by means of election and the zeal of France's new rulers for frequent application of the electoral principle also prompted numerous polls. In the early years of the Revolution annual renewals of personnel, not to mention by-elections called on account of resignations and irregularities, only compounded the problem.

All communities experienced at least eight elections between 1790 and 1792 but, in the case of Toulon, there were no less than fourteen contests, six of them in the course of 1791.[49] During that *annus horrendus* the death of the mayor brought an unexpected election in March, quickly followed in April by the election of thirty deputy-councillors, since so many of them had resigned. In June the legislative primaries took place and, hard on their heels, the first polls for justices of the peace which, twice suspended in July and August, were finally settled in December. By then, a renewal of the municipal council had occurred and the first elections had been held for the command of the National Guard. The assemblies met on fifty-one days of the year, not to mention those occasions when the sections had been convened to discuss local issues rather than to elect personnel. The voters could be excused for suffering from polling fatigue, though one or two of these close-fought contests produced some of the highest turnouts of the revolutionary decade at Toulon.

The timing as well as the frequency of elections also had a bearing upon abstention. The primary elections of 1790, which took place between April and August, had generally attracted a high turnout, but there were many complaints about the inconvenience. The assembly at Ruffec, in the Charente, was typical in protesting that 'the current season does not really allow huge numbers of farmers to abandon their pressing agricultural concerns'.[50] The makers of the Constitution subsequently selected the month of March for primary elections and November for municipal polls. These were times when reasonable weather could be expected and agricultural activity was relatively slack. Unfortunately, the first and only legislative elections under their constitution took place in June 1791, as deputies in the Assembly completed their constitutional business. Disgruntled voters at Plouzoch in the Finistère bemoaned 'the abandonment of their domestic tasks', requesting 'recompense and payment' from the government, as a 'reward for their great sacrifice'.[51]

---

[49] M. Crook, 'The People at the Polls: Electoral Behaviour in Revolutionary Toulon, 1789–1799', *French History*, 5 (1991), pp. 172–4.
[50] AD Charente L1678, Procès-verbal d'élection, May 1790.
[51] A. du Châtelier, 'Essai de monographie électorale pour les années 1790–91 et 92', *Bulletin de la Société académique de Brest* (1882), p. 25.

Disaffection rather than apathy and indisposition led many to abstain in 1791. To participate was to endorse the regime, for an oath of allegiance was required before a citizen could cast his vote. This test of loyalty was too demanding for many tender consciences. Examples of voters appearing at the assemblies, only to withdraw rather than swear the oath, are legion. In the canton of Pont-de-Salars in the Aveyron, in June 1791 for instance, fifty-four voters decided to leave when instructed to comply, leaving just thirty-three of their fellow citizens to conduct the primary election.[52] These Aveyronnais dissenters were objecting to the Civil Constitution of the Clergy, a comprehensive reform of the Church which a majority of the department's priests had refused to accept. One local historian claims that these elections were 'completely dominated by the growing religious schism'.[53]

In the west of France the connexion between abstention and religious discontent is also evident. Parish clergy had frequently been elected as presidents or secretaries of the cantonal assemblies in 1790: in the Morbihan, for example, some 40 per cent of presidents and 25 per cent of secretaries were priests.[54] Participation plummeted the following year as non-juring priests absented themselves from the polls and took their flocks with them. In the Morbihan, where several elections were annulled because oaths were taken *on behalf* of the Church, turnout slumped by almost two-thirds. Abstention was especially apparent in the canton of Saint-Avé, where the *procès-verbal* of the previous year had stated, 'the general wish of the canton . . . is that the Roman Catholic religion be decreed (by the National Assembly) the sole religion in France', in response to rumours already circulating that legislators were planning to 'abolish this most holy religion'.[55] At Saint-Avé turnout dropped from 48.2 per cent in 1790 to just 1.4 per cent the following year. The District of Pontivy where participation held up best was, by contrast, an area where most priests accepted the Civil Constitution.[56]

Electoral assemblies usually took place in churches (in the absence of any practical alternative) and began after mass on a Sunday. In 1791, in

---

[52] AD Aveyron 1L591, Procès-verbal d'élection, June 1791. See also Le Gall, Les consultations générales, II, p. 551.
[53] L. Mazars, *La Révolution en Rouergue, District d'Aubin, 1789–1795*, 2 vols. (Villefranche-de-Rouergue, 1976–78), I, p. 101.
[54] R. Dupuy, *De la Révolution à la chouannerie. Paysans en Bretagne, 1788–1794* (Paris, 1988), p. 94. [55] AD Morbihan L233, Procès-verbal d'élection, May 1790.
[56] T. Tackett, *Religion, Revolution and Regional Culture in Eighteenth-Century France. The Ecclesiastical Oath of 1791* (Princeton, 1986), p. 344. A similar pattern has been noted in the neighbouring Côtes-du-Nord by H. Pommeret, *L'esprit public dans le département des Côtes-du-Nord pendant la Révolution, 1789–1799* (Saint-Brieuc, 1921), p. 143.

Biting on the ballot 73

the absence of priestly benediction, many desisted from what had become a profane ritual in sacred space.[57] In the Loire-Inférieure, where such a connexion between abstention and loyalty to the Church is evident, one historian has gone so far as to insist: 'there can be no doubt . . . that abstention from these elections was the consequence of clerical instructions'.[58] Religious dissidents boycotted the polls rather than contest them, with the result that in the confessionally divided Gard predominantly Protestant cantons voted much more heavily than their Catholic counterparts.[59] Conversely, the Var, which saw the general level of electoral participation rise in June 1791, was an area of overwhelming acceptance of the Civil Constitution. It is interesting to note that elsewhere in the Midi, in one section of Toulouse, ten out of thirty-seven voters were juring priests.[60]

Evidently this correlation should not be pressed too far; no single or universal factor was responsible for declining turnout. There were often specifically local reasons for the boycott of electoral proceedings. In the Aveyron, for example, voters from the commune of Le Brusque refused to attend the primaries in 1790, because their village had not been chosen as a *chef-lieu de canton*.[61] It was the same in the Morbihan, a year later: not a single voter turned out from Elven, because the *chef-lieu* of the canton had been transferred to a more central location.[62]

The travelling required by inhabitants of outlying villages, who wished to take part in the primaries, is not to be underestimated either. Adverse weather could prevent attendance, even in the summer months.[63] If the assembly lasted for more than one day, there was the expense of an overnight stay or the prospect of making the same journey again the next day. Yet, despite the belief of some historians that 'distance from the *chef-lieu de canton*' was a major cause of abstention, this was not always the case, at least in 1790.[64] In the canton of Céret in the Pyrénées-Orientales, for instance, the hamlet of Las Illas polled twice as heavily as the *chef-lieu*,

---

[57] Du Châtelier, 'Essai de monographie électorale', p. 20.
[58] A.-F. Lallié, *Les assemblées primaires de la Loire-Inférieure en 1790, 1791 et 1792* (Vannes, 1902), p. 66.
[59] Gueniffey, *Le nombre et la raison*, pp. 236–7.
[60] Fournier, 'La participation électorale en Haute-Garonne', pp. 56–7.
[61] AD Aveyron 1L578, Procès-verbal du Pont-de-Camarès, June 1790.
[62] AD Morbihan L236, Procès-verbal d'élection, June 1791. At Ur, in the Pyrénées-Orientales, a dispute over the location of the *chef-lieu de canton* erupted into violence in 1791. One unfortunate voter was beaten up and 'great clumps of hair were torn from his head': M. Brunet, *Le Roussillon face à la Révolution française* (Perpignan, 1989), pp. 99–100.
[63] AM Fréjus D1, Délibérations du conseil municipal, 13 June 1790.
[64] F. Rouvière, *Histoire de la Révolution française dans le département du Gard*, 4 vols. (Nîmes, 1887–89), II, p. 428.

which managed only a 14 per cent turnout (but still dominated the assembly with fifty-three out of the seventy-seven citizens who were present).[65] Likewise, in the canton of Vence in the Var, five out of eleven registered voters turned out from the tiny hillside community of Gerbières, which was nine hours away on foot. However, since there were only solitary representatives from three other villages, the *chef-lieu* still mustered 136 of the 144 citizens who attended.[66]

The *chefs-lieux* did not always have their own way. The village of Coupenne in the Landes complained bitterly that two other communes in the canton had joined forces to ensure that all of the delegates to the departmental assembly belonged to them.[67] Rural-urban hostility was much in evidence, not least in the west. There was an obvious anxiety to secure a voice at the electoral college in the primary elections of 1790; it was necessary to grit one's teeth and see out the lengthy sessions. As villagers in the canton of Castanet (Haute-Garonne) put it, 'those who quit the assembly lose all influence'.[68] In 1791, by contrast, it was a different story. The more distant villages tended to show the highest degrees of abstention; it did not seem worth making the same effort for the second time in twelve months.

At least during these early years of the Revolution there was little evidence of the organised intimidation that frequently occurred later. To be sure, for respectable citizens, noisy, over-crowded assemblies could be off-putting in themselves, especially if spectators were allowed into the nave of the churches where voters met. The conservative journalist Mallet du Pan reported a certain reluctance to attend on account of 'the frightful effect which these electoral assemblies have upon peaceful citizens'.[69] In 1790 there were isolated attempts to eject particular individuals from the assemblies, usually because they were members of the former privileged classes or deemed to be their lackeys. A good example of this behaviour is furnished by the canton of Cazères, in the Haute-Garonne, where:

> the greater part of the decent folk who were present did not vote and were obliged to withdraw from the assembly . . . among them . . . the former seigneur . . . the parish priest and his curate . . . This was mainly the result of a pamphlet produced by a citizen from Toulouse that encouraged participants to exclude all members of the former privileged classes from the electoral assemblies.[70]

[65] AD Pyrénées-Orientales L428, Procès-verbal d'élection, May 1790.
[66] AD Alpes-Maritimes L542, Procès-verbal d'élection, June 1790.
[67] AD Landes 11L8, Procès-verbal d'élection, May 1790. Likewise at Guémené in the Morbihan, in 1790, where inhabitants from the *chef-lieu* denounced a cabal cooked up by outlying villages as 'the proscription of urban voters pronounced by those from surrounding rural areas': AD Morbihan L233, Procès-verbal d'élection, May 1790.
[68] AD Haute-Garonne L239, Procès-verbal d'élection, July 1790.
[69] *Mercure de France*, 51, 18 Dec. 1790, p. 226.
[70] AD Haute-Garonne L238, Procès-verbal d'élection, July 1790.

Fournier adds that in this department big property-owners, who were chiefly resident in neighbouring towns, usually bore the brunt of villagers' hostility.[71]

Long-standing local rivalries also surfaced in the assemblies, which provided ample scope for the conduct of factional as much as ideological dispute. An especially potent source of discord in these early years lay in enmity between different communes, which found themselves sharing the same canton. In the Aude, for instance, the hamlet of Pépieux complained about the overbearing conduct of voters from the *chef-lieu* of Azille. The electoral proceedings of 1790 had, it was alleged, been deliberately prolonged so as to deter neighbouring villagers from returning the next day. Protests at the assembly had been ignored so the good citizens of Pépieux were seeking a transfer to another canton, where they would no longer have to suffer 'injustices at the hands of the lawyers of Azille'.[72]

Government envoys were called in to arbitrate in another intercommunal dispute in the Aude, this time at Villepinte in the District of Castelnaudary. They decided to divide the canton into separate sections to avoid further trouble, since different villages were 'at daggers drawn, going back three generations, divided so deeply that they come to blows each time that they come into contact with one other'.[73] The commune of Vauzeron in the Cher had already arrived at a similar solution, meeting independently from Neuvy-sur-Branjon, 'so as to avoid any nasty business'; separation was also a means of settling matters in a speedier fashion.[74] A disenchanted priest in the Meuse also suggested devolving primary assemblies to village level. He was concerned that when rival communes came together, only to 'argue in a vulgar fashion', they were profaning the churches in which meetings were held.[75]

The eruption of rivalry, whether political, parochial or even personal (it is impossible to disentangle these twisted skeins of ill-feeling), raised the level of participation as often as they reduced it. A good example is provided by the case of Toulon, where a bitter struggle between opposing political clubs lifted turnout to unprecedented heights in 1791, only for interest to subside in 1792 after the more conservative faction was defeated. For when the result was a foregone conclusion voters showed

---

[71] Fournier, 'La participation électorale en Haute-Garonne', p.53.
[72] AD Aude L356, Commune de Pépieux, 31 May 1790. An identical complaint about the activities of 'so-called men of the law' emanated from La Gacilly in the Morbihan: AD Morbihan L233, Procès-verbal d'élection, May 1790.
[73] AN F¹cIII Aude 1, Rapport des commissaires, 28 May 1790.
[74] Bruneau, *Les débuts de la Révolution*, p. 140. See also AD Haute-Garonne L239, Procès-verbal d'élection, Montastruc, 25 July 1790.
[75] AN DIV 43, Curé de la Meuse, 6 June 1790.

little urgency about voting. Modern psephologists refer to this behaviour as 'consensual' rather than 'alienated' abstention.[76] In other words, many citizens were content to accept the choice of the minority who did turn out. After all, in the absence of declared candidatures, it was not possible to return a popular representative unopposed. Though evidence is hard to come by, it would appear that elections were often decided in advance, so that the actual assembly was merely employed to ratify a generally agreed decision.

There was little point in wasting precious time endorsing a foregone conclusion; the business could safely be left to those who had the leisure and experience to deal with such matters, to the men who were interested in being elected themselves. The composition of the departmental colleges will be considered below, but it is evident that the habit of leaving electoral politics in the hands of the notables was an enduring one. It was often persons already serving in the villages and towns, as municipal officers or judicial personnel, who were chosen as delegates to the electoral colleges. There were protests, not least in the west, where the 'bourgeois aristocracy' of town-dwellers was much resented. Voters at Douarnenez, in the Finistère, denounced 'a small number of persons, comprising the wealthy bourgeoisie, who are used to dominating the locality and who have always managed to substitute their own interests for those of the community'.[77] In some towns in the Midi, like Toulon, bourgeois control of the primaries came under attack in 1791, but it was not usually until the following year that more popular elements were elected instead.

The retention of the complex, antiquated electoral mechanism of the *ancien régime*, by the well-heeled deputies of the Constituent Assembly, was no accident. Lengthy proceedings played into the hands of the notables, who could afford to participate heavily in the system. Poorer citizens voted with their feet by failing to appear, or leaving after the first session. One simple test is to distinguish the respective turnout of those who were eligible for office – and by definition more wealthy – from those who were merely voters. In the District of Arras, in the Pas-de-Calais, some 50 per cent of voters registered as eligible participated in the primaries of 1790, as opposed to 20 per cent or less of those who were merely active citizens.[78] In the Loire-Inférieure, the following year, the

---

[76] E. Todd, *The Making of Modern France. Politics, Ideology and Culture*, trans. (Oxford, 1991), p. 209.
[77] AN DIV 28, Habitants de Douarnenez, 11 Feb. 1791. See also D. Sutherland, *The Chouans. The Social Origins of Popular Counter-Revolution in Upper-Brittany, 1770–1796* (Oxford, 1982), pp. 154–62.   [78] Jessenne, 'De la citoyenneté', p. 830.

procès-verbal of Pontchâteau indicated that all those present were eligible for election. In another six cases where data are available for the same department, less than 20 per cent of those who took part can be identified as active but not eligible citizens, though according to the tax rolls they represented nearly 50 per cent of the electorate.[79]

Robespierre was quick to protest that limitations upon eligibility for office constituted a major reason for low turnout: 'Those who pay only the equivalent of three days' wages in taxation will show little enthusiasm for leaving their businesses and their households in order to participate in the electoral assemblies where they do not possess the same rights, nor entertain the same expectations as their more wealthy counterparts...'[80] His concern was shared by a lawyer from Dax, in the Landes, who was shocked that so few artisans were attending the assemblies in 1790. Those who did appear were mostly 'spoilt children of the *ancien régime*... such indifference on the part of those who have been oppressed for so long saddens my civic soul'.[81] The example of Toulon, where universal eligibility for all posts was in operation from 1790 onwards, as well as a democratic suffrage, suggests that poorer citizens did not necessarily vote, even when they could be elected.

The exceptional series of *procès-verbaux* preserved at Toulon, with its precise record of almost every individual who attended the electoral assemblies, from 1790 to 1792, provides some remarkable sociological evidence in this regard. In the first mayoral election of February 1790, just over one-third of all voters were bourgeois (*rentiers*, merchants, or members of the liberal professions), though these groups comprised less than one-sixth of entries on a register for National Guard service (a prerequisite for active citizenship).[82] As turnout plummeted later in the year, so their presence grew more marked: they made up 43 per cent of the participants in the June primaries and almost 50 per cent in the partial municipal polls of November 1790.[83]

The popular classes were grossly under-represented at these assemblies, which they progressively deserted the longer the proceedings went on. In the popular quarter of Saint-Jean for example, in February 1790, the twenty-three citizens who attended the very last session were all bourgeois. This lower-class propensity to abstention was challenged in 1791, when the Jacobin club of Toulon actively encouraged the artisans, sailors

---

[79] Le Gall, Les consultations générales, II, pp. 557–8.
[80] *AP* XI, p. 324, 25 Jan. 1790.
[81] AM Bordeaux K1, Motion faite aux assemblées primaires de Dax, 1790.
[82] AM Toulon L572, Procès-verbal d'élection, Feb. 1790, L392, Inscription pour le service de la garde nationale, 1791 and Crook, *Toulon*, p. 34.
[83] AD Var 1L218, Procès-verbaux d'élection, June 1790 and AM Toulon L574, Procès-verbal d'élection, Nov. 1790.

and dockyard workers of this naval town to use 'their precious rights of citizenship'. Efforts to mobilise the Toulonnais masses began to produce popular majorities at the polls, yet fully enfranchised unskilled workers, like rural labourers residing in the city, still showed a tremendous reluctance to vote. Their failure to do so helps explain why percentage turnout at Toulon was rather low, compared to towns which operated a restricted franchise.[84]

The bourg of Vence, in the eastern Var, also introduced an extremely broad suffrage from 1790 onwards yet, once again, the bourgeoisie easily dominated the assemblies. In the first municipal elections, over 40 per cent of registered bourgeois cast a vote, compared to just 14 per cent of artisans and 5 per cent of rural labourers. The bourgeoisie comprised only 12.5 per cent of the electorate, yet it provided 32 per cent of the participants when a mayor was chosen and increased its relative share of the vote as interest waned for other posts.[85] Fournier has made a similar point regarding rural turnout in the Haute-Garonne: poorer peasants did participate in 1790, but it was they who abstained markedly when turnout fell the following year.[86]

During the Revolution, as today, the lower classes were far less likely to participate in elections than their better-off counterparts. It was not enough to give people the vote, they had to be encouraged and enabled to utilise it. The restricted franchise was not responsible for weak and declining turnout, as the advent of a wider suffrage in 1792 would show. An overdemanding electoral system, an inexperienced electorate and a deteriorating political climate were the main reasons for rising abstention. The assembly mechanism was, in fact, a means of exclusion rather than integration for many citizens. In 1791, electoral participation had become a test of loyalty to the regime which many voters, in rural areas in particular, were unwilling to take. Opponents of the new order chose to abstain from polling and began to look beyond the ballot box for ways of making their opinions known.[87] The advent of quasi-universal suffrage in 1792, in a context of deepening disorder, war and economic dislocation, would only exacerbate the crisis of legitimacy that was developing and which the electoral system was patently unable to resolve.

[84] Crook 'The People at the Polls', p. 170.
[85] AD Alpes-Maritimes, AM Vence III K1, Procès-verbal d'élection, Feb. 1790 and G. Castellan, *Une cité provençale dans la Révolution. Chronique de la ville de Vence en 1790* (Paris, 1978), p. 51.
[86] Fournier, 'La participation électorale en Haute-Garonne', p. 56.
[87] Dupuy, *De la Révolution à la chouannerie*, pp. 235–7.

4 One man one vote? The experiment with electoral democracy in 1792

On 11 August 1792 fiscal restrictions on the franchise were swept away along with the Constitutional Monarchy in France. This 'second revolution', as historians have dubbed it, ushered in a phase of great political experimentation, yet where voting was concerned the changes were of limited scope and application. Since the celebrated Constitution of 1793 was not actually implemented the suffrage never became universal for adult males; some restrictions persisted and elections above the local level remained indirect. Nor was the renewed turbulence into which the Revolution plunged conducive to high turnout during this period. Nevertheless, two plebiscites or constitutional referenda aside, the primary and municipal elections held in the latter part of 1792 were the most democratic of the decade. Their conduct offers a number of vital insights into the more radical forms of electoral politics that revolutionaries had already been advocating via press and political clubs since 1789.

It was violence on the streets of Paris, not votes in the ballot box that brought down Louis XVI and the Constitution of 1791. Yet the importance attached to the electoral process was demonstrated by a general anxiety to legitimise the *de facto* Republic with the election of a new constituent assembly as quickly as possible. The day after the momentous events of 10 August 1792, the rump of 284 deputies, who remained on duty in a Legislative Assembly much-reduced by desertion and resignation, began to prepare for the convocation of a National Convention.[1] Primary assemblies were to meet at the end of the month and the departmental electoral colleges, where the deputies themselves would be chosen, were to open a week later at the beginning of September.

It was unanimously decided to retain the two-tier electoral system already in place, but the tax requirements previously necessary to vote and to be elected were abolished. Many contemporaries, like second-degree electors in the Côte-d'Or, hailed this as the beginning of a new era:

[1] *AP* XLVIII, p. 28, 11 Aug. 1792.

'At last a National Convention will erase the lingering remnants of our former servitude . . . it will establish the right sort of government for a society of free men.'[2] Most historians have likewise interpreted these changes as the advent of universal suffrage in France. Albert Soboul has stated: 'By means of universal suffrage . . . this "second revolution" really integrated the people into the nation and signalled the advent of democracy.'[3] On the assumption that all adult males were enfranchised, it has been calculated that some 25 per cent of a population of 28 millions could now participate in elections. Bouloiseau, closely following Lefebvre, declared that 'at a stroke, 3 or 4 millions of 'passive citizens' acquired voting rights for which they scarcely seemed to be prepared' and, he concludes, the electorate expanded to some 7 million voters as a consequence.[4]

Other historians, like Sydenham and Doyle, have acknowledged the important qualifications that must be attached to statements about this franchise, which was extended but not to the point of universality.[5] A close scrutiny of the decree of 12 August 1792, which convened the primary assemblies two weeks later, reveals limits to the suffrage, even among adult males. It began promisingly enough, 'The division of the French people into active and non-active citizens is abolished', but added, 'In order to exercise the franchise it is necessary to be a Frenchman, aged twenty-one years old, resident in the canton for a year, *living upon an income or from the proceeds of employment, and not working as a domestic servant* [my emphasis].'[6] In other words the door was still closed against all women and those men who were deemed dependent, either in the absence of a regular income or as a result of servitude; the threshold had been lowered, but not completely removed.

The rump of the Legislative Assembly had declined an invitation to formally adopt the principle of universal manhood suffrage. On 11 August, a committee headed by Guadet had proposed the removal of all constraints save servile status.[7] To vote at the forthcoming elections it should suffice to be twenty-five years old, of French nationality, domiciled in the canton for a year and not a servant. In the ensuing debate deputies dropped the voting age to twenty-one and even debated a further reduction to eighteen (though to be elected one still had to be twenty-five). However,

---

[2] AD Côte-d'Or L210, Procès-verbal de l'assemblée électorale, 2 Sept. 1792.
[3] A. Soboul, *La Révolution française* (Paris, 1965), p. 63.
[4] M. Bouloiseau, *La République jacobine, 10 août 1792–9 thermidor an II* (Paris, 1972), p. 56.
[5] Doyle, *The Oxford History of the French Revolution*, p. 193 and M.J. Sydenham, *The French Revolution* (London, 1965), p. 112.
[6] J.-B. Duvergier, ed.*Collection complète des lois* (Paris, 1825–28), IV, p. 297.
[7] *AP* XLVIII, pp. 28–9, 11 Aug. 1792.

having significantly expanded the electorate in this respect, it was decided to proceed more cautiously where a voter's financial circumstances were concerned.

It was Marant, an obscure, conservative deputy from the Vosges (unlike most remaining *législateurs* he had voted against the impeachment of Lafayette, for example, and he was not subsequently re-elected to the Convention), who put forward an amendment which inserted the exercise of 'a profession of some kind' among the franchise requirements. This proposal was reminiscent of the existing 'taxes equivalent to three days' labour', or more properly the criterion of taxpaying applied to the Estates General of 1789, because it continued to stress the importance of making a contribution to society as a condition of voting. Those reliant upon others for their means of subsistence continued to be excluded from most aspects of public life. It was only in the still-born Constitution of 1793, adopted by the Convention almost a year later, that voting became a right, conferred upon all adult males regardless of their personal status.

In practice, even after the momentous events of 10 August, surviving deputies in the Legislative Assembly were unwilling to countenance too many radical steps forward. Direct elections to all posts and the replacement of the written ballot with voting out loud (*à haute voix*), or by acclamation, had all been placed on the political agenda, as well as universal manhood suffrage. Yet none of these other issues were debated in the assembly (despite an anonymous member's abortive attempt to raise them on 11 August); the electoral procedures employed in 1790 were to be repeated in 1792.

In their address to the French people on 13 August, deputies stressed the exceptional nature of the forthcoming elections. The franchise extension was only a provisional arrangement and great care was taken not to give any hostages to fortune where it was concerned:

> The Legislative Assembly has not retained any of the conditions for eligibility, nor any restrictions on the right to elect or to be elected, which were established by earlier laws, because those laws represent a limitation upon the exercise of sovereignty. *They are not therefore applicable to the election of a National Convention, when the rights of sovereignty must be employed with complete freedom.* [my emphasis][8]

Local elections later in the year were another matter. In December 1792 the departmental administration of the Ain insisted that in municipal elections, only formerly active citizens should be allowed to participate, pending the promulgation of a new constitution.[9] In the same way, in October, the Convention itself demanded the written ballot in Parisian

---

[8] *Moniteur*, XIII, p. 417, 13 Aug. 1792.
[9] Cited in Gueniffey, La Révolution française et les élections, p. 160.

municipal elections, though at primary assemblies in the capital, a couple of months earlier, the practice of voting out loud had been tolerated.[10]

In the vacuum created by the collapse of the 1791 Constitution, members of the Legislative Assembly acknowledged that they lacked 'the authority to submit the exercise of the people's sovereignty to binding rules, because a constituent assembly was being elected'. They could only *invite* citizens to observe existing electoral procedures in the interests of expediting the business in a uniform fashion. Most assemblies responded favourably to this appeal, but it went unheeded in some quarters. Not surprisingly there were voters at Paris who were determined to make the most of the fluid situation. Some sections in the capital had already begun admitting 'passive citizens' during the months which preceded Louis XVI's downfall and the events of 10 August seemed to sanction their initiative.[11] The Halle-au-Blé section was soon proudly announcing, 'the restitution . . . of full political rights to *all* citizens' and categorically refused to impose any restrictions upon the suffrage.[12] Faced with a critical situation that required urgent resolution, the authorities had no real alternative but to leave each assembly free to decide whom to admit to vote and how to do so.

Local administrators in the more distant provinces had only a week to notify the electorate; that they managed to organise the assemblies so rapidly was a significant achievement in itself. Only Paris, where primaries were still being held when the departmental college of the Seine opened, failed to keep abreast of a demanding timetable.[13] There were complaints in some cantons that changes in the franchise were being ignored: the township of Vitteaux in the Côte-d'Or was accused of restricting access to former active citizens and its second-degree electors were denied entry to the departmental electoral college. Few assemblies followed the example of Moulins-la-Marche in the Orne, which clearly stated it was accepting, 'active citizens *and all others now admitted by law*'.[14]

It was obviously impossible to compile new electoral registers before polling day in August 1792, especially since tax rolls could no longer be pressed into service to list the *ayant droit de voter*. When fresh population surveys were undertaken the following year they revealed the difficulty of arriving at any reliable figures. The disruption of war and further upheaval, not to mention legislative uncertainty, militated against a satisfactory degree of numerical accuracy regarding potential voters. Where

---

[10] Genty, *Paris 1789–1795*, p. 192.   [11] Rose, *The Making of the Sans-Culottes*, pp. 58–9.
[12] Charavay, ed., *Assemblée électorale*, III, pp. vii-ix.
[13] *Ibid.*, III, p. vii.   [14] AD Orne L377, Procès-verbal, 26 Aug. 1792.

statistics do exist for 1793 and 1794, they often represent a repetition of earlier sets, exhumed by hard-pressed administrators, or record huge, unrealistic fluctuations in the electorate.[15]

The Côte-d'Or sheds some interesting light upon the problem. A score of *procès-verbaux* emanating from the primary assemblies of August 1792 actually mention the total of those entitled to vote, yet indicate an increase of only 7 per cent upon the electorate of 1790.[16] Does this reflect the modest impact of the legislative changes, or merely a routine adjustment which fails to address the abolition of the electoral *cens*? The rich archives of the Côte-d'Or also possess registers dating from 1793 which suggest that the percentage of the population enfranchised had now risen to 21.6 per cent, as opposed to 18.4 per cent under the constitutional monarchy; this was scarcely an overwhelming advance.[17] A further survey, conducted in 1794 (or the Year II according to the revolutionary calendar), apparently with a view to implementation of the Constitution of 1793, suggests another rise, with 25.9 per cent of the population now accorded the right to vote, but this time on the basis of universal manhood suffrage.[18]

Demographic calculations indicate that if *all* adult males over the age of twenty-one had been enfranchised, this would have amounted to roughly 28 per cent of the population.[19] Yet in 1792 not *all* adult males had been given the vote, so a somewhat lower percentage should be anticipated. On the basis of figures from the Côte-d'Or and a dozen other departments besides, it seems reasonable to conclude that voters eligible to elect the Convention represented between 20 and 25 per cent of the population, or roughly 6 million Frenchmen. Compared to 1791, the electorate had thus grown by almost half. Though differentiation between poorer and richer departments persisted, there was much greater uniformity than before. Departments like the Loire-Inférieure, which had previously recorded low proportions of active citizens, enjoyed larger increases than departments like the Var, which already exhibited a relatively high proportion of potential voters.[20] Similarly, towns like Toulouse which had been penal-

---

[15] AN Série F^{20}, Population, contains a good set of surveys for the different departments and some lacunae can be filled with copies to be found in the AD. See the comments of Fournier in 'La participation électorale en Haute-Garonne', pp. 57–9.
[16] AD Côte-d'Or L234–5, Procès-verbaux d'élection and see M. Edelstein, 'L'établissement de la République en Côte-d'Or: étude électorale et politique', in M. Vovelle, ed., *Révolution et République: l'exception française* (Paris, 1994), pp 226–7.
[17] AN F^{20} 318, Tableaux de la population, Aug. 1793 and AD Côte-d'Or L497, Tableau de la population, 1790.
[18] AD Côte-d'Or L506, Tableaux de la population, 29 Pluv. II (17 Feb. 1794).
[19] Blayo and Henry, 'La population de la France de 1740 à 1860', pp. 102–4.
[20] Le Gall, Les consultations générales, III, Annexe II: Population et citoyens actifs.

ised by the fiscal criterion employed in 1790 and 1791, witnessed a proportionately greater increase in the electorate than neighbouring rural cantons in the Haute-Garonne.[21]

In the absence of any clear idea of the numbers able to vote, calculations for turnout in August 1792 are extremely hazardous. Any exaggeration of the size of the electorate will produce a lower degree of participation than is actually warranted, a mistake made by more than one historian. The table which follows is based upon the more conservative figures of 1793, rather than those of 1794, but there can be no pretence at any great precision. Not only are these figures sometimes suspect, but turnout has once again been calculated on the basis of one particular vote – the first round of balloting for second-degree electors – which was only one of several votes and not necessarily the best supported. Moreover, as in the past, available lists refer to those *ayant droit de voter*, potential voters who had to fulfil other criteria before they could actually be admitted to the electoral assemblies.

Scrutiny was rather less stringent than before. It is unlikely that many authorities opened civic registers for inscription by old and new voters in the week or so between calling the election and the opening of the polls. At Paris, however, the Section de 1792 (formerly Bibliothèque) did insist upon issuing *cartes de civisme* (passes needed for voting) and only 1,462 individuals signed up before the primaries took place. This total was only slightly in excess of the number of active citizens listed a year earlier.[22] Similarly, though the electoral decree of 12 August did not mention the requirement of National Guard service, there was some dispute over this point in the Loire-Inférieure.[23] Proof of tax-payment was another vexed question. At Toulon, the departmental administration of the Var replied that tax-receipts were not necessary for admission to the assemblies, but the Hôtel-de-Ville section at Paris (now renamed Maison-Commune) adopted the opposite point of view.[24]

The elections to the Convention in 1792 were held under difficult conditions and *procès-verbaux* are lacking, or defective, in many departments. Hence the smaller size of the sample used to gauge turnout on this occasion, only 4 per cent of the estimated national electorate. These scarce

---

[21] AD Haute-Garonne L237, Tableau général, Aug. 1790 and *ibid*. L203, Tableau de la population, Aug. 1793.
[22] AN F7 2483, Livre des serments, Section de 1792, Aug.-Sept. 1792.
[23] Le Gall, Les consultations générales, II, p. 604.
[24] E. Poupé, *Le département du Var, 1790–an VIII* (Cannes, 1933), p.189 and AN BI 14 Procès-verbal de la section Maison-Commune, Sept. 1792.

Table 9 *Turnout in primary elections, August 1792*

Department	Total of *ADV* in sample	Voters at first round for electors	Percentage turnout
Orne	6715	1717	35.6
Charente	7380	2360	32.0
Côte-d'Or	7075	1846	26.1
Aveyron	34028	7030	20.7
Marne	53664	10216	19.0
Basses-Alpes	15899	2374	14.9
Pyrénées-Orientales	8680	1296	14.9
Morbihan	40431	4536	11.2
Var	22797	2557	11.2
Seine	49831	4158	8.3
Total	246500	38090	15.5

Sources: AD Alpes-Maritimes L550; AD Aveyron 1L599; AD Basses-Alpes L199–203; AD Charente L532/1679; AD Côte-d'Or L234–5; AD Marne 1L297–304; AD Morbihan L237; AD Orne L375–7; AD Pyrénées-Orientales L430; AD Var 1L223; and AN BI 14

data, which are at least drawn from various points of the compass, suggest a level of participation which averaged only 15.5 per cent. The removal of Paris, with its abysmally low score, would inflate the average turnout to 17.3 per cent, but at the cost of lowering the sample to a mere 3 per cent of the notional 'national' electorate. The attendance was evidently not quite as low as Bouloiseau claimed, when he stated that 'On 26 August no more than a minute proportion of the electorate attended the primary assemblies: at best a tenth of those entitled to do so'.[25] The figure advanced here is closer to Alison Patrick's informed guess that 'perhaps one in five' took part.[26]

When compared to similar percentages for the primaries of 1791 (and still more so 1790), figures for 1792 represent a continuing decline in turnout. While the percentage fell, however, given the increase in the size of the potential electorate the *absolute numbers* of participants had often *grown* in comparison with totals for the previous year. In the tabulated sample numerical attendance actually rose in a majority of cantons in five departments. Increases of this sort also occurred in the Gard, Haute-

[25] Bouloiseau, *La République jacobine*, p. 56.
[26] Patrick, *The Men of the First Republic*, p. 152.

Saône, Loire-Inférieure and Seine-et-Oise, if not the Oise, to judge by the unverified findings of other historians.[27]

It seems reasonable to conclude that more voters were mobilised than a year earlier, though the contribution of newly enfranchised young men and former 'passive' citizens appears to have been limited. Evidence is not easily obtained but, in the case of Toulon, meticulously recorded details in the *procès-verbaux* reveal that only ten out of 741 citizens who voted for second-degree electors in the first round of voting were aged under twenty-five, which is to say little more than 1 per cent of all participants.[28] Yet rough calculations would suggest that more than 500 of these young Toulonnais adult males had been presented with the opportunity of attending the electoral assemblies for the first time (assuming they were properly informed).

At Toulon, fiscal restrictions on the franchise were never applied in the absence of personal tax returns, so their removal had no impact upon the size of the Toulonnais electorate. In spite of their entitlement to do so, few of the less well-off voters in the naval town had previously participated in elections and they showed little more inclination to do so in 1792.[29] Evidence from elsewhere casts similar doubt on the willingness of the poor to vote, even when offered the chance. Turnout in August 1792 was negligible among those hitherto excluded for paying insufficient tax. Le Gall reckons that in five cantons of the Loire-Inférieure for which data are available just over 90 per cent of the participants in 1792 were already listed as active citizens in 1791; of the remainder, only 4.3 per cent can be positively identified as 'ex-passives'.[30] In the canton of Bouaye not a single, newly enfranchised voter appeared, though the electorate had almost doubled in size. Evidence relating to one section in the city of Nantes, however, suggests that former 'passive' citizens there were more willing to turn out in 1792 than most rural counterparts.[31]

Gueniffey's research confirms these tenuous conclusions. At Chevreuse, in the Seine-et-Oise, only nineteen voters out of 126 who appeared at the primary assembly on 26 August 1792 had not possessed the right to participate before.[32] One is obliged to conclude that members

---

[27] Rouvière, *Histoire de la Révolution française dans le département du Gard*, II, p. 428; J. Girardot, *Le département de la Haute-Saône pendant la Révolution* (Vesoul, 1972–1974, II, p. 182; Le Gall, Les consultations générales, III Annexe III: La participation; M.E. Auvray, 'Les élections à la Convention nationale dans le département de la Seine-et-Oise (26 août-2 septembre 1792)', *Actes 78ᵉ con. nat.* (1953), p. 240; and Baumont, 'Les assemblées primaires et électorale de l'Oise', p. 149.
[28] AD Var 1L223, Procès-verbaux de Toulon, 26–7 Aug. 1792.
[29] Crook, 'The People at the Polls', pp. 170–1.
[30] Le Gall, Les consultations générales, II, p. 612.
[31] *Ibid.*, II, pp. 608–10.   [32] Gueniffey, *Le nombre et la raison*, p. 176.

of the old, limited electorate generally turned out more heavily in the primary stages of elections to the National Convention than they had a year earlier for the Legislative Assembly. This was no mean feat considering the turbulent circumstances afflicting France at the time. One explanation for the limited upturn in participation lies in the foundation of the Republic, the creation of a new regime attracting more interest than the perpetuation of an existing one in June 1791. This factor had operated favourably in both 1789 and 1790, with the election of the Estates General and the establishment of local administrations, not to mention even stronger turnout for the first municipal polls at the beginning of 1790.

There were also practical considerations for a recovery of interest in electoral participation two years later. In 1792 matters were generally conducted more expeditiously as a result of further modifications to voting procedure. In 1791 the cumbersome 'double-list' system for the selection of second-degree electors had already been abandoned as a redundant, time-consuming process. As Brissot had written, 'the double list of names complicates the business of counting votes, crucifies the scrutineers and does not have the alleged effect of preventing electoral cabals'.[33] In 1792 it was decided to speed up the election of the assembly's president, secretary and scrutineers by authorising their nomination *en bloc* and by means of a relative majority.[34] One single vote replaced a possible nine ballots, because members of the assembly's *bureau* had hitherto been elected separately and by absolute majority. As a result most assemblies could fulfil this formality on the first morning and begin, if not actually complete, the election of their delegates to the departmental assembly on the same day.

Such celerity contrasts markedly with the primaries of 1790, for example, when only one-third of the cantons completed their operations in two days. Of course, in 1792 not *all* assemblies were able to commence and conclude their proceedings so quickly. Le Gall has detected a tendency towards prolongation in the Loire-Inférieure, especially in the city of Nantes. There, ten sections out of eighteen took three or four days to complete the electoral business, but turnout still rose dramatically. However, in this instance the polls were deliberately left open so as to encourage more citizens to cast a vote. There was no immediate closure of voting once the roll call had been taken and the length of the session consequently served to attract rather than deter heavier participation.[35]

---

[33] Cited in Charavay, ed., *Assemblée électorale*, I, p. xi.
[34] Duvergier, ed., *Collection complète*, IV, p. 297
[35] Le Gall, Les consultations générales, II, pp. 603–4.

While most assemblies were content to follow prescribed procedures, some exploited the latitude permitted by the Legislative Assembly to tailor arrangements to suit themselves. Since the legislation only 'invited' compliance with the existing arrangements, there was little fear of annulment on these grounds, as had been the case beforehand. In some instances such freedom might prolong the proceedings, as in the Théâtre-Français section at Paris, where five ballots were held in pursuit of an absolute majority for all second-degree electors.[36] Elsewhere short-cuts were taken to expedite matters. Some assemblies accepted a relative majority on the first or second ballot for delegates in order to finish early. There was also an effort to conclude matters at a single session regardless of the hour: in the case of Troissereux, in the Oise, balloting continued through the evening until 3.00am the following morning.[37]

The adoption of voting out loud, or by unanimous accord (*haute voix* and *acclamation*), was justified by the principle of openness, as opposed to the secrecy of balloting. Yet it contributed towards a speedier resolution of business, since there was no need to engage in the arduous task of counting ballot papers. Such devices were most widely practised in the Parisian sections, but they are also to be found in neighbouring departments like the Seine-et-Oise.[38] They made matters much easier for illiterates, who grew more numerous (at least in principle) with the extension of the franchise.

The level of participation in the primary elections of 1792 was generally higher in town than countryside all over France. This relatively stronger urban showing confirmed a trend already apparent in June 1791, when attendance rates in cities fell less sharply than in surrounding rural areas. In August 1792, for example, turnout in Nantes rose at a much greater rate than the departmental average. Likewise, in the Côte-d'Or, Edelstein has calculated that the *chefs-lieux* recorded a higher than average vote in three out of six districts for which documentation is available. Only one of them had done so in 1791 and none at all in 1790.[39] Gueniffey too reports that in five out of six districts in the Eure and Seine-Inférieure (Seine-Maritime), there was a heavier turnout in the *chefs-lieux* than in the cantons as a whole, whereas in 1790 and 1791 the reverse had been true.[40]

In many towns a militant minority was encouraging a stronger vote

[36] AN BI 14, Procès-verbal de la section Théâtre-Français, Sept. 1792.
[37] Baumont, 'Les assemblées primaires et électorale de l'Oise', pp. 138–9.
[38] Auvray, 'Les élections à la Convention', p. 241.
[39] Edelstein, 'L'établissement de la République', p. 4.
[40] Gueniffey, *Le nombre et la raison*, pp. 176–9.

among the popular classes. To be sure, a recent, comprehensive, statistical survey of political clubs in the Revolution denies they operated as 'electoral machines', pursuing a central party line.[41] It is equally evident that, though the south-east possessed a high density of Jacobin Clubs, turnout there remained low. Conversely, eastern areas of France were distinguished by a relatively high turnout in elections, coupled with a thinner spread of political societies. The relationship between the existence of clubs and electoral participation is evidently a complex one. What requires emphasis, however, is the uniform urban implantation of these associations and the relative improvement in levels of participation in towns. There is abundant evidence of club involvement in electioneering and some clear correlations can be made.

Indeed, Michael Kennedy devotes a whole chapter to the subject in the first tome of his multi-volume history of the Jacobin clubs. At the beginning of 1790, when the first municipal elections were held, few clubs had been founded and those which did exist were only in their infancy. With the primary elections of spring and summer members began to dip their toes in the electoral waters. The exhortation to vote was an obvious starting point: 'What is the loss of a single day, fellow citizens, when the well-being of the state demands this sacrifice', proclaimed the club at Verdun.[42] By the summer of 1791, when a Legislative Assembly was to be elected, the clubs pressed especially hard for a good turnout. The Jacobin society at Alençon in the Orne, for example, encouraged fellow-citizens to attend the primary assemblies: 'You are about to fulfil the most honourable and most majestic of functions in a system of representative government.'[43] The *société-mère* at Paris distributed addresses urging voters to use 'the most sacred of rights by taking part in polling'.[44]

The society at Douai, in the Nord, went further and offered advice on the choices to be made, proposing the selection of 'honest and enlightened' men as second-degree electors, while other clubs recommended citizens 'renowned for their patriotism'.[45] Reluctance to actually name names and engage in overt 'party' politics was gradually overcome. In 1791 the club at Beauvais (Oise) printed a slate of forty-eight names to be elected in the town's sections, while Lille, Toulouse and Tulle, by contrast, published lists of 'cowardly and unpatriotic electors' from 1790, who were to be avoided at all costs.[46]

---

[41] *Atlas de la Révolution française*, VI, *Les sociétés politiques*, ed. J. Boutier *et al.* (Paris, 1992), p. 33. [42] *Ibid.*, p. 216. [43] AD Orne L361, Adresse, 12 June 1791.
[44] F.-A. Aulard, ed., *Recueil de documents pour l'histoire du club des Jacobins de Paris*, 6 vols. (Paris, 1889–97), II, p. 520.
[45] M. Kennedy, *The Jacobin Clubs in the French Revolution* 2 vols. (Princeton, 1982–88), I, pp. 210–12. [46] *Ibid.*, I, pp. 220–1.

In the event this unprecedented Jacobin 'campaign' was disrupted by the Feuillant split and the emergence of rival societies. Nonetheless, the following year such electoral manoeuvres were deployed more widely than ever.[47] In the Gard a *comité central des clubs*, like the one formed in the adjacent Hérault, drafted a similar address on the importance of attending the assemblies and making the most of 'the important decisions to be taken where the composition of the National Convention is concerned'.[48] The Jacobin club at Nîmes, the departmental *chef-lieu*, went so far as to send *commissaires* 'into every commune ... to invite citizens to confer with them' and 'ensure a good choice' or, in other words, to rig the elections.

The example of Toulon furnishes especially detailed evidence of the clubs' growing electoral influence. Significantly enough, the first time local Jacobins clashed with the town council was over poor turnout in the partial municipal elections of November 1790. A mere 5 per cent of voters took part in the first ballot for councillors and returned solidly conservative bourgeois to office.[49] The club, disappointed by this outcome, protested that patrols of National Guard had been deliberately posted away from their neighbourhoods, so as to deter militia-men from participating. Low turnout in preceding elections lends little credibility to this complaint, yet the increasingly radical leadership at the club had clearly grasped the importance of mobilising the voters as a means to power.

These Jacobins soon embarked upon some active electioneering in pursuit of this end. In January 1791 they convened the sections of Toulon in a 'deliberative' capacity to debate a number of local political issues (the electoral assemblies naturally lent themselves to this purpose, permitted by the Constitution) and succeeded in generating a relatively good response.[50] A militant minority of the Toulonnais popular classes commenced their electoral apprenticeship in these neighbourhood assemblies and proceeded to participate more heavily than hitherto in subsequent elections during the course of 1791. In June, the club even sought permission from the naval authorities for dockyard workers and sailors to be allowed to finish work early so as to attend the primary assemblies.

The lesson was not lost on conservatives, content with the constitutional monarchy, who now formed a second club and soon sought to mobilise an electoral following of their own. The resulting struggle for power at Toulon eventually overflowed on to the streets, but it began in the electoral assemblies. The inaugural mayoral election of 1790 had scattered votes among a score of individuals, but that of November 1791 saw

[47] *Ibid.*, II, pp. 287–8.
[48] F. Rouvière, *Le mouvement électoral dans le Gard en 1792* (Nîmes, 1884), pp. 76 ff.
[49] AM Toulon L574, Procès-verbaux d'élection, Nov. 1790.
[50] Crook, *Toulon*, pp. 101 ff.

nearly all of them converge upon two 'candidates' from the rival clubs. The winner was a Jacobin who drew the greater part of his two-thirds majority from the popular quarters of the town, where dockyard workers and sailors resided.[51]

The concentration or division of votes is one way of teasing out organised electoral activity at a time when candidates, campaigns and canvassing were still viewed askance. In practice all three accompanied the electoral process, but it is extremely difficult to grasp these carefully camouflaged conflicts, personal and parochial as well as political, without detailed knowledge of local circumstances. Paul Hanson has demonstrated how, at the beginning of 1793, the Jacobins of Marseille met to draw up a slate of twenty names for the post of town councillor. In several sections they were able to muster substantial support behind these 'candidates', who were duly elected but only at the price of provoking allegations of illegal practice. Hanson remarks: 'these are electoral tactics we take for granted today . . . but for many Marseillais in 1792–93, in the midst of inventing a political culture . . . these tactics seemed decidedly undemocratic and threatening'.[52]

The same reticence where party allegiances were concerned was initially apparent in the political press which, together with clubs, added another vital dimension to the politics of the revolutionary decade.[53] In 1790 and 1791, anodyne exhortations to vote and choose 'good patriots' were to be found in most newspapers, like those which appeared in Jacobin circulars. There were some rare exceptions to this general rule: Desmoulins had suggested names for the election of judges in Paris in October 1790 and, the following year, Marat had published a list of 'bad citizens' who were to be removed as second-degree electors in the capital.[54] By the summer of 1792, however, the gloves were off. In Paris, at least, individuals were named, instead of the usual enumeration of the personal qualities required for office. The best examples of this emergent trend are furnished by two patriotic, but increasingly bitter journalistic rivals, Louvet and Marat.

On 15 August 1792 Louvet's *Sentinelle* confined itself to recommending the exclusion of priests and aristocrats from the primary assemblies: 'Reject all schemers, nobles, priests and men who made their money

---

[51] AM Toulon L579, Procès-verbaux d'élection, Nov. 1791.
[52] P.R. Hanson, 'The Federalist Revolt: An Affirmation or a Denial of Popular Sovereignty?', *French History*, 6 (1992), pp.339–40. I am grateful to the author for communicating an earlier version of this paper in which the quotation appears.
[53] J.D. Popkin, *Revolutionary News: The Press in France, 1789–1799* (Durham, 1990) for a good survey of recent work on the press. The role of newspapers in electoral politics, however, remains to be explored.
[54] Cited in Charavay, ed., *Assemblée électorale*, I, pp. xx and II, p. xii.

under the *ancien régime*.'⁵⁵ Six days later the same paper was explicitly proposing former deputies of the Legislative and Constituent Assemblies as members of the Convention. This ploy earned a severe rebuke from Marat who, in the *Ami du Peuple*, produced his own list of 'excellent patriots', headed by Robespierre and Danton, before denigrating many of Louvet's suggestions: 'Barère, a worthless individual lacking integrity; Rabaut Saint-Etienne, a false patriot; Boutidoux, an old soak; Cloots, a German spy; Lanthenas, a puppet of Madame Roland'.⁵⁶

The provincial press seems to have remained more cautious: at Strasbourg some personal comments were passed upon existing representatives of the Bas-Rhin, but little more.⁵⁷ In 1792, however, both government and deputies, hitherto conspicuous by their absence from the electoral arena, also joined the fray. Roland, who had just been reinstated as Minister of the Interior, not only issued circulars on behalf of his political associates but also despatched *commissaires* to the primary and departmental assemblies, where they competed with emissaries from the insurrectionary Commune of Paris.⁵⁸ Deputies from the Legislative Assembly, unlike their predecessors in the Constituent, refused to pass a self-denying ordinance and those who remained in post effectively declared themselves candidates for the Convention when, on 22 August, they urged voters to 'give preference to those who have constantly supported the principles of popular sovereignty, liberty and equality'.⁵⁹

These partisan appeals did not always succeed in securing the desired electoral results, still less in raising the level of participation. Paris, the focus of so much electioneering remained the area of lowest turnout; in 1792 the surrounding countryside was still voting more heavily than the capital itself.⁶⁰ On the whole, contours of attendance across the country reproduced the pattern of the two preceding years. There were inevitable exceptions like the Aveyron and the Charente but, generally speaking, south and west scored below the average while north and east tended to poll more heavily.⁶¹ Yet, whatever the variation, from region to region or town to countryside, abstention remained the choice of the vast majority of Frenchmen in 1792 as in 1791; it was extremely rare to find a canton where turnout exceeded 50 per cent.

⁵⁵ J.-B. Louvet, *La Sentinelle*, Reprint (Paris, 1981), 15 and 21 Aug. 1792.
⁵⁶ J.-P. Marat, *L'ami du peuple*, cited in Charavay, ed., *Assemblée électorale*, III, pp. 598–601.
⁵⁷ Marx, *Recherches sur la vie politique*, pp. 77–82.
⁵⁸ Gueniffey, *Le nombre et la raison*, pp. 433–4.
⁵⁹ Aulard, *Histoire politique*, p. 218.
⁶⁰ AN BI 14, Procès-verbaux d'élection, Sept. 1792.
⁶¹ For some additional figures on turnout, culled from other sources, see Gueniffey, *Le nombre et la raison*, p. 167 and, for the Aube, Horn, Elections and Elites, p. 220.

Contemporaries felt the elections had been held at an inconvenient moment for rural folk. The canton of Saint-Martin in the district of Epernay, in the Marne, excused its low turnout by commenting: 'While the number of voters who have taken part is rather disappointing, there is no need to look beyond the especially urgent tasks being undertaken in the countryside in order to find an explanation.'[62] One bourg in the canton of Ville-sur-Tourbe, in the same department, actually refused to allow workers to attend their primary assembly on account of such 'pressing commitments', only to be reprimanded by the District administration and obliged to reverse its decision.[63]

The oath to be sworn prior to voting in 1792 once again acted as a deterrent to those with tender consciences. On the suggestion of Gohier, the Legislative Assembly adopted the formulation 'I swear to maintain liberty and equality or to die in their defence', for use at both primary and secondary assemblies. It is not always clear how many assemblies actually insisted upon the observation of this requirement, but there are numerous examples of refusals to comply. At Chapelle-sur-Erdre, in the generally refractory department of the Loire-Inférieure for example, no less than 200 voters appeared, but only six voted for the canton's twelve second-degree electors; the vast majority left when instructed to swear the oath.[64] Similarly in the Aveyron, where this aspect of the electoral process had caused problems the year before, the canton of Marcillac saw attendance fall by over a third when the oath was administered.[65]

What was different in the summer of 1792, compared to twelve months earlier, was the climate of military crisis and political insecurity, which must have deterred a good many voters.[66] In the Marne, which recorded a relatively low turnout by its previous standards, both the districts of Sainte-Menehould and Vitry were subject to enemy incursions. The electoral assembly was transferred away from the affected areas to Reims, where the ensuing panic helped provoke September massacres similar in kind, if not degree, to those which sullied the capital.[67] Provence also witnessed an ugly upsurge of violence during the summer months of 1792 and such incidents kept numerous citizens well clear of the primary assemblies, not just conservatives whose colleagues had come to grief.

The intensity of electoral conflict certainly inhibited the participation

---

[62] AD Marne 1L298, Procès-verbal, 28 Aug. 1792.
[63] G. Laurent, *Les assemblées primaires et l'élection des députés du département de la Marne à la Convention nationale (26 août-6 septembre 1792)* (Reims, 1902), p. 31.
[64] Le Gall, Les consultations générales, II, p. 607.
[65] Mazars, *La Révolution en Rouergue*, I, p. 154.
[66] D. Sutherland, *France 1789–1815: Revolution and Counter-Revolution* (London, 1985), pp. 150–5 for the provincial context. [67] Laurent, *Les assemblées primaires*, pp. 5–6.

of political minorities in places like Paris and Toulon, lowering the turnout as a consequence. At Toulon there was no repeat of the fierce partisan struggle of 1791; instead, the withdrawal of the bourgeoisie handed an easy victory to the Jacobins in August 1792, at a much-reduced poll of only 15 per cent.[68] Evidence of orchestrated attempts to intimidate rivals is not hard to find. According to a correspondent of Brissot's newspaper, the *Patriote français*, citizens in cantons of the Eure-et-Loir expelled opponents with the cry 'For God's sake! no priests: they should be suspended from office; no nobles: they are just aristocrats; no administrators and no bourgeois: they are all royalists'.[69] At Villeneuve, in the Allier, one individual claimed he had been obliged to quit the assembly when fellow voters announced that 'they were not prepared to countenance bourgeois, bailiffs or merchants as second-degree electors'.[70]

In some places a quite deliberate policy of exclusion operated. At Versailles, for example, those who had recently signed petitions in support of Louis XVI were prevented from voting, while at Paris a similar fate befell those who had autographed the so-called 'petition of 8,000' aimed at preventing provincial volunteers (the famous *fédérés*) from coming to Paris in July.[71] Likewise at Tours, the Poissonnerie section decided that signatories to a petition on behalf of refractory priests should be denied admission.[72] Finally, in one section at Toulouse, 'a member proposed the motion that, in a situation where patriotism alone will save the *patrie*, the assembly should expel anyone tainted with antisocial behaviour'. At least four people were subsequently forced to leave on the grounds that they were 'unworthy to sit with good and upright citizens'.[73]

Not all these pressures were politically motivated. Inhabitants of the village of Gournay-sur-Aronde in the canton of Mouchy in the Oise withdrew from their assembly in August 1792, 'as a result of the appalling treatment they . . . have received from the citizens of Mouchy, the *cheflieu*'.[74] The commune of Dizy in the canton of Hautvilliers (Marne), meanwhile, protested against the employment of oral voting at their primary assembly, because they felt it had deprived them of their 'own' delegate to the departmental electoral college. When the election was restaged on 1 September 1792, as a consequence of this complaint,

---

[68] AD Var 1L223, Procès-verbaux de Toulon, 26–7 Aug. 1792.
[69] *Le Patriote français*, 22 Aug. 1792.
[70] AD Allier L137, Procès-verbal de Villeneuve, 26 Aug. 1792.
[71] Auvray, 'Les élections à la Convention', p. 241.
[72] Faye, *La Révolution . . . en Touraine*, p. 104.
[73] AD Haute-Garonne L241, Procès-verbal de la troisième section de Toulouse, 26 Aug. 1792.   [74] Baumont, 'Les assemblées primaires et électorale de l'Oise', p. 150.

inhabitants of Dizy were threatened with violence as they made their way to the polls.[75]

Lefebvre suggested that 'the revolution of 10 August inevitably excluded royalists . . . leaving those who had not voted disturbed and discontented'.[76] Many monarchists and supporters of the refractory clergy evidently desisted from participation in elections to the Convention, but there does not appear to have been any concerted attempt to organise an electoral boycott on their behalf. Though such instances are relatively rare, primary assemblies like that of Mouthe (in the Doubs) did seek to preserve the monarchy and some pronounced royalists were elected to the departmental assemblies, most notably in the Allier and Ardèche.[77] Nonetheless, the overwhelming abstention of conservatively minded citizens gave Jacobins a pretty free hand and, in this situation, the impetus for a large popular turnout was missing.

In this sense the primary elections of 1792 were the work of 'a determined minority', to borrow Mathiez's phrase.[78] Yet the few frequently acted with the tacit consent of the many. In the canton of Blaison in the Maine-et-Loire, for example, a handful of voters claimed to have 'the complete confidence of their fellow-citizens . . . for all that is done'.[79] The notion of proxy-voting, entrusted to those with time to spare, was encouraged by an assembly mechanism at which attendance might be a formality. At Bubry, in the Morbihan, six out of eight deputies to the departmental electoral college failed to appear at the primary assembly where they received unanimous endorsement; their election had presumably been decided in advance.[80]

During the primary elections of August 1792 sovereignty had effectively reverted to the people and a range of interesting as well as inhibiting electoral practices had been employed. While they are usually associated with the radical concept of direct democracy and the influence of Rousseau has been invoked, some of this behaviour harked back to traditions emanating from elections to the Estates General of 1789, which had never completely disappeared from the popular political consciousness.[81] Voting out loud, required at preliminary assemblies in 1789, was now

---

[75] Laurent, *Les assemblées primaires*, pp. 27–8.
[76] G. Lefebvre, *La Révolution française* (Paris, 1951), p. 272.
[77] Aulard, *Histoire politique*, pp. 245–6 and Patrick, *The Men of the First Republic*, pp. 153–4.
[78] A. Mathiez, *La Révolution française*, 3 vols., Editions Denoël (Paris, 1985), II, p. 52.
[79] Cited in Gueniffey, La Révolution française et les élections, p.274.
[80] AD Morbihan L237, Procès-verbal de Bubry, 26 Aug. 1792.
[81] Rose, *The Making of the Sans-Culottes*, p. 171, states that the doctrine was 'rooted originally in Rousseau's *Social Contract*'.

commended by Louvet as the only method 'worthy of free men'.[82] In several Parisian sections its use was demanded not only at primaries, but also at the departmental assembly of the Seine.[83]

There was also growing opposition to the indirect nature of legislative elections, which reached a peak when the sections convened in August 1792. Robespierre had been in the vanguard as usual, proposing direct elections for national deputies as early as July.[84] He was strongly supported by fellow-Jacobin Anthoine, who claimed that the 'unsatisfactory' composition of so many departmental administrations and law courts was a further justification for abolishing the electoral colleges; directly-elected municipal bodies had always been much more patriotic.[85] The Parisian press was quick to lambast the second-degree assemblies as 'useless intermediaries between people and legislators', though Brissot felt that time was too short to change the system for elections to the Convention and he earned a rebuke from Marat as a consequence.[86]

The cry was taken up by La Croix, a member of the Marseille section (formerly Théâtre-Français), who claimed the two-tier system was contrary to popular sovereignty and 'conducive to intrigue and cabals', because of the small numbers who composed the electoral colleges.[87] He demanded that 'the voters in the primary assemblies nominate their representatives directly, without the obligation to express their choice via the electoral colleges which have consistently distorted their wishes up until now'. There was also great annoyance, in Paris as elsewhere, that the number of second-degree electors had not been increased commensurate with the rise in the total of potential voters. The Halle-au-Blé section, which had nineteen delegates in 1791 now claimed thirty-two and the Place-Vendôme (Piques) section actually elected additional delegates, albeit in vain.[88]

The effort to overcome the obstacle of the electoral colleges led some primary assemblies to resurrect the principle of the mandate, as a means of influencing the later stages of the process. In Paris the practice of mandating delegates had a continuous history from 1789 onwards, when it was enshrined in the drafting of *cahiers de doléances*. The Cordeliers district had been condemned by the National Assembly for demanding an oath of obedience from deputies later in the year and one militant, Claude-Charles Martin, had been propounding the idea since 1788.[89]

---

[82] Louvet, *La sentinelle*, 21 Aug. 1792.
[83] AN BI 14, Procès-verbaux de la section de Place-Vendôme, for example, Sept. 1792.
[84] Aulard, ed., *Recueil de documents*, IV, pp. 169–70.
[85] *Ibid.*, IV, p. 198. [86] Aulard, *Histoire politique*, pp. 256–7.
[87] Charavay, ed., *Assemblée électorale*, III, pp. iii–iv. [88] *Ibid.*
[89] Rose, *The Making of the Sans-Culottes*, pp. 76–7 and 168.

In 1792 the concept, neatly summed up by the radical Varlet when he wrote, 'the first act of sovereignty is to elect, the second to define the powers, the mandates of those elected', had passed into common currency.[90]

The relevant legislation invited the primary assemblies to 'bestow unlimited powers upon their second-degree electors', but in the capital the tide of direct democracy was running too strongly to be stopped altogether. According to the Arcis section, for example, the departmental assembly of the Seine was simply 'the mandatory of the sections in which all sovereign power continues to reside'.[91] The Montreuil section issued its delegates with specific instructions and retained the right of recall if they abused their authority. For its part the Arsenal section promised to keep a watchful eye over 'the conduct of their mandatories', while the Quinze-Vingts even went so far as to replace a delegate who was failing to attend sessions of the electoral college in September.[92] A final attempt to exert control over second-degree electors was made by the Bondy section which claimed the power of veto over all deputies elected to the National Convention. This declaration echoed a similar proposal from the Place-Vendôme (Piques) and was endorsed by the Paris Commune, though ultimately to no effect.[93]

Outside the capital, despite the assembly of many sections *en permanence* during the summer of 1792, overt expressions of direct democracy remained muted, certainly at the level of the primary assemblies. In the Oise, at Ons-en-Bray, there was some discussion of drawing up a *cahier de doléances* to guide delegates, in an explicit association of the constituent elections of 1792 with those of 1789.[94] Meanwhile, in the Allier, a handful of conservative cantons instructed deputies to press for a retention of the monarchy.[95] Conversely, one of the sections of Caen expressed its hostile attitude towards the monarchy by putting a portrait of Louis XVI to the torch and binding delegates to a Republic.[96] Yet, once the disarray of the summer months was overcome, most politicians including those of Paris (who eventually refused to allow the sections of Paris a veto over the electoral college's choices) put their weight firmly behind the location of sovereignty in their hands.

Direct democracy foundered on the reef of poor attendance. The

---

[90] *Ibid.*, pp. 169–70.   [91] Cited in Genty, *Paris, 1789–1795*, p. 190.
[92] AN BI 14, Procès-verbal de la section des Quinze-Vingts, Sept. 1792.
[93] Charavay, ed., *Assemblée électorale*, III, pp. iv-v.
[94] Baumont, 'Les assemblées primaires et électoral de l'Oise', p. 142.
[95] L. Biernawski, *Un département sous la Révolution française, l'Allier* (Moulins, 1909), pp. 158–60.
[96] G. Lesage, ed., *Episodes de la Révolution à Caen racontés par un bourgeois et un homme du peuple* (Paris, 1926), p. 91.

Luxembourg section in Paris had declared in 1791 that 'small numbers ensured unanimity and purity of intention', but there was concern that enemies of the Revolution would regard abstention as an indication that the people were ready to relapse into slavery. It was suggested that the names of defaulters be published, while faithful attenders might be awarded a medal.[97] The Bondy section had actually issued a warning to recalcitrant voters that, if they failed to attend three sessions in a row, their names would be noted as 'bad citizens' and they would be denied *certificats de civisme*.[98] The Rue de Montreuil section, for its part, exhorted members to go and fetch their relatives and friends, 'by shaming them into attendance ... or even employing abuse, if necessary'.[99]

Few of these suggestions appear to have had much effect. In January 1793 the Gardes-Françaises section received, approved and distributed an address from colleagues at the Arsenal concerning 'the urgent need to persuade their fellow-citizens to attend their sectional assemblies and, in particular, to vote in the elections'. The 'overwhelming majority of citizens' had failed to participate in recent municipal polls. For the most part, or so it was alleged, those who did attend were 'among the less well-off; in the main they were manual workers who, having toiled all day, could have been excused for seeking some relaxation'. By contrast, 'better-off citizens' had failed to participate, only to complain later about the electoral outcome. It was decided that the names of these armchair critics would be noted as 'enemies of the people'.[100]

Contemporaries as well as historians were dismayed by the relatively low level of electoral participation in the summer of 1792 and local elections held towards the end of the year were scarcely more encouraging. The Convention decided, as numerous departmental electoral assemblies had already demanded, that local administrative bodies elected under the monarchy should be totally renewed now that France was a Republic. Data for municipal polls, held during the winter months from November to March, are not easily evaluated; given the continuing uncertainty about how many citizens were entitled to vote, any figures must be treated with extreme caution. Yet the percentage turnout reproduced here, which relates to the first round of voting for mayors, can be usefully compared with similar calculations for elections held a year earlier in November 1791.

[97] BN Lb⁴⁰ 1932, L'assemblée générale de la Section du Luxembourg, 21 Nov. 1791.
[98] BN Lb⁴⁰ 3238, Derniers mots de la section de Bondy aux insouciants (Paris, no date).
[99] AN BI 8, Procès-verbal de la Rue de Montreuil, June 1791.
[100] BN Lb⁴⁰ 1844, Section des Gardes-Françaises, 7 Jan. 1793. For the reaction in another section, see M. Slavin, *The French Revolution in Miniature. Section Droits-de-l'Homme, 1789–1795* (Princeton, 1984), pp. 93–4.

Table 10 *Turnout in municipal elections, November 1791 and December 1792–January 1793*

Location	Percentage of *ADV* voting at first round for mayor Nov. 1791	Percentage of *ADV* voting at first round for mayor Dec. 1792–Jan. 1793
Haute-Vienne:		
0–500 Inhabitants	59.2	44.5
500–1500	49.2	28.5
1000–1500	26.4	24.5
1500–2500	35.8	16.8
Côte-d'Or: 3 Rural Communities	44.9	31.0
Var: Grasse Dist. 0–2000 Inhabs.	20.2	17.2
2000 +	5.3	8.2
Aix-en-Provence	12.3	26.0
Strasbourg	66.8	25.1
Montpellier	20.0	17.4
Toulouse	7.1	16.7
Dijon	27.8	16.5
Paris	13.7	13.9
Bar-le-Duc	15.5	13.3
Toulon	25.2	13.3
Châlons-sur-Marne	9.3	6.9

Sources: Audevart, 'Les élections en Haute-Vienne', pp. 133–4; Fortunet *et al.*, *Pouvoir municipal et communauté rurale*, p.19; AD Alpes-Maritimes L548–51; Derobert-Ratel, *Institutions . . . à Aix-en-Provence*, p. 605; AM Strasbourg, Délibérations, vol. II; AM Montpellier K1/4; AM Toulouse 1K 10–11; AM Dijon 1D1 2–3; Genty, *Paris 1789–1795*, pp. 108 and 193; Aimond, *Histoire de Bar-le-Duc*, p. 315; AM Toulon L579–80; AD Marne E 5873–4

A downward trend in turnout is generally apparent, though some towns in the Midi produced strong returns, while their northern counterparts recorded rather feeble polling. Smaller rural communities continued to show a relatively greater interest in local affairs, despite a persistent decline in participation after 1790. Since the atmosphere of unrest and military threat that marked the summer months had been largely dispelled, it was doubtless the absence of much real competition for posts which lowered turnout in many places. At Toulon, for example, the incumbent Jacobin mayor, who had fought so hard for his election in

November 1791, was re-elected in December 1792 with 96 per cent of a low poll.[101]

Despite concern in the sections over persistent absenteeism, Paris turned out relatively well for its municipal elections, which proved to be a protracted affair, not to say a veritable marathon. Pétion had resigned as mayor in September after his election to the National Convention. Nonetheless, in the absence of declared candidates, he was re-elected in October and immediately refused to serve. It was only on 30 November 1792 that a willing, and moderate replacement was found after no less than seven ballots.[102] In the circumstances participation held up remarkably well and, on two occasions, over 15,000 Parisians voted in the best turnout so far recorded during the Revolution, in absolute if not relative terms. This total was halved when a new municipal council was elected, though a progressive decline in participation as the importance of posts diminished was an enduring feature of the revolutionary electoral system.

These municipal elections at Paris, the last time a mayor was elected in the capital for almost two hundred years, saw renewed demands for oral voting. The Champs-Elysées section was still insisting in October that 'the exercise of the right to vote should not be inhibited by any instructions which do not emanate from the assemblies themselves, for this is a privilege that can never be alienated'.[103] The Convention's ban on oral voting notwithstanding, at least thirteen sections persisted with *haute voix*. The 1792 section asserted its autonomy by allowing all adult males to vote, 'even if they are domestic servants'.[104] But authority was gradually being reimposed from the centre and public discussion of favoured contenders for office did not proceed as planned.

A final round of elections took place during the winter months of 1792–93, to elect *juges de paix* and their *assesseurs* in the cantons. In the Haute-Vienne turnout was generally lower than in recent municipal elections, while in the Var it was slightly higher.[105] As always, the more fiercely contested polls were better attended. Indeed, at Saint-Amans-des-Cots in the Aveyron almost half the electorate was persuaded to vote in a bitter battle for the nomination between rival communities.[106] With the exception of the occasional and poorly attended local by-election, to replace a deceased mayor or municipal councillor for example, these judicial elec-

---

[101] AM Toulon L580, Procès-verbaux d'élection, Dec. 1792.
[102] Genty, *Paris 1789–1795*, pp. 193–4 and S. Lacroix, 'L'élection du maire de Paris en 1792', *Rf*, 38 (1900). [103] Cited in Genty, *Paris 1789–1795*, p. 192.
[104] AN F¹cIII Seine 1, Section de 1792, 11 Oct. 1792.
[105] Audevart, 'Les élections en Haute-Vienne', p. 135 and AD Alpes-Maritimes L552, Procès-verbaux d'élection, Dec.–Jan., 1792–93.
[106] Mazars, *La Révolution en Rouergue*, I, pp. 47–9. See also Du Châtelier, 'Essai de monographie électorale', pp. 33–6, on similar parochial disputes in the Finistère.

tions were the last to be held for a couple of years. During the Terror and its Thermidorean aftermath, in the Years II and III of the revolutionary calendar (1793–95), the appointment of officials by *représentants-en-mission* from the Convention became the rule in many places.

The failure of so many Frenchmen to use the extended franchise of 1792 might suggest that few of them regretted this suspension of the electoral principle and the return to the practice of nominating officials. Yet turnout in the legislative elections of 1792 was not quite as disastrous as many historians have assumed. In terms of absolute numbers more voters participated in these primary assemblies than a year before, especially in the cities where there were signs that a greater political awareness was emerging. Although deputies in the Convention were generally opposed to the idea of direct democracy, it was agreed that the forthcoming republican constitution would be submitted to a popular vote. Elections were put on ice while the constitutional question was being decided, but citizens were invited to vote in two important referenda instead.

5 Voting the Constitution: The referenda of 1793 and 1795

The National Convention was first and foremost a constituent assembly and, during the three turbulent years of its existence, two Constitutions were drafted. The first, that of 1793 (or Year I of the republican era), was set aside 'until circumstances permitted'. It was never implemented because when stability of a sort did return, after Thermidor (July 1794), less radical ideas prevailed. A more conservative Constitution, that of 1795 (or the Year III), was devised to replace it. This time the document was put into immediate effect and the Convention finally separated. Between its creation in the summer of 1792 and its dissolution in the autumn of 1795 no legislative elections had taken place in France; only at the local level were a few assemblies convened for municipal and judicial purposes. The electorate was instead given an unprecedented opportunity to participate in two constitutional referenda, the first of which was held in the summer of 1793.

On 21 September 1792, the day after it assembled, the Convention boldly declared: 'Before it can be put into effect any constitution must be endorsed by the people.'[1] The idea of a popular consultation had been mooted in the Constituent Assembly by Pétion as early as September 1789. He suggested that the people should be called upon to arbitrate in the case of deadlock between king and assembly, by simply voting in favour of one side or the other.[2] His colleagues were unimpressed and subsequently refused to submit the Constitution of 1791 to the electorate for ratification. Demands for a 'referendum' of this sort were supported by conservative deputies like Malouet, but rejected on the grounds that the National Assembly already incarnated the will of the nation.[3]

By the time the Convention met, in the autumn of 1792, this concept of representation had been undermined by assertions of direct democracy, which flourished during the summer months of 1792 in the limbo left by

---

[1] *AP* LII, pp. 71–2, 21 Sept. 1792.   [2] *AP* VIII, pp. 581–4, 5 Sept. 1789.
[3] M. Fridieff, *Les origines du referendum dans la Constitution de 1793* (Paris, 1932), p. 229.

the collapse of royal authority and the Constitution of 1791. In the ensuing elections to the Convention, a number of primary assemblies had called for a constitutional referendum, most notably at Paris and a dozen or so departmental electoral colleges followed suit. In the Jura, for example, it was stipulated that 'the constitution . . . must not be implemented until it has been accepted by the people gathered in their primary assemblies'.[4]

Yet if the *conventionnels* ultimately bowed to demands for such a consultation (the terms plebiscite and referendum were not actually employed during the Revolution), it was out of expediency as much as conviction. On 16 October 1792 Manuel proposed a referendum on the recent declaration of the First Republic, but his suggestion was given extremely short shrift.[5] During the trial of Louis XVI, the Girondin deputy Vergniaud was similarly unsuccessful in arguing that the fate of the king should be submitted to the people. A substantial minority of 287 deputies voted in favour of the *appel au peuple* in January 1793, but Robespierre's observations on the impracticalities of a popular vote had won the day.[6] Lasource met similar resistance when he argued in April that the conduct of deputies condemned by the popular movement in Paris should be put to a vote of the whole nation.[7]

Two months later, however, the much-debated referendum finally materialised. The now-dominant Montagnard faction was anxious to rally support for a new Constitution, hastily issued in June after the expulsion of leading Girondin deputies from the Convention. The Constitution of 1793, drafted by Hérault de Séchelles and adopted by the assembly on 24 June, was carefully constructed from the democratic consensus that had emerged in recent months. Despite some significant modifications to earlier versions, it would be misleading to call it a 'Montagnard' Constitution, for tactical considerations were uppermost in the minds of its authors.[8]

All Frenchmen aged over twenty-one years old could vote and be elected, without further qualification save six months residence in the canton. These citizens would meet each year to directly elect a new Legislative Assembly on the basis of one deputy for 40,000 inhabitants. Condorcet's proposals for referenda were taken on board by the

---

[4] AN C179, Procès-verbal du Jura, 8 Sept. 1792 and Aulard, *Histoire politique*, pp. 257–8.
[5] *AP* LII, p. 525, 16 Oct. 1792.
[6] M. Walzer, ed., *Regicide and Revolution. Speeches at the Trial of Louis XVI* (Cambridge, 1974), pp. 178 ff. and D.P. Jordan, *The King's Trial. Louis XVI vs. the French Revolution* (Berkeley, 1979), pp. 143 ff.   [7] *AP* LXII, p. 196, 15 Apr. 1793.
[8] J. Godechot, ed., *Les constitutions de la France depuis 1789* (Paris, 1970), pp. 79–92 for the text.

Montagnards, though in an attenuated form which allowed the electorate to censure, but not initiate legislation. Moreover, this provision would only operate under stringent conditions which demanded a significant mobilisation of voters: a request for the primary assemblies to meet in a deliberative capacity required signatures from 20 per cent of the electorate, while discussion could only commence when at least 50 per cent were in attendance.

No wonder Aulard concluded that the Constitution of 1793 was 'unworkable' as it stood. According to this great historian the document represented 'a democratic programme, but for future rather than immediate application'. It was, in truth, an expedient designed for the current situation, an attempt to end the civil war which had erupted in several regions. Only a new Constitution, Aulard continued, would unite 'a people which was so deeply divided and at odds with itself'. Above all, 'the departments feared a Parisian dictatorship; by means of a referendum, the Convention was giving the final word to the provinces.'[9] A Constitution which conceded the principle of popular censure and the possibility of revision, at the behest of the electorate, was thus immediately put to the people following its adoption in the Convention.

On 27 June Barère proposed and the assembly decreed that 'within a week of receiving the present decree, the Declaration of Rights and the Constitution will be submitted to the primary assemblies'.[10] In order to 'reconcile the citizens and unite them around a common objective', it was also decided that delegates chosen at each primary assembly would meet in Paris on 10 August (the first anniversary of the overthrow of the monarchy) for a 'festival to celebrate the unity and indivisibility of the Republic'. The votes would be verified and counted, using the *procès-verbaux* these delegates brought with them. A public endorsement of the result would seal the '*rapprochement* of Paris and the provinces' and establish 'fraternity among the French people'.

This novel experiment with a referendum sprang from the particular circumstances of 1793, but it would be repeated in future, for authoritarian as much as democratic ends. There is no doubt that in 1793 it was welcomed by a substantial number of voters, whose enthusiasm was for the most part genuine rather than contrived. Even sceptics like the municipal councillors at Brest received the document warmly, on account of 'the urgent need for a constitution and the anxiety of the French people to be fully consulted upon the fundamental articles of its government'.[11] The constitutional vote offered the prospect of a fresh parliamentary assembly

---

[9] Aulard, *Histoire politique*, p. 308.   [10] *AP* LXVII, p. 557, 27 June 1793.
[11] AM Brest 1D2, Délibérations du conseil municipal, 22 July 1793.

and the renewed rule of law. In the short term at least, the consultation went a long way towards reducing conflict between rival republican factions in France.

The generally conciliatory effect of the referendum is reflected in the huge number of votes cast, despite the civil strife and enemy incursions which prevented assemblies from meeting in over 400 cantons (8 per cent of the total). For this reason the overall turnout cannot be compared to other elections, or even later referenda of the revolutionary and Napoleonic periods, without considerable qualification. Indeed, it is extremely difficult to obtain precise figures for participation at a departmental level. Some *procès-verbaux* are missing, while others were drawn up belatedly and served to confuse official calculations. Finally, almost 300 of the extant proceedings recorded a unanimous verdict, without offering any indication of the numbers who actually voted.[12]

This notion of unanimous endorsement is a reminder that, even when each individual vote counted towards the whole, many participants still preferred to make a collective response, which the maintenance of polling by assembly inevitably encouraged. The traditional concept of proxy voting, of those present speaking for those unable to attend, persisted too. It was clearly articulated at L'Arche in the Basses-Alpes, where 'the assembly declared it was unanimously accepting the constitution, on behalf of those who were absent as well as those citizens from the canton who were present'.[13] At Jaussier, in the same alpine department, three municipal officers stated that they represented 'the general will of their community' at the cantonal assembly. At Belin, in the Gironde, *commissaires* from the commune of Les Salles duly arrived bearing votes cast by fellow-villagers, only to have them ruled inadmissible.[14] Such thinking was by no means a monopoly of the Midi: at Ivoy in the Ardennes the president of the meeting was anxious to record that 'other citizens, unavoidably detained by cutting hay, were also entirely in favour of the new constitution'.[15]

The parliamentary *Commission des Six*, which was put in charge of the count, concluded on 20 August 1793 that 1,784,377 votes had been cast for the constitution and 11,531 against.[16] This declaration came too late to be announced at the *fête* of 10 August, yet it was still a trifle premature since many cantons had yet to make a return. In many areas the assem-

---

[12] AN BII 25, Tableau des votes, 20 Aug. 1793 and Aulard, *Histoire politique*, pp. 310–1.
[13] *Ibid.* BII 2, Procès-verbaux des Basses-Alpes, 28 July-4 Aug. 1793.
[14] *Ibid.* BII 12, Procès-verbal de Belin, 28 July 1793.
[15] *Ibid.* BII 2, Procès-verbaux d'Ivoy, 14 July 1793.
[16] *Ibid.* BII25, Tableaux des votes, 20 Aug. 1793 and 1 pluviôse II (20 Jan. 1794).

blies had not met until August and had consequently failed to send a delegate to Paris. A supplementary report on the referendum, issued in pluviôse II (January 1794), took the official score to 1,801,918 in favour and just 11,610 in opposition.

René Baticle, who made a splendid, comprehensive study of the voluminous documentation deposited in the *Archives nationales*, reckoned that even the later total published by the Commission was too low. He arrived at 1,869,004 votes overall, including negative responses, abstentions (i.e. a refusal to pronounce pro or con on the part of a citizen who was present) and invalid ballots, as well as affirmative opinions.[17] There is no doubt that, if the unanimous decisions recorded at many assemblies were turned into figures, the final total would approach 2,000,000 participants. This represents the biggest turnout of voters since 1790, perhaps of the entire revolutionary decade, even allowing for the inclusion in 1793 of newly created departments like the Alpes-Maritimes or Mont-Blanc, which added some 20,000 votes to the result.

Absolute numbers raise enough problems, but the calculation of percentage turnout is still trickier since the size of the electorate is so difficult to determine. According to the decree of 27 June 1793, the rules applied to the election of the Convention in August 1792 remained in force, pending adoption of the new democratic constitution. In other words, all adult males over twenty-one years old, resident in the canton for a year and exercising a profession, but not in domestic service, could vote.[18] Unfortunately no general assessment of the number of citizens *ayant droit de voter* is available for 1793; information of this sort was requested by the *Comité de Division*, but replies from the districts are fragmentary and frequently unreliable.[19] The informed guess made in the previous chapter would suggest that, as in the summer of 1792, perhaps 6,000,000 adult males could vote. So overall turnout in the plebiscite was in the region of 30 per cent, lower than 1790 but superior to any count taken thereafter. In the generally chaotic circumstances of summer 1793, with thousands of young men away on military service, it was a remarkable achievement.

An attempt can be made to compare turnout between departments, dividing the population by four in order to obtain a rough guide to the electorate of 1793.[20] The resulting order of grandeur applies right across the country, to an extent not feasible for earlier years of the Revolution.

---

[17] R. Baticle, 'Le plébiscite sur la Constitution de 1793', *Rf*, 57 and 58 (1909–10), Tableau.
[18] *AP* LXVII, p. 558, 27 June 1793.
[19] AN F^{20} 298–394, Tableaux de la population, 1793–an II, classified by department. Serge Aberdam is currently analysing this large corpus of material.
[20] Population figures from 1806 have again been employed on account of their reliablity but, since fewer than one in four inhabitants was enfranchised in 1793, their inflationary effect may be discounted.

Voting the Constitution 107

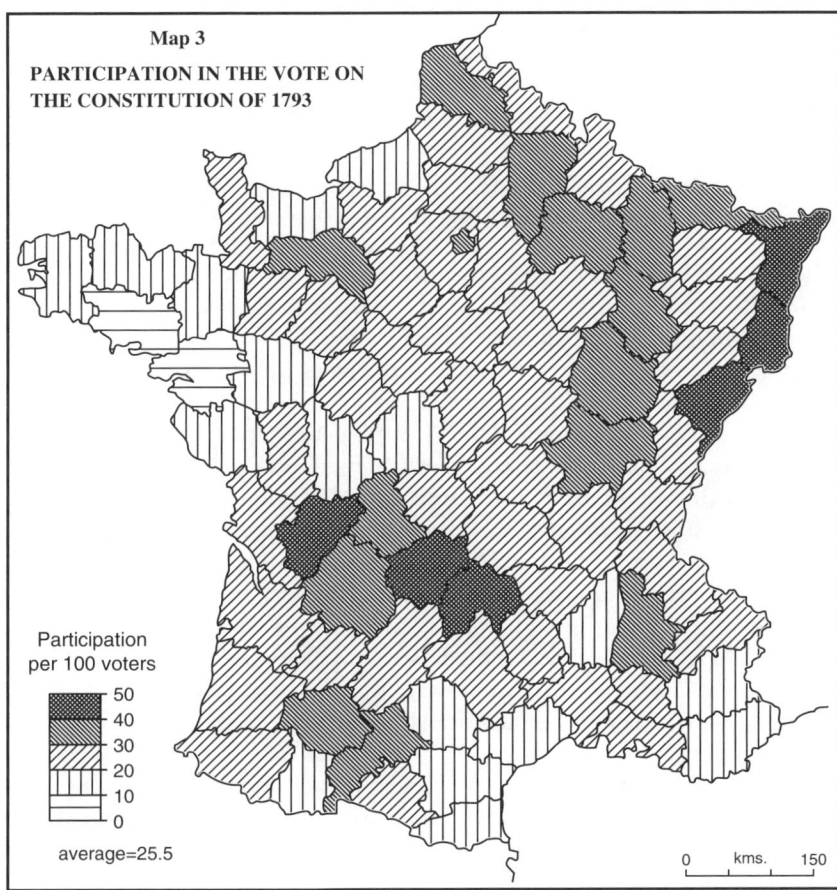

3 Participation in the vote on the Constitution of 1793

Leaving aside departments where disorder or invasion inhibited assembly, the pattern which emerges (on map 3) correlates closely with the preceding, much less comprehensive geography of turnout which this study has revealed. Polling was generally stronger in north and east than south and west. Only three departments with participation rates above 40 per cent were located below an imaginary line drawn from Lyon to Rouen. One of them, the Charente, has already been noted for its high levels of attendance in 1790 and 1791, while heavy polling in the Corrèze and neighbouring Cantal comes as more of a surprise. By contrast only one department above the Lyon-Rouen dividing line (the Seine-Inférieure) fell below a solid score of 25 per cent in this referendum.

Within departments huge and inexplicable variations were once more apparent from one neighbouring canton to another. In the Marne in the District of Châlons, for example, Jalons polled at 13.5 per cent, nearby Cernon at 57.4 per cent.[21] Yet one trend, apparent since 1791, was confirmed by the referendum of 1793: namely a generally heavier turnout in urban as opposed to rural areas. In the Côte-d'Or, for instance, five out of six district *chefs-lieux*, including Dijon, attracted a higher level of participation than the average for other cantons in the circumscription. The same was true of many *chefs-lieux de département*, from Châlons-sur-Marne to Vannes and Carcassonne.[22] The intense politicisation of the cities might offer an explanation for this differentiation between town and countryside, especially since copies of the constitution were sent to political clubs as well as local authorities. In 1793 even the sections of Paris polled strongly, with sixteen of them topping 1,000 participants, while the rural districts of Franciade (formerly Saint-Denis) and Bourg-l'Egalité (Bourg-la-Reine) recorded rather more modest totals.[23]

The lowest departmental turnouts can usually be ascribed to a failure to vote at all in many cantons. Not a single assembly was held in Corsica because the island had been plunged into civil war and was also suffering from enemy occupation. Spanish incursions likewise prevented all but one canton from convening in the District of Céret, in the frontier department of the Pyrénées-Orientales. In the Var it was resistance to the government which wrecked the poll: fourteen out of seventeen cantons in the rebel districts of Toulon and Hyères refused to meet.[24] At Toulon itself the arrival of the Constitution had not succeeded in dissipating anti-Montagnard sentiment. Indeed, on 1 August 1793, the document was rejected out of hand as the 'handiwork of the assassins who hold the Convention in thrall' and copies were ceremonially burned.[25]

The referendum was eventually held in some recalcitrant areas in September. Such was the case at Marseille, where the sections were convened as soon as the city had been recaptured by government forces. Only twenty-one out of thirty-two assemblies returned a numerical verdict, as opposed to unanimity in favour of the Constitution. Nonetheless, a massive turnout was clearly apparent, well in excess of the total vote in earlier Marseillais elections, doubtless in an effort to atone for the town's recent rebellion.[26] In the West, more deeply enmeshed in the toils of civil

---

[21] AN BII 18, Procès-verbaux de la Marne, July 1793.
[22] *Ibid*. BII 7, Procès-verbaux de la Côte-d-Or, July 1793 and Crook, '"Aux Urnes Citoyens!"', p. 158.   [23] AN BII 23, Procès-verbaux de la Seine, July 1793.
[24] Poupé, *Le département du Var*, pp. 518–20.
[25] AM Toulon, L2 I 5, Voeu des sections sur l'acte dit constitutionnel, 1 Aug. 1793.
[26] AN F¹cIII Bouches-du-Rhône 1, Procès-verbaux de Marseille, Sept. 1793.

war, it was not unusual for 'refugee patriots' to hold their own assemblies in hospitable republican cantons or the neighbouring departments to which they had fled. In the Loire-Inférieure, for example, patriots from the insurgent districts of Machecoul and Clisson assembled at Nantes in order to cast their votes.[27] In the Vendée, republicans from the Mouilleron canton initially voted at La Rochelle, where they had sought sanctuary, while others voted later on home ground when it had become safe to do so.[28]

Assemblies were rarely held on the same day, even in the same department. The decree of 27 June simply stated that the electorate should meet within a week of receiving instructions and there were inevitable delays in more remote areas. Paris polled first, at the beginning of July, while most departments convened their cantons on Sundays 14, 21 or 28 July, but dates in August were not uncommon. Some assemblies were deliberately adjourned in an effort to attract a higher turnout: the proceedings at Besse, in the Var, finally commenced on 2 August, but since only twenty-seven citizens were present it was decided to reconvene nine days later; this occasion proved equally unsatisfactory and it was only on 12 September, in the presence of sixty-seven voters, that a decision in favour of the Constitution was eventually recorded.[29]

Eyguières, in the Bouches-du-Rhône, experienced similar difficulties in securing a good turnout, but in this case postponement served to diminish rather than increase attendance.[30] The most curious case of a deferred vote in the referendum emanates from Brasparts in the Finistère, where a verdict was not recorded until 15 germinal II (4 April 1794), though without any accompanying explanation.[31] In one or two cases communes met separately having missed the cantonal assembly, while others used the latitude permitted by the decree (which, in the absence of a Constitution, *invited* rather than instructed conformity with past electoral practice) to convene an independent meeting. Citizens of Saint-Savourin, which formed part of the canton of Auriol in the Bouches-du-Rhône, declared themselves unwilling to tramp the 'two whole leagues' to their *chef-lieu* on a hot summer's day and voted *chez-eux* instead.[32]

---

[27] AN BII 15, Procès-verbaux de la Loire-Inférieure, districts de Clisson et Machecoul, 22 July 1793 and Le Gall, Les consultations générales, II, pp. 657–8.
[28] *Ibid.* BII 31, Procès-verbal de Mouilleron, 23 frimaire II (13 Dec. 1793).
[29] *Ibid.* BII 31, Procès-verbal de Besse, 2 Aug.-12 Sept. 1793.
[30] *Ibid.* BII 4, Procès-verbal d'Eyguières, 4 Aug. 1793.
[31] *Ibid.* BII 10, Procès-verbal de Brasparts, 15 germinal II (4 Apr. 1794).
[32] *Ibid.* BII 4, Procès-verbal de Saint-Savourin, 1 Sept. 1793.

Electoral idiosyncrasies abounded in 1793, not least where the actual business of casting a vote was concerned. Over 100 assemblies, including many in the capital, adopted the Constitution by *acclamation*. In the section of Maison-Commune (formerly Hotel-de-Ville) at Paris, for example: 'The president announced that each citizen is free to cast his vote upon the constitution as he sees fit . . . [and] since not a single objection was raised, the constitution was put to the vote and adopted, unanimously and to applause from all quarters . . .' In the Arsenal section, as at Molière-et-La-Fontaine (*ci-devant* Fontaine-Montmorency), 'everyone stood up to give spontaneous approval to the constitutional document' though here, as elsewhere, the president of the assembly subsequently demanded a head count.[33]

The decree on the referendum, like article 16 of the Constitution itself, allowed each voter to choose between a vote by ballot or out loud. Baticle has unearthed twenty-one cases where a 'mixed regime' for voting was tolerated. In the fourth section of Brest, for example, 145 participants voted verbally (144 pro and just one con), while 275 were in favour and nineteen against in a written ballot. This isolated case suggests that negative verdicts were more likely to be recorded where greater secrecy was guaranteed, though Baticle is unwilling to accept this argument.[34] In most cases a collective decision was made on procedure and in one instance this involved voting with peas and beans; the peas secured a majority for the Constitution!

The majority of *procès-verbaux* simply record that a vote on the Constitution was held, without indicating the manner of taking it. Oral voting was certainly more widespread in 1793 than in the summer of 1792, for the consultation lent itself to a straightforward yes or no. Above all, as the Droits de l'Homme (Roi-de-Sicile) section in Paris emphasised, this method was 'the most appropriate one' for dedicated republicans. Some interesting variations were introduced on the theme of openly expressing an opinion. Quite literally standing up to be counted, *assis et levé*, was not uncommon and nor was raising hands, taking off hats or moving to one side of the meeting place.[35] At Marigny, in the Manche, participants were invited to leave the premises if they accepted the Constitution, voting with their feet more than a century before Lenin's celebrated dictum on the subject.[36]

[33] *Ibid.* BII 23, Procès-verbaux des sections de Paris, July 1793.
[34] AM Brest 1K7 16, Procès-verbal de la 4ᵉ section, 24 July 1793 and Baticle, 'Le plébiscite', pp. 12–13.
[35] AN BII 23, Procès-verbal de la section des Droits-de-l'Homme, 3 July 1793.
[36] Baticle, 'Le plébiscite', p. 14.

In Paris and other big cities the level of participation was increased by leaving the polls open for several days. The Fraternité section at Paris, for instance, recorded 327 votes on Tuesday 2 July but, eleven days later, the total accepting the Constitution had risen to 669.[37] In these circumstances citizens were asked to inscribe their opinions in a register, thus anticipating a procedure later utilised for referenda and other elections under Napoleon – albeit in the complete absence of assemblies and under rather different circumstances.

The use of assemblies in the constitutional referendum of 1793 encouraged varieties of electoral behaviour which flourished as never before or afterwards. On this occasion, unlike 1791 or 1792, no oath of loyalty was required, but this did not stop some meetings prescribing their own. An especially lengthy one was devised at Carentan in the Manche, which began: 'I swear to live free, without a king, or to die in the attempt.'[38] As always there were speeches galore, urging reconciliation between citizens or hostility to enemies of the Republic in the most flowery language. One orator, who compared the Constitution of 1793 to Noah's Ark, rescuing France from the flood of anarchy, betrayed his ecclesiastical background in the process. Since constitutional clergy continued to officiate at many cantonal assemblies it is no surprise to find an abundance of religious language, nor that proceedings should end with a *Te Deum*.[39] Most meetings were still held in churches, often on a Sunday after mass, though the one held at Peyrolles in the Bouches-du-Rhône took place *al fresco*, under the tree of liberty![40]

Assemblies also afforded ample opportunity for displays of fraternal affection. It was not unusual for the exchange of 'republican embraces' to occur, as at the Piques section in Paris.[41] Elsewhere emotions ran even higher. At Saint-Nicholas-de-la-Grave in the Haute-Garonne the president's speech provoked such a sensation among participants that several of them, transfixed by 'transports of the most sublime enthusiasm . . . their eyes swimming with tears of joy, threw themselves into each others' arms to share a fraternal kiss'. Some 250 *citoyennes* were allowed to join in the collective ecstasy and acclaim the Constitution before this particular *jour de gloire* ended, in typical southern fashion, with a *farandole* being danced around the town.[42] Women and children

---

[37] AN BII 23, Procès-verbal de la section de la Fraternité, 2–13 July 1793.
[38] Baticle, 'Le plébiscite', p. 518.   [39] *Ibid.*, pp. 514–15.
[40] AN BII 4, Procès-verbal de Peyrolles, 4 Aug. 1793.
[41] *Ibid.* BII 23, Procès-verbal de la section des Piques, 2 July 1793.
[42] *Ibid.* BII 11, Procès-verbal de Saint-Nicolas-de-la-Grave, 28 July 1793. At Lamballe, in the Côtes-du-Nord, 'women swarmed into the assembly to offer their assent to the Constitution', according to Pommeret, *L'esprit public dans le département des Côtes-du-Nord*, p. 225.

were admitted to several assemblies, usually as observers, though at Laon (Aisne) and Pontoise (Seine-et-Oise) their votes were counted too.[43] In cases like these the electoral ritual became the affair of the entire community.

Above all the assembly mechanism facilitated discussion of the Constitution and other related issues at almost a third of the 6,000 assemblies. Debate on such occasions was already a well-established practice, reinforced because the constitutional document made provision for it and the decree on the referendum actually recommended it. Both the Declaration of Rights and the Constitution of 1793 were to be read out to the assembled citizenry and debate would precede the vote. This procedure provoked criticism in some cantons: a section of Mugron, in the Landes, objected to the time such a reading would take and moved straight to a decision.[44] In the non-francophone departments there were frequent demands for translation: at Carhaix, in the Finistère, peasants requested that it 'be read out and explained in Breton', while Saint-Girons in the Ariège sought the employment of 'the language of the fields'.[45]

In a few cases, like the Bondy section at Paris or Les Sables-d'Olonne in the Vendée, Declaration and Constitution were voted upon article by article.[46] Though it was rare to proceed in so time-consuming a fashion, roughly a tenth of all assemblies sought modifications to one or more item. Article 35 of the Declaration, which enshrined the right to insurrection, was a favourite target of criticism, as was article 4 of the Constitution, which generously awarded foreigners the franchise after a year's residence. Where the suffrage was concerned many voters in the Midi were anxious to raise the minimum age requirement back to the traditional majority of twenty-five years.[47] The assembly at Ramouillet (Yonne), for its part, objected to the enfranchisement of servants, while there were scattered calls for a reimposition of fiscal criteria to vote or to be elected.[48] On the other hand, Lourdes and Bagnères, in the Hautes-Pyrénées, sought an end to all indirect elections and, exceptionally, the neighbouring canton of Mauleon wanted to make voting compulsory, despite its own high turnout.[49]

[43] Baticle, 'Le plébiscite', p. 511.
[44] AN BII 15, Procès-verbal de Mugron, 21 July 1793.
[45] Ibid. BII 2, Procès-verbal de Saint-Girons, 28 July 1793, ibid. BII 10, Procès-verbal de Carhaix, 28 July 1793 and Baticle, 'Le plébiscite', p. 7.
[46] AN BII 23, Procès-verbal de la section de Bondy, 3 July 1793 and ibid. BII 31, Procès-verbal des Sables-d'Olonne, 4 Aug. 1793.
[47] Ibid. BII 3, Procès-verbal de Saint-Symphorien, 21 July 1793.
[48] Baticle, 'Le plébiscite', pp. 223–4.
[49] AN BII 25, Procès-verbaux de Mauleon, Lourdes and Bagnères, 28 July 1793.

A less impressionistic approach to debate at the assemblies of 1793 brings to light three particular issues, none of which was directly linked to either the Declaration or the Constitution.[50] The first of these was a demand for repeal of the recent law on equal testation, which had already provoked a fierce reaction from political clubs in the Midi, the territory of Roman law and primogeniture. Such protest was naturally confined to the southern half of the country and a geographical division was also in evidence where the 4 May 1793 'maximum', or control on grain prices, was concerned: the south was hostile, while cantons in the Parisian basin were solidly in favour of restrictions.

As one might expect, demands for the restoration of traditional Catholicism emanated from predominantly non-juring areas, that is to say departments hostile to the Civil Constitution of the Clergy. The canton of Ploudiry in the Finistère demanded the removal of all legislation 'which represents a direct or indirect attack upon the free exercise of our holy, Catholic, Apostolic and Roman religion', while La Ferrière (Calvados) sought an end to divorce and a ban on priests marrying.[51] Cantons from all points of the compass, however, save the centre of France, spoke up on behalf of the constitutional clergy, especially where regular payment of their stipends was involved. In such cases priestly influence was doubtless at work, helping to turn the *procès-verbal* into something of a *cahier de doléances*, to be taken up to Paris by the cantonal delegate.

One final aspect of the process of engaging in debate and drawing up comments in the referendum of 1793 deserves particular attention. This was the political discussion that took place in those departments which had espoused 'federalism', or rather protested against the purge of the Convention on 2 June 1793. Few negative votes were cast against the subsequent 'Montagnard' Constitution which was deliberately designed to pacify the provinces, though there was a significant concentration of noes in the West. Abstention might have represented a more appropriate response from 'federalists' yet, if failure to turn out is easy to tabulate, it is notoriously difficult to interpret; in fact, anti-Montagnards tended to vote in order to hasten adoption of the Constitution and thus the formation of a new legislature.

In these circumstances study of the more overtly political amendments that were passed by many assemblies reveals the geography of republican opposition more effectively. No less than 5 per cent of the *procès-verbaux*

---

[50] Vovelle, *La découverte de la politique*, pp. 203–5.
[51] AN BII 4, Procès-verbal de la Ferrière, 28 July 1793 and *ibid.* BII 4, Procès-verbal de Ploudiry, 28 July 1793.

contained 'federalist' amendments.[52] From the Jura to the Gironde and from the Basses-Alpes to the Finistère emerged a series of demands for immediate elections and the ineligibility of existing *conventionnels* for reelection. In the Basses-Alpes, for example, no less than sixteen cantons out of forty-five included these points in their *procès-verbaux*.[53] Here and elsewhere, such stipulations were accompanied by calls for removal of the national assembly from Paris and a sympathetic attitude towards anti-Montagnard local authorities which had campaigned against the Convention in recent weeks.

Conversely, the absence of hostile comment or constitutional amendments in areas which had flirted with 'federalism' in June, reflects the success of the referendum in pacifying erstwhile opponents. In the Haute-Garonne, cantons which had met in June to coordinate action against the Montagnards now meekly fell into line.[54] In the Calvados numerous assemblies even used the opportunity of voting on the new Constitution to denounce the departmental *Committee for Resistance to Oppression* which they had earlier helped create.[55] One section at Brest appears to have deleted its original demands for fresh elections, excluding existing *conventionnels*, in the copy of the *procès-verbal* that was taken to Paris.[56] Pommeret, historian of the Côtes-du-Nord, concludes that the vote was 'a means of recanting ... of disculpation from the charge of federalism', though in this department a large number of negative verdicts were recorded and villagers from Saint-Donan were expelled from their cantonal assembly, apparently for demanding a restoration of the monarchy.[57]

Still more interesting is the retraction of an initially negative response to the constitution at the canton of Buis in the Drôme. A petition was drafted so that the assembly could reconvene and unanimously adopt the constitutional document, 'as a means of unifying the nation'.[58] Hopes of renewed harmony were widespread, as the example of the Loire-Inférieure clearly demonstrates. After the referendum two *représentants en mission* from the Convention, Gillet and Cavaignac, admitted to the Committee of Public Safety in Paris that federalist sympathisers among the inhabitants of Nantes, 'had been misled for a moment' but, they

---

[52] M. Crook, 'La Constitution de 1793 et le fédéralisme', forthcoming in *Les fédéralismes*.
[53] AN BII 2, Procès-verbaux des Basses-Alpes, Aug. 1793.
[54] *Ibid*. BII 11, Procès-verbaux de la Haute-Garonne, July 1793 and Fournier, 'La participation électorale en Haute-Garonne', pp. 59–61.
[55] AN BII 4, Procès-verbaux de Cambremer and Mézidon, 28 July 1793.
[56] AM Brest 1K7 18, Procès-verbal de la 6ᵉ section, 24 July 1793.
[57] Pommeret, *L'esprit public dans le département des Côtes-du-Nord*, pp. 222–5.
[58] Baticle, 'Le plébiscite', p. 16.

asked, 'was it not possible to forget the mistake they had made, in view of the good they had done in voting massively for the constitution?'. Sadly these conciliatory hopes were dashed; the mayor of Nantes and numerous 'federalists' were subsequently arrested and over 100 individuals were executed. Instead of a period of peace and harmony, based upon the new Constitution, it was Carrier's Reign of Terror which ensued.[59]

Those who voted for the implementation of a new republican regime were cruelly deceived. Though the Constitution was officially accepted on 10 August, and notwithstanding the promise that 'immediately after publication of the decision taken by the French people, the Convention will arrange a date for the primary assemblies to meet . . .', no elections were announced. As the deputy Delacroix pointed out on 11 August 1793, carving out new single-member constituencies and compiling fresh electoral registers would require a prolonged period of grace.[60] Then, on 28 August, Barère mounted the tribune to declare that the crisis facing the Republic necessitated further delay, for this was scarcely a propitious moment to embark upon polling at all levels of the administration.

When Terror became 'the order of the day', in October 1793, the elections were postponed for an indefinite period. Implementation of the Constitution receded into the distant future yet, even after Thermidor (July 1794) and the downfall of the Montagnards, it was by no means certain that the Constitution of 1793 would be consigned to the scrapheap, or that the cedar box in which a copy had been placed for safe-keeping would become its tomb. In 1795, the republican Year III, a few remaining radicals still pressed for application of the ill-starred document. Now it was moderates in the Convention who dragged their feet, preferring to rely upon the maintenance of emergency measures to defeat their political opponents.

When a constitutional commission was finally appointed on 14 germinal III (3 April 1795), on the morrow of disturbances in Paris, it merely proposed modifications to the Constitution of 1793.[61] Only after the comprehensive defeat of the Parisian *sans-culottes*, who rose up in a second abortive insurrection demanding 'bread and the Constitution of 1793' at the beginning of prairial III (late May 1795), did a declaration of less democratic intent become politically feasible. Now minds were concentrated upon the matter, a new Constitution emerged quite rapidly. There was general agreement on the need to avoid the excesses of the past

---

[59] Le Gall, Les consultations générales, II, pp. 670–1.
[60] *AP* LXII, pp. 19–20, 11 Aug. 1793 and Aulard, *Histoire politique*, p. 313.
[61] Aulard, *Histoire politique*, pp. 543 ff.

and, as Thibaudeau put it, steer 'a middle way between monarchy and demagoguery'.[62] Boissy d'Anglas presented a statement of principle on 5 messidor (23 June 1795) and two months later the Constitution of the Year III was completed. A five-man Directory, from which the regime took its name, would be chosen by members of a bi-cameral parliament, who were elected on a tax-payers' franchise.

Visions of equality were cast aside by the constitutional commission. Boissy d'Anglas, himself a repentant democrat, set the tone in his infamous *Discours préliminaire*, when he declared: 'We must be ruled by the best . . . a country governed by property-owners is within the social order, that which is dominated by non-property-owners is in a state of nature.'[63] Few were prepared to challenge an emerging conservative consensus. Tom Paine, idealism undimmed by incarceration during the Terror, was the only *conventionnel* to stand up for universal manhood suffrage in the chamber. Yet his speech, read out on 19 messidor (7 July), sank like the proverbial lead balloon and publication was refused.[64] One or two more cautious colleagues queried the wisdom of the tax-payers' franchise, only to express satisfaction that non-payers could make a voluntary contribution (equivalent to three days' local wages, of fond memory) in order to vote.

Radical pamphleteers were thin on the ground too. Lanthenas, a rare Girondin who refused to renounce his egalitarianism, repudiated all limitations on the suffrage in his *Droit de Cité*.[65] Souhait, an obscure Montagnard deputy from the Vosges, made an especially impassioned plea that: 'All citizens, regardless of whether they are rich or poor, should be admitted to vote in both the primary and secondary assemblies.'[66] All men deserved to exercise the franchise, he argued, since even the humblest of wage-earners had given their lives for the *patrie*. Those who had served in the armed forces were subsequently exempted from the fiscal requirement, but appeals to the principle of one man one vote, which were generally endorsed in 1793, now found precious few defenders.

Lanjuinais had swum with the democratic tide during constitutional discussions two years earlier, yet on 21 messidor (9 July) he responded vigorously to Paine's defence of the rights of all men: 'The time for toadying to the people is past . . . which of us wants to witness for a second time the spectacle of political assemblies given over to crass ignorance, to

---

[62] Cited in D. Woronoff, *La République bourgeoise de thermidor à brumaire 1794–1799* (Paris, 1972), p. 40.
[63] *Moniteur* XXV, pp. 81 ff., 5 messidor III (25 June 1795).
[64] *Ibid.*, XXV, pp. 171–2, 19 messidor III (7 July 1795).
[65] BN Le[38] 1620, Droit de cité, thermidor III (July 1795).
[66] *Ibid.* Le[38] 1553, Opinion de J. Souhait sur le droit de suffrage, thermidor III (July 1795).

contemptible greed or vile drunkeness . . . the sort of thing we had to endure under the rule of the men of forty sous?'[67] This allusion to the payment made to *sans-culottes* for attendance at section meetings conjured up the unacceptable face of democracy, the popular dictatorship of the Year II.

The 'new realism' of 1795 should not occasion too much surprise. Few bourgeois revolutionaries had initially advocated universal manhood suffrage. In 1789 it was the *marc d'argent* imposed upon national deputies that had generated most debate. Mistrust of the poor was now freely reiterated; as Merlin de Douai put it: 'I cannot believe that you would wish to entrust the direction of the state to men who own nothing and produce nothing, to those men who are nothing but a burden upon society.'[68] The sense of *déjà vu* in this debate was confirmed when Dupont (de Nemours), former deputy in the Constituent Assembly, re-emerged from the political shadows to dust down his physiocratic principles in a pamphlet entitled *Observations sur le projet de Constitution*.[69] 'It is quite evident that property-owners are citizens *par excellence*, because without them no-one in the country would be fed or sheltered', he wrote. The time had come for the natural rulers of France to return to their rightful place at the helm.

In these circumstances it was surprising that limitations on the basic franchise were not more severe.[70] The reduced voting age of twenty-one was retained, though one year's residence in the canton was reimposed and the liberal naturalisation laws of 1793 were reversed. Domestic servants, who had won brief acceptance in the preceding Constitution were once again excluded, together with members of cosmopolitan corporations like religious orders and all who had served foreign powers. An interesting novelty in 1795 was the stipulation that all newly enrolled voters should be able to read and write, but this provision was not to come into operation until the Year XII (1805). There was a practical argument in favour of a literacy requirement in a system which once more insisted upon voting by written ballot. Yet the delay in instituting this cultural *cens* also reflected a confidence in the progress of education under the Republic.[71]

The reappearance of a fiscal requirement is, however, the best known feature of electoral arrangements under the Directory. To be sure, while they resurrected the shades of *citoyen actif* and his counterpart, *citoyen passif*, the Thermidoreans were careful to avoid the terminology; voters

[67] *Moniteur* XXV, p. 196, 21 messidor III (9 July 1795).   [68] *Ibid.*
[69] BN Lb⁴¹ 4447, Observations sur le projet de Constitution, messidor III (July 1795).
[70] Godechot, ed., *Les constitutions*, pp. 191–4 for the text.
[71] B. Baczko, *Comment sortir de la Terreur. Thermidor et la Révolution* (Paris, 1989), pp. 345–9.

were simply referred to as *citoyens*. To achieve this status payment of 'a direct personal or property tax' was certainly required. Historians have always assumed that this hurdle, which recalled the criteria employed in elections to the Estates General of 1789, debarred rather fewer males than the three days' local wages in taxation of 1791. Suratteau, for example, has estimated that roughly six out of seven million adult Frenchmen were enfranchised by the Constitution of 1795, representing well over 20 per cent of the population.[72]

Members of the Legislature estimated that only one person in five could vote and detailed research suggests that the total of *ayant droit de voter* was nearer 5 million.[73] In five departments for which a reasonably reliable set of statistics can be assembled, and using the census of 1806 as a yardstick, the proportion of inhabitants *ayant droit de voter* in 1797 did not exceed 20 per cent in a single case. The average of less than 18 per cent does not in fact represent a substantial advance upon the situation six years earlier. The overall increase, between 1791 and the Year V (1797), could be almost entirely attributable to a lower voting age. The Constitution of 1795 was not, therefore 'far less restrictive than its predecessor of 1791', even at the level of the basic franchise.

Eligibility to the electoral colleges, where departmental administrators and national deputies were chosen, was much more exclusive under the Directory than during the early years of the Revolution. The re-establishment of secondary assemblies, decided after lengthy debate in the Convention, prompted a reconsideration of the qualifications required for election.[74] In the end, the criteria belatedly inserted into the Constitution of 1791 (but not actually employed) were resurrected in 1795, with just one minor amendment. Possession, lease of property or sharecropping yielding between 100 and 200 days' labour in revenue *per annum* was demanded of second-degree electors, depending upon the size of the community they inhabited.

Few lists of those eligible under this system, which represented the Thermidoreans' efforts to 'end the Revolution', by basing it squarely upon a propertied elite, remain in the archives. Little more than 10 per cent of the electorate seem to have qualified. The distribution of property and lease-holding influenced the outcome locally, with larger towns housing larger numbers of *éligibles* than rural areas. Better-off artisans and wealthier peasants retained some access to the departmental assemblies, not simply 'well-heeled bourgeois and large property-holders', as Godechot

[72] J.-R. Suratteau, 'Heurs et malheurs de la sociologie électorale pour l'époque de la Révolution française', *Annales ESC*, XXIII (1968), p. 560.
[73] *Moniteur* XXVII, p. 3, 24 frimaire IV (15 Dec. 1795).   [74] *Ibid.*, XXV, pp. 306–8.

Table 11 *The right to vote in 1791 and the Year V (1797)*

Department	1791	1791	AN V (1797)	AN V (1797)
	Number enfranchised	Percentage of 1806 population	Number enfranchised	Percentage of 1806 population
Aveyron	57,841	17.5	61,707	18.6
Charente	57,224	17.5	60,377	18.5
Gironde	77,372	15.0	94,435	18.3
Meurthe	53,861	14.7	65,575	17.9
Somme	63,366	12.8	78,678	15.9
Total/Average	309,664	15.2	360,772	17.7

Sources: *AP* XVI, pp. 532–3; AN F¹cIII Aveyron 1, Tableau général des assemblées primaires, 17 ventôse V (7 Mar. 1797); AN F²⁰ 313/333/386, Tableaux des votants, an V (1797); and Clémendot, *Le département de la Meurthe*, p. 223

has claimed.[75] Yet less than 1 million Frenchmen were eligible to serve on the electoral colleges after 1795, compared to roughly 3 million in 1790 and 1791 (on the basis of ten days' wages in taxation, the criterion which operated before the Constitution of 1791 came into effect).

Even so, this estimated total of *éligibles* under the Directory is much larger than most textbooks imply. Once again the number of second-degree electors actually chosen in a given year is frequently confused with the bigger pool from which they were fished.[76] After 1795 the annual membership of the departmental assemblies was in fact reduced in comparison with the earlier years of the Revolution. Then, one elector was delegated for every 100 registered voters, but this ratio was now reduced to one for every 200 *ayant droit de voter*. In other words, national deputies were to be elected by roughly 30,000 college members, as opposed to some 45,000 at the outset of the revolutionary decade. Having restricted access to the departmental colleges in this manner, the *conventionnels* saw no need to add further fiscal requirements for men elected to the Legislative Councils. Though the electoral colleges could choose any registered citizen as a deputy, in practice they were unlikely to look beyond their own ranks. There was no need to exhume the infamous *marc d'argent*, which had been buried beneath so much obloquy in 1791.

[75] Godechot, *Les institutions*, p. 462.
[76] Doyle, *The Oxford History of the French Revolution*, p. 319 fails to make this distinction clear, while G. Lewis, *The French Revolution. Rethinking the Debate* (London, 1993), p. 50, confuses second-degree electors and primary voters.

The Constitution of 1795 also reduced the space available for political activity by removing elements of direct democracy enshrined in its ill-fated predecessor of 1793. Save for the relatively remote possibility of participating in the process of constitutional revision, the primary assemblies were to play no role in either ratifying or initiating legislation, still less in controlling their delegates. The practice of mandating deputies and assembling outside of elections, which had flourished between 1790 and 1793, was now explicitly forbidden. Indeed, discussion of any sort was banished from the assemblies, primary and secondary, which were only allowed to meet for a *décade* (the ten-day week of the revolutionary calendar), whether their business was completed or not.

The Constitution of 1795 which contained these stringent regulations was submitted to the people, for the same pressing political reasons as its immediate predecessor. This second referendum represented another attempt to overcome divisions in French society that the Terror had driven still deeper. Since the Constitution of 1793 had never been implemented, its successor was likewise put to the quasi-universal electorate established in August 1792: 'Those Frenchmen admitted to the last primary assemblies will be able to vote again on this occasion'.[77] Exactly how many citizens were accordingly enabled to legitimise the new constitutional arrangements must remain a matter of conjecture in most cases. Perhaps 6 million voters were entitled to pronounce upon a document which would effectively reduce their political rights. Yet, though restrictions on the franchise and eligibility were conveyed to the assemblies, when the text of the Constitution was read aloud, few objections were raised against them.[78]

Meetings of the primary assemblies were hastily convened during fructidor (September 1795) and once more it is difficult to advance any completely reliable figures for turnout. Results were printed and circulated in a handsomely bound volume published on 6 vendémiaire IV (28 September 1795), but this was intended to reassure the public that votes were being honestly counted rather than to provide a final set of returns.[79] Historians have unwisely accepted the total this tome offers as an accurate record, stating that 1,057,390 voted in favour of the Constitution and

---

[77] *Moniteur* XXV, p.561, 5 fructidor III (22 Aug. 1795). Suratteau, 'Heurs et malheurs de la sociologie électorale, p. 567, mistakenly suggests that the universal suffrage of the 1793 Constitution was employed.

[78] A. Lajusan,, 'Le plébiscite de l'an III', *Rf*, 60 (1911), p. 107.

[79] Some primary assemblies, like one section at Châlons-sur-Marne (AN BII 52 for the *procès-verbal*) had demanded publication since the counting of votes was unsupervised and there were fears of fraud.

49,978 against, or 1,107,368 participants in all.[80] In fact *procès-verbaux* from many departments had yet to arrive, while even more assemblies than those of 1793 produced a unanimous verdict without further qualification.

So far no one has undertaken the unrewarding task of totting up votes in all the *procès-verbaux* eventually deposited at the *Archives nationales*. A scrupulous recount for the Var yields 8,883 votes rather than the official 8,485, even ignoring eight cantons which simply recorded unanimity.[81] Participation in the Vaucluse has also been underestimated by several hundred and the discrepancy discovered for the Pyrénées-Orientales is still greater: 2,089 votes cast instead of 1,141 in the printed volume.[82] In these circumstances it would not be unreasonable to suggest that perhaps 1,300,000 Frenchmen voted in the consultation of 1795. This was certainly fewer than the 2 million who turned out for the referendum of 1793, but it was a creditable achievement in view of the continuing turmoil afflicting areas of the West and the Midi.[83] If the electorate is put at around the 6-million mark, then the level of participation was roughly 20 per cent. This is higher than usually thought and compares favourably with elections since 1790; indeed this figure was scarcely surpassed during the period that followed.

Though turnout was generally a third or more lower in 1795 than in 1793 there were some notable increases. At Paris, for example, over 40 per cent of the estimated electorate voted on the Constitution of the Year III, as opposed to roughly 30 per cent a couple of years earlier.[84] Heavier polling was equally apparent at Châlons-sur-Marne, Nantes and Vannes but, whether figures were up or down on attendance in 1793, it is clear that turnout in the referendum of 1795 was significantly higher in urban areas than in the countryside.[85] The greater involvement of town dwellers compared to their rural counterparts was already evident in 1793 and two years later the disparity had widened further.[86]

A willingness to vote was far more pronounced in the cities, despite the wholesale closure of clubs and the dissolution of revolutionary commit-

---

[80] AN BII 74, Tableau du dépouillement et recensement du voeu des assemblées primaires, 6 vendémiaire IV (28 Sept. 1795).
[81] Poupé, *Le département du Var*, pp. 515–20.
[82] AN BII, Procès-verbaux des Pyrénées-Orientales, fructidor III (Sept. 1795) and P. Vaillandet, 'Le plébiscite de l'an III en Vaucluse', *AhRf*, IV (1932), p. 508.
[83] Vaillandet, 'Le plébiscite de l'an III', pp. 501–3.
[84] AN BII 61, Procès-verbaux de la Seine, fructidor III (Sept. 1793).
[85] A. Troux, *La vie politique dans le département de la Meurthe d'août 1792 à octobre 1795*, 2 vols. (Nancy, 1936), II, p. 852 for further examples.
[86] M. Crook, 'Aux Urnes Citoyens!' 'Rural and Urban Electoral Behaviour during the French Revolution, 1789-1799', in A. Forrest and P. M. Jones, eds., *Reshaping France. Town, Country and Region in the French Revolution* (Manchester, 1991), p. 158.

Table 12 *Urban and rural turnout in the referenda of 1793 and 1795*

Town and district	Percentage turnout in 1793	Percentage turnout in 1795
Carcassonne	18.7	13.6
Rural Cantons	17.9	12.5
Châlons-sur-Marne	35.0	47.5
Rural Cantons	18.3	8.3
Dijon	56.5	48.0
Rural Cantons	39.8	22.9
Vannes	12.8	18.6
Rural Cantons	3.9	2.5

Sources: AN BII 34 and 74, Tableaux du dépouillement et recensement du voeu des assemblées primaires, 1793 and 1795

tees. Leaving the polls open for several days also helped to improve the level of participation. By contrast, rural areas in the North were affected by harvesting, while exceptionally bad weather was hitting the South. Yet peasant disenchantment with the Revolution, especially over religious issues, was a basic cause of relatively poor attendance in the countryside.[87] The demise of the constitutional church took its toll, for juring clergy who had played an important role in the preceding referendum were conspicuous by their absence in 1795. In departments of the West many cantons failed to assemble: at Péaule in the Morbihan, for example, only ten citizens gathered out of over 1,000, but they decided not to constitute themselves formally due to 'the fear of exposing ourselves to the fury of evil-doers and enemies of the public good'.[88] In the Midi, meanwhile, the White Terror deterred republicans from appearing at assemblies which were dominated by reactionaries.[89]

Not surprisingly the Breton departments polled badly but, with the exception of Paris, so did the Ile de France and Picardy, where turnout rarely exceeded double figures. The overall geography of participation in 1795 contrasts sharply with that of 1793: in the Year III ten of the departments with above-average participation were situated south of an imaginary line drawn from Lyon to Rouen, while only five were located to the North. Two years earlier heavier turnout was nearly always to be found in northern and eastern regions of France.

---

[87] Fournier, 'La participation électorale en Haute-Garonne', pp. 61–5.
[88] AN BII 55, Procès-verbal de Péaule, 20 fructidor III (6 Sept. 1795).
[89] Vaillandet, 'Le plébiscite de l'an III', p. 507.

Voting the Constitution

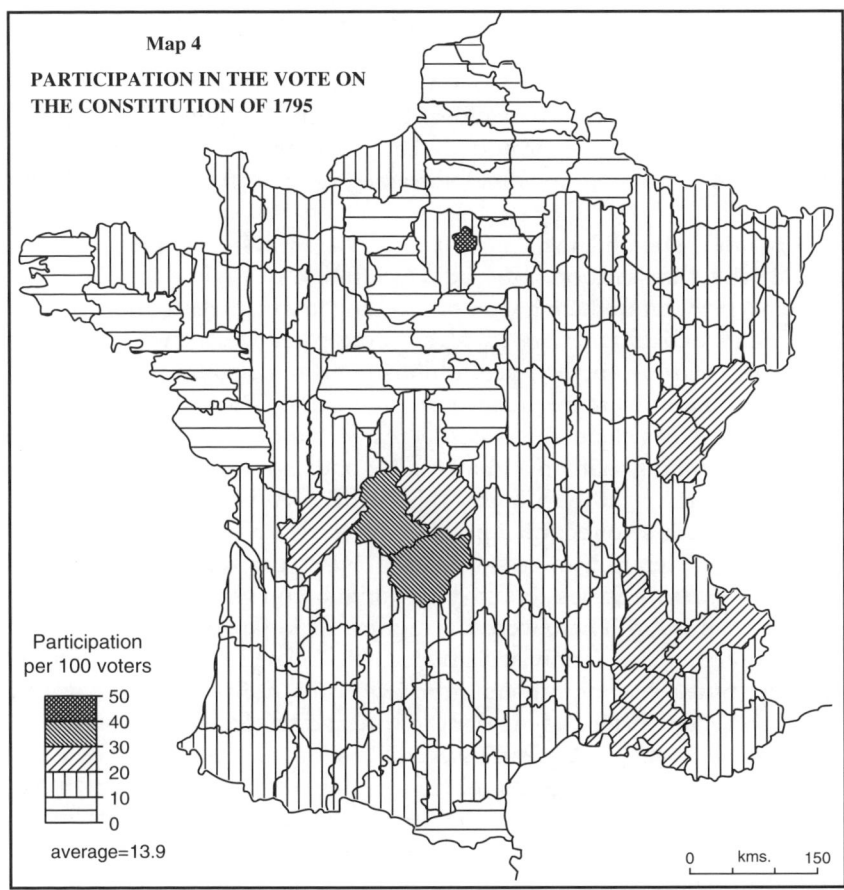

4 Participation in the vote on the Constitution of 1795

The cartography of voting in the 1795 referendum bears a more evident political imprint than its predecessor, with committed republican areas turning out in greater numbers than conservative ones. In 1795, unlike 1793, negative votes also represented a significant proportion of the total cast: 5 per cent at the later date, as opposed to less than 1 per cent on the earlier occasion. Those departments where substantial numbers of voters rejected the Constitution of the Year III were nearly all located in the Parisian basin; indeed, in the Eure-et-Loir almost half of the participants recorded a negative verdict. In the West the number of rejections was low, because opponents seem to have boycotted the polls while the republican minority made a determined effort to vote.⁹⁰ Once again abstention is difficult to interpret. It should not be automatically equated with 'royalism' in 1795; on the contrary, in some areas it was a manifestation of Jacobin sympathies. At the section of Pont-Neuf in Paris, dominant conservatives protested that 'anarchists' had not been prevented from attending: they had abstained because they knew their day was over.⁹¹

For those who did take part, it was not always a simple matter of hearing the Constitution, plus the Declaration of Rights *and* Duties of Citizens, read out to them before proceeding to a vote; discussion of these documents and other, unrelated issues often followed. In 1795, unlike 1793, instructions on the referendum sought to discourage any debate, but amendments were frequently put nonetheless. The tradition of 'deliberation' as well as election was boldly reasserted by several assemblies, in resolutions stating that 'no administrative body nor even the national legislature' had the right to withdraw this facility.⁹² As in 1793, more general grievances were also recorded in the *procès-verbaux*, relating to the status of the Catholic church and testamentary laws in particular.⁹³

To this extent it is possible to gauge opinion on various aspects of the 1795 Constitution. There were few arguments in favour of universal suffrage, though the assembly at Saint-Jean-de-Losne in the Côte-d'Or did cite 'the bitter disappointment experienced by the poor at discovering they had been deprived of the right to vote and be elected' as a reason for its negative vote.⁹⁴ At Paris several ballot papers demanded the Constitution of 1793 (just as others mentioned that of 1791 and advocated monarchy), but it was the strict eligibility requirements which attracted most adverse comment. At Issy-sur-Seine the assembly declared that 'the qualifications to be met by second-degree electors are contrary to the principle of equality and they are particularly irksome in the countryside, where there are many wise and enlightened citizens who lack the income required to become one . . .'.⁹⁵ A section of Limoges, a Jacobin stronghold, opined: 'We are deeply disturbed to see the wealthy supplanting all other categories of citizen.'⁹⁶ Echoes of direct democracy also cropped up here and there. At Triel (Seine-et-Oise) it was recorded: 'The deputies should not be called Representatives of the Nation . . . they are

---

⁹⁰ Vovelle, *La découverte de la politique*, p. 207, gives an extremely misleading impression of where opposition to the Constitution lay.
⁹¹ AN BII 61, Procès-verbal de la section du Pont-Neuf, 21 fructidor III (7 Sept. 1795).
⁹² Lajusan, 'Le plébiscite de l'an III', p. 13.   ⁹³ *Ibid.*, pp. 113–26.
⁹⁴ AN BII 41, Procès-verbal de Saint-Jean-de-Losne, 20 fructidor III (6 Sept. 1795).
⁹⁵ *Ibid.*, BII 61, Procès-verbal d'Issy, 20 fructidor III (6 Sept. 1795)
⁹⁶ Lajusan, 'Le plébiscite de l'an III', p. 108.

merely mandatories of the section which has elected them and can recall them if necessary.'⁹⁷

Shades of the Year II were also apparent where voting methods were concerned. The instructions of 5 fructidor III offered each participant a choice of 'the manner of voting that suits him best', pending implementation of the 1795 Constitution which only recognised vote by ballot. Some mixed regimes combining oral voting and the written ballot were allowed but, generally speaking, a decision was made in favour of one or the other. Voting 'out loud' was less widespread in Paris than it had been in 1793, but more frequent in rural departments like the Morbihan, or the Aveyron where the canton of Nant proudly declared that its decision had been made 'collectively and unanimously'.⁹⁸ In the capital the use of written ballots in 1795 allowed individuals to indicate their dissent in a way that had rarely been possible in 1793.

Hostility towards the Convention and its deputies was much in evidence in the Year III. Above all there were understandable fears that, as in 1793, implementation of the new Constitution might be unduly delayed. To be sure, the *conventionnels* had tried to allay these misgivings by stipulating that second-degree electors should be chosen as soon as the referendum was completed. However, no date had been set for convocation of the departmental assemblies and two sections at Châlons-sur-Marne declared that if the colleges were not convened by 15 vendémiaire (7 October 1795) they would take further (unspecified) action.⁹⁹ In fact both sections agreed to meet on a weekly basis to review the situation in the meantime, an example followed elsewhere in the area around Paris.

It is difficult to avoid the conclusion that many voters accepted the 1795 Constitution *faute de mieux*, because it was preferable to have a settlement than not. Resignation rather than enthusiasm was the order of the day. At Belleville (Seine) the *procès-verbal* noted disappointment with the document on offer, which was only accepted in order to restore 'regular government', while Asprières in the Aveyron desperately sought 'an anchoring point' in storm-tossed conditions.¹⁰⁰ There was little rejoicing and one firm republican sadly remarked: 'The counter-revolutionaries believe that their apparent acceptance of the constitution will provide a cloak of respectability for their dastardly projects.'¹⁰¹ The most widespread desire was for fresh elections and a new regime to succeed a discredited Convention.

---

[97] *Ibid.*, p. 110.   [98] AN BII 38, Procès-verbal de Nant, 20 fructidor III (6 Sept. 1795).
[99] *Ibid.* BII 52, Procès-verbaux de Châlons-sur-Marne, 20 fructidor III (6 Sept. 1795).
[100] *Ibid.*, BII 61, Procès-verbal de Belleville, 20 fructidor III (6 Sept. 1795) and *ibid.* BII 38, Procès-verbal d'Asprières, 20 fructidor III (6 Sept. 1795).
[101] Vaillandet, 'Le plébiscite de l'an III', p. 516.

In the light of this comment the wave of resistance which greeted the infamous 'law of the two-thirds' is quite comprehensible. Contained in the electoral instructions of 5 and 13 fructidor (22 and 30 August 1795) was the proviso that: 'All the deputies currently serving in the Convention are re-eligible. The departmental assemblies must choose at least two-thirds of them to form the new Legislature.' The address which accompanied the supplementary decree of 13 fructidor, made a strong case for this unusual measure.[102] The self-denying ordinance adopted by members of the Constituent Assembly in 1791 was widely held to have helped scupper the first revolutionary Constitution since none of its authors was entrusted with its execution. It was rightly feared that, presented with a free choice, many electoral colleges would choose deputies hostile to the Constitution of the Year III, if not to the Republic itself.

The address also attempted to salve the *conventionnels*' consciences by inviting the primary assemblies to deliver a verdict on the 'two-thirds'; if the sovereign people agreed to limit their own electoral freedom then no violation of democratic principles would occur. The problem was that most voters were unaware of the decree, which was not effectively conveyed to them.[103] Even the address issued on 13 fructidor was rather vague where the need to test opinion on the 'two-thirds' was concerned. In any event, it arrived too late to influence the referendum in outlying departments, like the Côtes-du-Nord, where the primary assemblies had already dispersed. In other instances, where the infamous decrees were mentioned, no vote was taken because administrators, like those of the Aude or the Pyrénées-Orientales (which cast a mere 206 and 173 votes respectively on the 'two-thirds'), believed that the legislation was not open to question. Only rarely, and mostly in the Parisian basin, did a vote on the *deux-tiers* approach 50 per cent of figures for the Constitution itself. Most departments initially responded like the Aveyron, where just five out of ninety-four cantons recorded a verdict.[104]

All was confusion, a reflection of the Convention's uncertainty as to how to handle the contentious issue of re-electing itself. There is no doubt that some voters felt that endorsing the Constitution was tantamount to approving the associated decrees. The belief that another referendum was not required was explicitly stated in one solidly republican section of Dijon.[105] Naturally this favourable interpretation was eagerly seized upon

---

[102] *Moniteur* XXV, pp. 637–8, 13 fructidor III (30 August 1795).
[103] Lajusan, 'Le plébiscite de l'an III', pp. 237–40.
[104] AN BII 38, Procès-verbaux de l'Aveyron, 20 fructidor III (6 Sept. 1795).
[105] *Ibid*. BII 41, Procès-verbaux de Dijon, 20 fructidor III (6 Sept. 1795).

by deputies in the Convention, who were extremely worried by the adverse response the 'two-thirds' was attracting.

It was boldly asserted on 22 fructidor (8 September 1795), that the *deux-tiers* had been accepted by 'the overwhelming majority' of assemblies that had already met. Indeed, the speaker in the Convention added, 'there are even some primary assemblies which would like to see all the *conventionnels* remain in post'.[106] This was whistling in the dark, for deputies could hardly have been unaware that most of the Parisian sections had unanimously rejected the 'two-thirds' over the past couple of days. Worse was to follow; ignorance or silent assent often dissolved into opposition as assemblies took up the issue when choosing their second-degree electors, or deliberately reconvened to discuss the matter. At Marseille, for example, many sections met again at the beginning of vendémiaire (end of September), to reject the law (most aptly!) by a two-thirds majority.[107] In the neighbouring Vaucluse citizens of Sainte-Cécile, fearful that their earlier silence would be interpreted as approval, reassembled on the fourth complementary day (20 September) to announce: 'in accepting the Constitution the assembly did not wish to imply any endorsement of the decree of 5 fructidor ... which it considers to be an assault on the sovereignty of the people'.[108]

When the results of the consultation were published on 6 vendémiaire (28 September 1795), these belated votes were certainly not taken into account. Nor were unanimous rejections of the two-thirds, which had been especially common in Paris, where only thirteen out of forty-seven sections had put figures to their rejection of the *deux-tiers*. As a consequence, though most of the 67,000 Parisian participants in the referendum had cast a negative vote on the decrees, little more than 20,000 were recognised as having done so. Certainly positive affirmations of support for the 'two-thirds' were extremely rare. Neufchâtel in the Seine-Inférieure went out on a limb when it suggested that: 'It is essential to the general well-being of the Republic that a majority of those who have conceived, considered and voted for the constitution should oversee its implementation and guide its application'.[109] Endorsement of the decrees was usually couched in more grudging terms. The canton of Seurre in the Côte-d'Or 'accepted the two-thirds law, but purely out of concern for the public good, rather than any confidence in the current deputies'.[110]

Lajusan, author of the only general study of the 1795 referendum,

---

[106] *Moniteur* XXV, p. 700, 22 fructidor (8 Sept. 1795).
[107] AN BII 38, Procès-verbaux de Marseille, 1–8 vendémiaire IV (23–30 Sept. 1705).
[108] Vaillandet, 'Le plébiscite de l'an III', p. 514.
[109] AN BII 61, Procès-verbal de Neufchâtel, 20 fructidor III (6 Sept. 1795).
[110] *Ibid.* BII 41, Procès-verbal de Seurre, 20 fructidor III (6 Sept. 1795).

states that 'these decrees ... were distasteful to the vast majority of citizens', though his assertion is impossible to verify.[111] Were all the separate votes on the *deux-tiers* to be added together they might produce a majority hostile to the legislation, rather than the two to one majority in favour (205,498 to 108,784) which appears in the officially published returns. On the other hand, there is a strong case for arguing that many voters in areas which polled heavily for the Constitution would have supported the 'two-thirds' rule had they been given the opportunity to do so.

Refusals were concentrated in departments north of a line drawn from the Jura to the Calvados. Apart from Paris, thirteen departments returned a hostile verdict of more than half the votes cast on the 'two-thirds'. All of them, save for the Doubs and the Bas-Rhin (where only a small minority of participants expressed an opinion on the *deux-tiers*), were located in an arc around the capital. Elsewhere, favourable votes were focused in the towns: in the Côte-d'Or, for example, almost three-quarters of the department's positive responses to the decrees came from the (soon-to-be-abolished) *chefs-lieux de district* while, in the Loire-Inférieure, Nantes provided the bulk of the support.[112]

Many of the recalcitrant assemblies were willing to consider returning members of the Convention to the next legislature (though the Panthéon section in Paris believed that an *assemblée constituante* should not perpetuate itself), but they would not tolerate 'obligatory re-election'.[113] The assembly at Châtillon, near Paris, refused 'to prescribe the choice which their second-degree electors were to make', while Sainte-Cécile, in the Vaucluse, gave its delegates *carte blanche*: 'We are awarding them unlimited scope when the selection of deputies to the Legislature is made at the departmental assembly; individuals can be chosen from current members of the Convention or among any other persons who are deemed satisfactory, without regard for the decree of 5 fructidor III.'[114]

Opposition did not end with protests in the *procès-verbaux*; in the heartland of resistance to the *deux-tiers*, in and around Paris, it developed into a general rebellion. It was the good old days of 1793 again, as opponents of the decrees seized upon the rhetoric of popular sovereignty to justify their action. Sections in the capital proclaimed their right to assemble every day (*en permanence*), to remain in session as long as they saw fit, and to communicate with other assemblies in the name of the 'unity and indivisibility of the Republic'. The section of Lepeletier, which had taken the initiative, stated that 'the authority of all public bodies must yield to the

---

[111] Lajusan, 'Le plébiscite de l'an III', p. 240.
[112] AN BII 41, Procès-verbaux de la Côte-d'Or and Le Gall, Les consultations générales, II, pp. 707–9.   [113] AN BII 61, Procès-verbaux de la Seine, fructidor III (Sept. 1795).
[114] Vaillandet, 'Le plébiscite de l'an III', p. 514.

sovereignty of the people'.[115] The 'primary and permanent assembly' of the Théâtre-Français declared that forty-six out of forty-eight sections in the capital were supporting the campaign (only the Quinze-Vingts had accepted the *deux-tiers*, while Popincourt held aloof from further action).[116] Cantons in the surrounding departments of the Oise, Seine-et-Oise, Eure-et-Loir, Aube and Marne hastened to join 'the struggle between the people and its mandatories'.[117]

The Convention, however, having published results which revealed large majorities for both Constitution and decrees, was in no mood to compromise. Messages of support were received from committed republicans like those at Dijon who castigated the sections in the capital as 'the last resort of the enemies of the people'; there was even a whiff of 'federalism' to their accompanying suggestion that deputies should quit Paris, 'an ungrateful and inhospitable city'.[118] The protesters were inevitably presented as royalist wolves in sheep's clothing seeking to ravage the Republic, though it would appear that most of them were opposed to the Convention rather than to the Republic *per se*. To this allegation the section of Bonne-Nouvelle replied: 'A great number of wage-earners and artisans have regularly attended the sessions of this assembly in an enthusiastic fashion; you will find in our midst neither royalists nor assassins (*septembriseurs*), nor that handful of troublemakers who have been denounced in your chamber as perverting the actions of every primary assembly in Paris.'[119] Royalists were doubtless involved, but it was the purge of the Convention on 31 May 1793 which the sections found so unpalatable, not the overthrow of the monarchy on 10 August 1792.

Led by bourgeois, with a measure of popular support, a number of sections persisted in their opposition even when presented with the stark choice between submission or suppression. The ensuing revolt of 13 vendémiaire (5 October 1795) was put down without too much difficulty and the infamous sections were subsequently abolished, but the episode was hardly an auspicious start for the new system of government.[120] At best the choice of the electorate had been unduly circumscribed, at worst voters had been cheated in what virtually amounted to a *coup d'état*. Some Thermidoreans, it transpired, had been thinking of cancelling the departmental assemblies and choosing the new deputies themselves. Though the electoral colleges soon met and followed instructions on the 'two-

---

[115] Genty, *Paris 1789–1795*, p. 251.
[116] AN BII 61, Procès-verbal de la section du Théâtre-Français, 21 fructidor III (7 Sept. 1795).   [117] Lajusan, 'Le plébiscite de l'an III', p. 259.
[118] J. Brelot, *La vie politique en Côte-d'Or sous le Directoire* (Dijon, 1932), pp. 26–7.
[119] AN BII 61, Procès-verbal de la section de Bonne-Nouvelle, 22 fructidor III (8 Sept. 1795).   [120] H. Zivy, *Le 13 vendémiaire an IV* (Paris, 1898).

thirds', the birth of the Directory had been blighted. Not for the last time the popular will was frustrated by a regime which attempted to govern normally in abnormal circumstances, to end the Revolution in a revolutionary situation. Yet in spite of these difficulties, as much as because of the new Constitution, the remainder of the decade marked a further stage in the electoral apprenticeship of the French people. In this respect, as in others, the Directory is not to be scorned or ignored, but should be taken seriously.

6 Parties, schisms and purges: Elections under the Directory, 1795–1799

The Constitution of 1795 was inaugurated in an inauspicious fashion and enjoyed a charmed existence until it was overturned four years later. This was longer than either of its predecessors, but because the Directory came to an ignominious conclusion historians have been only too willing to write it off as a bad job and to overlook its achievements, especially in the political sphere. The significance of the electoral apprenticeship that was conducted during the second half of the revolutionary decade has largely escaped attention as a result. It is seldom recognised that the franchise remained a very broad one, or that in two of the annual elections which were held the level of participation was reasonably high. An interesting experiment with declared candidatures was also undertaken, despite a dogged reluctance to endorse the existence of parties, which were more effectively organised than ever. If government intervention of the most blatant sort brought the electoral system into disrepute, the unprecedented involvement of the executive was nonetheless a reflection of the crucial role that elections now played in the political process.

The Directory is rarely viewed in a positive light and its electoral contests are usually regarded as fiascos which attracted only a derisory turnout. A general history of Upper Normandy during the Revolution furnishes a typical example of this prevailing outlook:

An analysis of electoral returns, from 1795 to 1798, reveals a process of disaffection. The mass of the people shunned political activities from which they were mostly excluded ... In the Year VII (1799) participation in elections diminished further, dropping to only 9 per cent of those entitled to vote. In these circumstances the revision of the constitution was as much the secret wish of the nation as the intention of a small number of conspirators preparing a *coup d'état* at Paris.[1]

Perspectives like these are distorted by a failure to acknowledge some equally low levels of electoral participation in 1791 and 1792. Set in the context of the revolutionary decade the polls of 1797 and 1798 attracted

---
[1] Comité régional d'histoire de la Révolution, *La Révolution en Haute-Normandie, 1789-1802* (Rouen, 1989), p. 147.

5 The Departments of France under the Directory, 1795–1799 (excluding Corsica)

some relatively heavy turnout, even though attendance at the initial round of elections, in September 1795, was generally disappointing.

Only too conscious of the lessons of recent history the authors of the Constitution of the Year III decided upon the immediate, indeed instant implementation of their efforts. In 1793 no firm date had been set for fresh legislative elections and, in the event, none were held. In 1795, by contrast, voting for second-degree electors, who would sit in the departmental colleges, was to begin as soon as votes on the Constitution had been cast. It was assumed that the primary assemblies would deliver a positive verdict. Even those which did not were expected to proceed to operate a system they had just rejected, though one refractory canton in the Meurthe stubbornly refused to do so.[2] All adult males who had voted on the constitutional document were invited to remain present, notwithstanding the reinstatement of restrictions upon the basic franchise, a concession occasionally ignored at local level.[3]

In fact many voters decided to leave before the choice of second-degree electors was made. The available *procès-verbaux* suggest a fall in attendance of up to half compared to the already modest turnout in the preceding referendum. There were inevitable exceptions to this rule, most notably in cantons of the Aude and Aveyron where inclement weather had delayed the arrival of participants. Over the country as a whole average turnout barely exceeded 11 per cent. At Candiès, in the Pyrénées-Orientales, the national agent wrote that he had 'never witnessed such disdain' for so important a task.[4] It was mid-September, still harvest-time, and voters excused themselves on the grounds of urgent agricultural business. The selection of second-degree electors did, after all, demand a second, or in cases where a vote had been taken on the two-thirds decree, a third successive round of balloting; enthusiasm always waned the longer a session went on, so the comparison with other legislative elections is not entirely fair.

Of course, this calculation for 1795 must be treated with the same measure of caution as all revolutionary electoral statistics. Participants themselves expressed uncertainty over the numbers entitled to vote, which had a crucial bearing upon the number of second-degree electors to be chosen (at the rate of one for every 200 active citizens), as well as upon the level of turnout. To judge by the cantons sampled here, Bordeaux was unique in conducting a fresh count of *ayant droit de voter* before the issue was decided.[5] Elsewhere estimates, or informed guesses were employed and there was naturally a great temptation to inflate the figures in order to obtain an extra delegate or two. Having said that, at Rivesaltes (Pyrénées-Orientales) voters had to reconvene because they had chosen one elector too few.[6] There is no disputing, however, that the data reveal a generally poor turnout north and south, roughly following the contours of participation in the plebiscite. No longer were north-eastern areas of France polling more heavily than the Midi: the Aveyron scored best, while even the Pyrénées-Orientales pipped the once heavily voting Marne, and the formerly poll-shy Basses-Alpes outstripped both Meurthe and Meuse.

[2] Troux, *La vie politique*, II, p.859.   [3] Roquette, *J.-J. Roquette*, II, p. 248.
[4] AD Pyrénées-Orientales L431, Procès-verbal de Candiès, 21 fructidor III (7 Sept. 1795).
[5] AM Bordeaux, Procès-verbal de la section 5, 22 fructidor III (8 Sept. 1795).
[6] AD Pyrénées-Orientales L431, Procès-verbal de Rivesaltes, 22 fructidor III (8 Sept. 1795) and 15 vendémiaire IV (7 Oct. 1795).

Table 13 *The vote on the Constitution and the primary elections of the Year III (1795)*

Dept.	Vote on Constitution			Primary elections		
	ADV	Voters at 1st round	Percentage	ADV	Voters at first round	Percentage
Aude	52127	6025	11.6	18079	1783	9.9
Aveyron	60007	10519	17.5	18773	2909	15.5
Basses-Alpes	10364	1417	13.7	13906	1568	10.4
Côte-d'Or	12363	1846	14.9	14145	1616	11.4
Marne	64817	8497	13.1	59727	6391	10.7
Meurthe	76000	11405	15.0	16989	1680	9.9
Meuse	58173	8924	15.3	17575	1587	9.0
Morbihan	18899	2422	12.8	19604	2001	10.3
Orne	83748	12612	15.1	24435	3637	14.9
Pyrénées-Orientales	10600	1380	13.0	11400	1228	10.8
Total	447098	65047	14.5	214656	24400	11.4

Note: This comparison is not strictly accurate, since the sample for the vote on the Constitution is twice as large as the one for the primaries, but the order of grandeur remains instructive.
Sources: AN BII 74 Tableau du dépouillement et recensement du voeu des assemblées primaires; AD Aude L375–6; AD Aveyron 1L620–2; AD Basses-Alpes L199–203; AD Côte-d'Or L238–9; AD Marne 1L297–304; AD Meuse 356; AD Morbihan L239; AD Orne L391–6; AD Pyrénées-Orientales L431; and Clémendot, *Le département de la Meurthe*, p.98

A much clearer contrast can be drawn between town and country. In the Marne, for example, all six (former) district *chefs-lieux* outshone not just the average score, but every single canton within the circumscription; in the case of Châlons, the departmental capital, voting was four times the local mean.[7] This pattern was repeated in the Côte-d'Or, where Dijon achieved a turnout of almost 60 per cent, as opposed to an average of 11 per cent elsewhere in the department.[8] The same can be said of Perpignan in the Pyrénées-Orientales or Nantes in the Loire-Inférieure, while at Brest the poll of just under 40 per cent was the highest of the entire

[7] AD Marne 1L297, Procès-verbaux du district de Châlons, fructidor III (Sept. 1795).
[8] AD Côte-d'Or L238–9, Procès-verbaux, fructidor III (Sept. 1795).

Table 14 *Urban and rural turnout in primary elections under the Directory, Year III to Year VII (1795–1799)*

Town and area	Year III (1795) percentage turnout	Year V (1797) percentage turnout	Year VI (1798) percentage turnout	Year VII (1799) percentage turnout
Carcassonne	10.9	44.9	31.5	18.6
district	10.6	12.6	22.3	11.2
Châlons s/Marne	38.5		37.8	13.1
district	8.0		15.0	6.1
Dijon	58.1	42.1	39.2	18.6
department	10.3	18.3	16.9	8.7
Vannes		25.8	22.9	17.9
district		8.5	5.4	3.2
Troyes		53.8		17.2
department		15.8		8.3

Sources: AD Aude L375–86; AD Marne 1L305–11; AD Côte-d'Or L238–50; and AD Morbihan L241–6

decade.[9] Rural cantons were decisively worsted, their superior performance of earlier years firmly consigned to the past. In some cases derisory figures were recorded in the countryside, the wooden spoon going to Peyrefitte in the Aude, where only 2 per cent of the *ayant droit de voter* took part.[10]

When local elections were held in the autumn turnout was little better at cantonal level, but improved significantly in the villages. The Constitution of 1795 abolished mayors and amalgamated smaller communities into cantonal municipalities, so that the cantons became administrative as well as judicial and electoral units.[11] Rural inhabitants assembled at the *chef-lieu de canton* to elect justices of the peace and presidents for the new *municipalités de canton* on 10 brumaire (1 November). Only a few figures are available, but they confirm that rural inhabitants were not travelling well: in the Loiret there were sometimes insufficient persons present to organise the gathering, let alone proceed to a vote.[12]

[9] AD Pyrénées-Orientales L431, Procès-verbaux, fructidor III (Sept. 1795), Le Gall, *Les consultations générales*, II, pp. 712–14 and AM Brest 1K7 11–9, Procès-verbaux, fructidor III (Sept. 1795).
[10] AD Aude L376, Procès-verbal d'élection, 21 fructidor III (7 Sept. 1795).
[11] Godechot, ed., *Les constitutions*, pp. 121–2.
[12] C. Bloch, 'Le recrutement du personnel municipal en l'an IV', *Rf*, 46 (1904), p. 156.

This business completed, country folk then retired to their respective communes and, on 15 brumaire (6 November), they separately elected their own *agents* and *adjoints municipaux* to represent them at cantonal level. They were far more inclined to vote in their own communities than at the *chef-lieu de canton*, not only in 1795 but in subsequent years as well. Turnout in excess of 30 per cent was often recorded, especially in smaller villages, a level of participation rarely matched in municipal elections in the urban areas.

Larger towns of over 5,000 inhabitants retained their own councils, though these were much reduced in size after 1795. In the initial elections held on 10 brumaire turnout was generally poorer than it had been a couple of months earlier. At Toulon representatives-on-mission denounced the citizens' 'criminal lack of interest in exercising the most sacred of civic tasks'.[13] Voting had not been included among the list of duties appended to the new Constitution, but urban voters showed a good deal more enthusiasm for approving it than choosing new town councillors. At Brest, for instance only 28 per cent turned out in November compared to 40 per cent in September, while at Dijon there was a huge drop from almost 60 per cent in fructidor to less than 30 per cent in brumaire.[14]

This psephological pattern would prove an enduring one under the Directory too: urban voters generally displayed greater assiduity in the annual choice of second-degree electors, which preceded the election of justices of the peace and municipal officers at the polls. To judge by the sample examined here, voting for town councillors rarely surpassed the 20 per cent mark after the Year IV and often fell to single percentage figures in the Year VII. Toulouse offers an outstanding exception to this general rule, doubtless on account of a delicate balance between the city's political parties which mobilised large numbers of voters as they jostled for power. At Marseille a bitter battle for control of the town in the Years IV and V produced unprecedented electoral participation, but interest waned once the Jacobins were firmly in command.

The Constitution of 1795 had in fact imposed a different type of municipal régime upon the great cities of Marseille, Bordeaux, Lyon and, of course, Paris. In an attempt to reduce their regional influence these metropoli had been broken down into *arrondissements*, each of which was endowed with a seven-man council and coordinated by an unelected *bureau central*. Elections for municipal councillors were delayed until the summer of 1796, because the Directory feared a recrudescence of the

---

[13] AM Toulon L115, Arrêté de Niou et de Servière, 15 brumaire IV (6 Nov. 1795).
[14] AM Brest 1K7 11–9, Procès-verbaux d'élection, brumaire IV (Nov. 1795) and AD Côte-d'Or L240, Procès-verbaux de Dijon, brumaire IV (Nov. 1795).

Table 15 *Turnout in municipal elections under the Directory, Year IV to Year VII (1795–1799)*

Percentage participation in the first round of voting for town councillors, or municipal agents and their deputies

(a) Villages and small towns of less than 5,000 inhabitants: A sample of municipal agents and their deputies

Locality	Year IV (1795)	Year V (1797)	Year VI (1798)	Year VII (1799)
Côte-d'Or	34.8	33.5	36.6	18.4
Meurthe	23.4	19.8	23.4	25.4
Rural canton of Toulouse	34.6	43.1	35.9	36.0
Vence (Var)		55.1	32.6	23.1

(b) Larger towns of over 5,000 inhabitants: Municipal councillors

Town	Year IV (1795/6)	Year V (1797)	Year VI (1798)	Year VII (1799)
Aix-en-Provence	10.0	22.9	11.6	9.4
Bar (le- Duc)		12.8	25.3	9.5
Bordeaux	24.4	12.0	10.2	9.6
Brest	28.5	13.8	18.9	14.4
Châlons s/Marne	17.7	19.6	24.6	
Marseille	35.3	32.3	20.8	10.8
Nancy	7.4	13.5	12.7	
Toulon		31.3	16.1	18.0
Toulouse	27.7	71.5	50.6	44.2

Sources: (a) Smaller Towns and Villages: AD Côte-d'Or L275–8, Procès-verbaux d'élection, ans IV-VII (1795–99); AD Haute-Garonne L249–56; AD Alpes-Maritimes, Vence III K1; and Clémendot, *Le département de la Meurthe*
(b) Large Towns: AM Bordeaux K5–11, Procès-verbaux d'election, ans IV-VII (1796–99); AM Brest 1 K7–19; AD Marne Supplément E 5875–6; AM Marseille K3 9–11; AM Toulon L586–8; AM Toulouse 1 K13–16; Derobert-Ratel, *Institutions et vie municipale à Aix-en-Provence*, p.605; C. Aimond, *Histoire de Bar-le-Duc*, new ed (Bar-le-Duc, 1982); and Clémendot, *Le département de la Meurthe*

138   Elections in the French Revolution

unrest that had erupted in Paris in vendémiaire of the year IV (September 1795). The cooling-off period would, it was hoped, 'encourage citizens to approach the electoral process in a calmer frame of mind'.[15] In the event there were no disturbances in Paris, where the level of participation was under 10 per cent.[16] Yet while apathy reigned in the capital, a mighty turnout at Marseille was accompanied by widespread violence which produced a fatality.[17]

Under the Directory municipal, judicial and departmental bodies, like the Legislature, were subject to partial, annual renewal. A single electoral cycle was prescribed, beginning on 1 germinal (21 March) in the cantons, where business was to be concluded within ten days. Voters from the smaller communes reassembled separately on 15 germinal to choose *agents* and *adjoints*. Finally, second-degree electors were awaited at the departmental *chef-lieu* five days later for a session of ten days' duration. The whole process was completed within a month and no provision was made for by-elections; positions that became vacant were to be filled by cooption or simply left empty. Three sets of regular elections subsequently took place on this basis in the Years V, VI and VII, from 1797 to 1799. Calculations for turnout have been taken from the first round of voting for electors, in a sample of cantons from a dozen departments with a good series of *procès-verbaux* (see table 16).

As always the figures are rather less precise than they appear. They should be taken as indicating an order of grandeur rather than a high degree of statistical accuracy, because reliable voter-registration was beyond the grasp of most officials. From the Year V onwards new lists of potential voters, the *ayant droit de voter*, were to be compiled each year according to the tax-payers' franchise established in the Constitution of the Year III. It is extremely unusual to find a department like the Meuse where fresh sets of figures were drawn up for each of the years that followed. Indeed, many departments struggled to produce any lists at all under the Directory.

In the newly created Alpes-Maritimes, for instance, administrators admitted: 'It has proved impossible to distinguish citizens who pay taxes from those who do not . . . thus all adult males have been given the vote regardless of their fiscal status.'[18] Next door, in the Var, a table for the Year V looks suspiciously familiar and on closer inspection it turns out to be an exact replica of a register drawn up in 1791, presumably resurrected *faute*

[15] BL FR99, Sur les élections municipales, 27 messidor IV (15 July 1796).
[16] AN BI 16, Procès-verbaux d'élection, 1 thermidor IV (19 July 1796).
[17] AM Marseille K3/9, Pocès-verbaux d'élection, 1 thermidor IV (19 July 1796).
[18] AN F¹cIII Alpes-Maritimes 1, Commissaire au ministre, 30 nivôse V (19 Jan. 1797).

Table 16 *Turnout in primary elections under the Directory, Year III to Year VII (1795–1799)*

Percentage participation in the first round of voting for second-degree electors

Department	Year III			Year V			Year VI			Year VII		
	ADV	PART	Percentage	ADV	PART	Percentage	ADV	PART	Percentage	ADV	PART	Percentage
Basses-Alpes	13906	1568	10.4	13992	2395	17.1	13971	4667	33.4	13997	2650	18.9
Aude	18079	1783	9.9	21341	3136	14.7	13920	3489	25.1	17121	2478	14.5
Aveyron	18773	2909	15.5	32105	7683	23.9	28581	5128	17.9	36203	4105	11.3
Charente							21472	4759	22.2	9517	893	9.4
Côte-d'Or	14145	1616	11.4	12945	3354	25.9	10695	3061	28.6	14168	1691	11.9
Finistère							19006	2346	12.3	20424	1361	11.0
Haute-Garonne				32468	14324	44.1	12453	3501	28.1	11995	2423	20.2
Marne	59727	6391	10.7				35856	6243	17.4	35659	2731	7.7
Meuse	17575	1587	9.0	15835	1709	10.8	17937	3046	17.0	18105	1334	7.4
Morbihan	19604	2001	10.3	23216	3911	16.8	19557	2773	14.2	19917	1914	9.6
Orne	24435	3637	14.9	5154	1453	28.2	26330	4356	16.5	35673	3107	12.1
Pyrénées-Orientales	11400	1228	10.8	11977	1635	13.7	9909	1781	18.0	9237	753	8.2
Total/Average	197644	22720	11.5	169033	39600	23.4	229687	45150	19.7	232016	25440	11.0

PART = Participants

Sources: AD Basses-Alpes L199–203; AD Aude L375–86; AD Aveyron 1L620–687: AD Charente L126–7; AD Côte-d'Or L238–50; AD Finistère 10L81–94; AD Haute-Garonne L241–7; AD Marne 1L297–311; AD Meuse L356–60; AD Morbihan L241–6; AD Orne L390–418; and AD Pyrénées-Orientales L431–3

de mieux.[19] Even in the unusually efficient Côte-d'Or officials succumbed to the temptation of despatching to Paris lists they had originally compiled in the Year II.[20] In this exemplary department, however, many primary assemblies maintained the tradition of recording numbers eligible to vote in their *procès-verbaux*. Such a practice was rarely employed elsewhere but, if needs be, rough calculations can be made from the total of second-degree electors chosen in the canton in the ratio of one for every 200 *ayant droit de voter*.

Hard-pressed officials in the Landes owned up to their sleight of hand with the new electoral registers of the Year V, blaming cantonal administrators for their predicament: 'Up to now we have received lists from only fourteen cantons out of twenty-six . . . Among those which have arrived the majority contain huge inaccuracies . . . Consequently we have decided to make adjustments to the general table drawn up in 1790 because it was compiled with much greater exactitude.'[21] As a result of this expedient the total of *ayant droit de voter* in the Landes in 1797 was scarcely greater than it had been seven years earlier, yet it was reduced again the following year to serve party-political interests. Resurgent republicans of the Year VI claimed their royalist opponents had engaged in some gerrymandering, creating additional assemblies 'in places dominated by priests, nobles and former seigneurs . . .', thus inflating the number of voters in areas favourable to their cause.[22] In 1798 republicans reversed this situation with the award of additional votes to Jacobin strongholds and a sharp reduction in conservative cantons.

Such partisan interference threatened to undermine the entire electoral process. There had certainly been disputes over entitlement to vote in the past, but systematic manipulation on behalf of a particular party was symptomatic of the intensity of political conflict under the Directory. Constantly changing legislation, which excluded or admitted different political categories from the franchise, offered further scope for sharp practice, besides provoking endless disputes at the electoral assemblies themselves.[23] A law of 1 fructidor III (18 August 1795), for example, had deprived *émigrés* of the franchise until their return to the country was officially sanctioned. More important were the subsequent laws of 19 fructidor V, 9 frimaire and 5 ventôse VI (5 September and 29 November 1797 and 23 February 1798), which removed voting rights

---

[19] AN C 482, Procès-verbal de l'assemblée départementale, vendémiaire IV (Oct. 1795) and *ibid.* F^{20}388, Tableau des cantons, 3 prairial V (22 May 1797).

[20] AD Côte-d'Or L497, Division des assemblées primaires, 4 nivôse V (24 Dec. 1796).

[21] AN F^{1}cIII Landes 1, Distribution des assemblées primaires, 5 ventôse V (23 Feb. 1797).

[22] AN AFIII 239, Administration départementale au ministre, 18 ventôse VI (8 Mar. 1798).

[23] Aulard, *Histoire politique*, pp. 583–7 and Le Gall, *Les consultations générales*, I, pp, 187–201.

from *émigrés*' relatives, nobles and, finally, all those who had served with rebel forces. As conservatives in the Landes protested, lists of *émigrés* were deliberately extended in order to remove their relations from electoral contention.[24]

With these exceptions the registers of *ayant droit de voter* comprised all adult males entered on the tax rolls, notwithstanding cases of prolonged absence such as military service. As in the past, all listed persons had certain formalities to fulfil before they could actually exercise their right to vote. Enrolment in the National Guard remained essential, though how faithfully this requirement was followed is a matter of doubt. In the Finistère, for instance, it was reported in the Year V that only a fraction of the peasantry had signed up with the militia; in theory the majority had surrendered the franchise by failing to do so.[25] A declaration of citizenship was also demanded from those entitled to vote, but on 15 ventôse V (4 March 1797), only a fortnight before elections were due to begin, the municipal agent at Guiquelleau in the same department complained that 'no one had come to register'.[26] Nor was this problem of non-registration confined to rural areas: at Nantes only a quarter of eligible voters were actually *inscrits* in 1797, at Nancy less than half.[27] Under the Directory as before, if only properly registered citizens were taken into account, as opposed to the much larger numbers *ayant droit de voter*, the turnout in elections would immediately double.

Whatever these persistent uncertainties where the figures are concerned there is little doubt that electoral participation in the Year V topped the 20 per cent mark. Politicians in the Convention had declared that the primary assemblies of 1795 were 'in anticipation of those scheduled for 1796 (the Year IV), when none would be held'.[28] Resurgent royalists seeking a parliamentary road to power, if not an immediate monarchical restoration, were thus obliged to wait some eighteen months for the next

---

[24] AN AFIII 239, Electeurs de Dax au Directoire, 19 germinal VI (8 Apr. 1798). For similar protests at Marseille, in the Year IV, which allegedly affected some 2,500 individuals and led to annulment of the elections, see AN F¹cIII Bouches-du-Rhône 8, Adresse des Marseillais, 30 thermidor IV (17 Aug. 1796).
[25] AN F¹cIII Finistère 5, Commissaire de Landerneau au ministre, 30 nivôse V (19 Jan. 1797).
[26] AD Finistère 10L86, Commissaire au ministre, 14 ventôse V (4 Mar. 1797) and see also, P. Bourdin, 'Les paysans et le pouvoir directorial dans le Puy-de-Dôme', *AhRf*, LIX (1987), pp. 315–16.
[27] Le Gall, Les consultations générales, I, pp. 168–72 and C. Pfister, ed., *Les assemblées électorales dans le département de la Meurthe le district, les cantons et la ville de Nancy. Procès-verbaux originaux* (Nancy, 1912), p. xxvii.
[28] *Moniteur* XXV, p. 561, 5 fructidor III (22 Aug. 1795).

round of legislative elections. They put the interval to good use to prepare an effective campaign and mobilise the electorate.[29]

D'André, a former member of the Constituent Assembly endowed with substantial funds from Britain, tried to devise a coordinated strategy, to which the pretender Louis XVIII was persuaded to give his blessing. Agents were despatched into the provinces where royalist associations and *Instituts philanthropiques* were being established. In the Sarthe, for example, a *comité royaliste* was created, which issued a broadsheet with the unfortunate title *Le Préservatif de l'Anarchie*.[30] Right-wing newspapers promoted the election of candidates sharing their political ideas, but the pulpit was probably more influential than the press in encouraging voters to attend the primary assemblies.[31] At grassroots level the role of refractory clergy, aided and abetted by local landowners, was crucial in guiding rural political choices.

This royalist offensive produced a relatively high turnout in reactionary departments and cantons. The Orne, in Lower Normandy, is a good case in point: worried patriots at Le Sap, to the north of the department, wrote to the Minister of the Interior to report that one commune in the canton, which had contributed a mere six voters to the constitutional vote of 1795, was now represented by over one hundred.[32] A non-juring parish priest was apparently pulling the strings in this case, while elsewhere royalist agents were touring the countryside 'their pockets stuffed full of lists' bearing the names of *honnêtes gens* (respectable persons) they wanted to implant as second-degree electors.

In 1797 voters were allowed to hand their own ballot papers to the tellers, instead of writing or having them written at the officials' desk. This experiment was not repeated the following year because it was held responsible for a great deal of electoral fraud as illiterate peasants were conned by royalist agents. Bribery was apparently rife in the Seine-Inférieure in Upper Normandy, where a monarchist slogan, 'It is not five rulers we want, just one', was enjoying wide circulation. It was even alleged that a forest guard recruited by the royalists was blackmailing poachers into voting, by threatening them with exposure if they failed to take part in the election.[33]

---

[29] W.R. Fryer, *Republic or Restoration in France? 1794–1797* (Manchester, 1965), pp. 189–203 and H. Mitchell, *The Underground War against Revolutionary France. The Missions of William Wickham 1794–1800* (Oxford, 1965), pp. 140–9.

[30] M. Reinhard, *Le département de la Sarthe sous le régime directorial* (Saint-Brieuc, 1935), p. 251.

[31] J.D. Popkin, *The Right-Wing Press in France, 1792–1800* (Chapel Hill, 1980), pp. 89–90.

[32] AN F¹cIII Orne 1, Commissaire au ministre, 5 germinal V (25 Mar. 1797).

[33] Comité régional d'histoire de la Révolution, *La Révolution en Haute-Normandie*, pp. 147–8.

Where the royalist challenge was less evident, in the Meurthe or the Meuse for example, or in republican cantons of reactionary departments, the level of participation remained relatively low. However, in those areas where patriots made a determined effort to stem the anti-republican tide, the resulting battle produced some of the best-attended assemblies of the entire decade. The Haute-Garonne, for instance, was the cockpit of patriotic resistance in the South-West and violent incidents erupted at more than a third of the primary assemblies in this department.[34] Some of these were parish pump disputes of the familiar variety, opposing rival clienteles or communes. Peter Jones is right to remind us that elsewhere, beneath the 'air of ideological grandeur . . . the abiding impression is one of doggedly secular rivalry for local office'.[35] Yet Fournier reckons that divisions were increasingly occurring within, rather than between communities and assuming a strong political hue in the process. At Bazièges a fiercely fought contest of this sort was responsible for a 70 per cent turnout, with constitutional clergy doing their utmost to rouse republican ardour.

Toulouse, *chef-lieu* of the Haute-Garonne, managed a poll in excess of 70 per cent too and all over France towns tended to vote more strongly than the surrouding countryside.[36] At Toulon, in the Var, polling was in the region of 35 per cent, prompting the municipal administration to comment: 'Since the beginning of the Revolution the primary assemblies have never been so well attended.'[37] Yet official claims that these elections had been conducted, 'with all the calm, order and propriety that one could wish for', were rejected by some 400 individuals who had been prevented from voting. According to them:

> Solid citizens were replaced by a dreadful horde of anarchists who, having been chased out of neighbouring departments, have discovered a refuge from their criminal past in our city. Here they have found local officials more than willing to grant them a certificate attesting a year's residence, when in fact their appearance in the town only dates from a couple of months ago.[38]

Factional strife of this sort, which disrupted the polls all over the Midi in the Year V, was a grim reminder of the divisions wrought by Terror and Counter-Terror in recent years.[39] Neither side was willing to give the other access to power without putting up an exceptionally strong fight.

---

[34] Fournier, 'La participation électorale en Haute-Garonne', pp. 65–8.
[35] Jones, *Politics and Rural Society*, p. 205.
[36] AM Toulouse 1K14, Procés-verbaux d'élection, germinal V (Mar. 1797) and Crook, '"Aux Urnes Citoyens!"', pp. 159–60.
[37] AN F¹cIII Var 1, L'administration municipale au ministre, 7 germinal V (27 Mar. 1797).
[38] *Ibid.*, Protestation des habitants, 2 germinal V (22 Mar. 1797).
[39] Poupé, *Le département du Var*, pp. 430–2, for the situation in the Var in particular.

The unprecedented campaigning which accompanied the elections in 1797 was encouraged by the institution of declared candidatures.[40] Despite a number of earlier proposals to this effect it was only in the Year III that legislators took the plunge and decreed that names of candidates could be registered prior to the annual round of voting. More detailed regulations assured citizens that: 'This open manner of offering oneself to the electorate is the most worthy of a republican and, when all is said and done, it is preferable to the secret intrigue and obscure manoeuvres of scheming ambition.' During the month of nivôse (December–January) individuals were invited to submit their own names, or those of worthy compatriots, for the various offices to be filled at local, departmental and national level. Assuming that the candidature was in order, it would be publicised when the relevant assemblies met a couple of months later in the spring.

Though there was a better response when it came to the departmental electoral colleges, interest at municipal and primary level proved rather lukewarm. Many villages either did not bother to open registers or failed to record any names. When the president of the cantonal assembly at Riez in the Basses-Alpes asked for the lists of candidates, he was told there were none.[41] The same was true in rural cantons of the Finistère; where the matter was mentioned at all it was only to report a nil return.[42] In the Loire-Inférieure only Nantes seems to have received any proposals for municipal office or second-degree electors.[43] Likewise in the Bas-Rhin, only Strasbourg mustered any candidates willing to serve at the departmental assembly.[44] The innovation was half-hearted, since voters could still nominate whoever they wished on their ballot papers, yet many republicans blamed the system of candidatures for royalist success at the polls. The experiment was jettisoned the following year, though the elections of the Year VI demonstrated that party-politics were a growth industry, regardless of electoral legislation.[45]

Equally revealing in the Year V was the emergence of a partisan provincial press, which began to abandon its anodyne injunctions about voting for 'good' or 'virtuous' citizens and at last stood up to be counted.[46]

[40] Gueniffey, 'Revolutionary Democracy'.
[41] AD Basses-Alpes L202, Procès-verbaux d'élection, 1 germinal V (21 Mar. 1797).
[42] AD Finistère 10L85, Procès-verbal de Guerlesquin, 1 germinal V (21 Mar. 1797).
[43] BN Le[40] 129, Tableau des citoyens de la commune de Nantes, indiqués comme candidats (no place, no date) and Le Gall, Les consultations générales, II, pp. 744–7.
[44] Marx, Recherches sur la vie politique, p. 164.
[45] Pons de Verdun, Rapport fait ... sur la suppression des candidats (Paris, an VI).
[46] H. Gough, 'National Politics and the Provincial Jacobin Press during the Directory', History of European Ideas, 10 (1989), pp. 447–50. Despite considerable interest in the press, the treatment of elections by provincial newspapers has received little attention; I hope to pursue the matter myself in the near future.

The example of Toulouse offers an especially vivid illustration of this development. In the Year V the town was served by two rival sheets, the republican *Journal de Toulouse* and the reactionary *Anti-Terroriste*. In 1797, both devoted a huge number of column inches to the elections.[47] Coverage commenced well before the assemblies opened, with a good turnout being solicited on both sides. The *Journal* urged: 'Patriots, don't forget about germinal . . . remember to appear *en masse* at the primary assemblies.' The *Anti-Terroriste* carried a similar message, adding the sombre warning that in Sparta those who failed to vote had faced the death penalty and threatening to print the names of those who abstained.

Though the advice that was offered continued to place principles above personalities, the taboo upon naming names was cast aside as the respective merits of the men of 1789 and those of 1793 were recommended to readers. Once the polls had opened regular reports were made upon their progress. The *Journal* was confident that a majority of voters were republican in outlook and suggested that indications elsewhere in the department were just as favourable. Its rival's initial rejoicing over the exceptionally high level of participation quickly turned into alarm. The disappointing choice of second-degree electors for Toulouse was attributed to outbreaks of violence at the assemblies, perpetrated by 'anarchists'. The recent revision of section boundaries within the town, a piece of gerrymandering which had allegedly adjusted voting wards to the Jacobins' advantage, was also blamed for the conservatives' *débâcle*.[48] Popkin, historian of the right-wing press under the First Republic, is doubtful that provincial newspapers could 'dictate the choice of particular individuals', but he misses the novelty of their attempt in the Year V to do so.[49]

Of course, journalistic comment reflected as much as generated partisan conflict, which was most graphically illustrated by the increasing number of electoral schisms. The ploy was not a new one, for isolated instances of minorities splitting away to form another assembly, conduct separate elections and draw up their own *procès-verbal*, can be found as far back as 1789.[50] Most of the earlier examples stemmed from village rivalry over control of the cantons. Such was the dispute between Cabasse and Carcès, which led to the despatch of two delegations to the departmental electoral college of the Var in 1792.[51] This parochial dimension never dis-

[47] *Le Journal de Toulouse*, 20 ventôse-4 germinal V (10–24 Mar. 1797) and *L'Anti-Terroriste*, 12 ventôse-6 floréal V (2 Mar.-25 Apr. 1797).
[48] H. Ramet, *Histoire de Toulouse*, new ed. (Marseille, 1977), p. 52.
[49] Popkin, *The Right-Wing Press*, p. 90. Marx, *Recherches sur la vie politique*, pp. 82–5, is equally sceptical where the role of the press in the elections of the Year V is concerned.
[50] For example, in Brittany. See Signor, *La Révolution à Pont-l'Abbé*, pp.85–6.
[51] Poupé, *Le département du Var*, p. 189.

appeared entirely, but it was overlaid by party-political animosities: schisms even began to erupt at village level in communal elections. Only a few occurred in the Year IV, but they became more widespread the following year and threatened to divide the departmental assemblies, when they decided which of the opposing delegations to admit to their proceedings.

The practice of electoral schism, or secession, is extremely well-documented because both assemblies, the original *assemblée mère* or *assemblée scissionnée*, just as much as the breakaway *assemblée scissionnaire*, always sought to justify their conduct. Republicans asserted not only the right but the duty of secession, 'whenever the Constitution was being violated'. The complexity of the rules governing elections certainly offered plenty of scope for allegations that irregularities were being engineered by the other side. An official in the Basses-Alpes despaired of the endless infractions he was obliged to report, while one individual in the Haute-Garonne had suggested a course of studies on the Constitution to reduce the incidence of such problems.[52]

A schism either took place after the creation of the assembly *bureau*, or when participants' credentials were being discussed. In both cases the strength of the respective parties was tested and the likely outcome of the contest became clear. President, secretary and scrutineers would chair, record, count and consequently influence the result, while the admission of additional voters might tip the balance between rival forces. The *Anti-Terroriste* of Toulouse urged its readers to: 'Remember how important it is that you participate in choosing the *bureau* . . . and determining *bona fides* . . . the success of your efforts depends upon it'.[53]

A classic illustration of the *genre* is furnished by a section of Blain, in the troubled Loire-Inférieure, where a schism occurred in the Year V.[54] In this instance the assembly was besieged by a host of would-be voters who claimed the local authorities had refused their registration. When it became evident that a majority of those already present supported their right to attend, the republican minority quit to proceed separately in another building. Those in charge of the *assemblée mère* discovered that inkstand and paper had been removed by departing officials, but they were able to muster 159 participants as opposed to a mere forty-three at the rival assembly. The latter had been established at the *hôtel de ville* by complaisant municipal administrators, though secessionists did not always find alternative accommodation so easily. At Entrevaux in the Basses-Alpes one seceding group found itself in competition with a

---

[52] AN F¹cIII Haute-Garonne 1, Lalanne de Toulouse au ministre, 28 nivôse V (17 Jan. 1797) and *ibid*. F¹cIII Basses-Alpes 2, Tableau des irrégularités, 12 prairial VII (31 May 1799). [53] *L'Anti-Terroriste*, 28 ventôse V (10 Mar. 1797).
[54] Le Gall, *Les consultations générales*, II, pp, 764–6.

wedding party and had to leave the *maison commune* to reassemble at the local hospital.[55]

Presented with a choice between rival delegations, the departmental college might invalidate the operations of both primary assemblies. In the Loire-Inférieure, once again in the Year V, electors from the *assemblée mère* of Vertou were refused admission for employing violence against their political opponents.[56] Yet beleaguered republicans who had formed an *assemblée scissionnaire* fared no better, on the grounds that they lacked a mandate to convene separately, even when 'the constitution had been brought into disrepute'. Perhaps if more schisms had been treated in this fashion the practice would have lost its attraction. Instead these electoral splits multiplied to reach staggering proportions: Suratteau has estimated that in the Year VI at least 600 cantons were divided, or roughly one primary assembly in ten.[57] The Landes, Haute-Garonne and Basses-Alpes were among the departments most badly affected.

Far from being outlawed, the tactic of secession was actually endorsed by the Directory in its effort to influence the composition of the electoral colleges. In the Year V, while the government had made some attempts to counteract the royalist campaign, it was caught off balance by the depth of hostility to the regime. The only means of reversing this disaster was to resort to a purge of personnel which the elections had brought to power. The infamous *coup d'état* of 18 fructidor V (September 1797) not only struck deputies in the Legislature, but also scores of departmental and local officials.[58] Some embattled republicans like the patriots of Vannes, in the Morbihan, had urged the executive to act in this fashion and congratulary addresses subsequently poured in from the provinces.[59] Yet if the *coup* was an effective way of redressing unwelcome electoral returns, it was an extremely crude one. The Directory naturally hoped to avoid so draconian a measure in future by promoting more favourable results in the first place.

Thus the government entered the electoral arena in the Year VI to an extent that it had never even contemplated before. With the establishment of centrally appointed *commissaires du directoire exécutif* suitable agents had been implanted in the localities. A *commissaire* was attached to each cantonal administration, under the command of a *commissaire central*

---

[55] AN F¹cIII Basses-Alpes 1, Commissaire au ministre, 9 germinal VI (29 Mar. 1798).
[56] Le Gall, *Les consultations générales*, II, pp. 790–1.
[57] Suratteau, *Les élections de l'an VI*, pp. 227–31.
[58] C. Derobert-Ratel, *Institutions et vie municipale à Aix-en-Provence sous la Révolution, 1789 – an VIII* (Millau, 1981), pp. 171–4, for a typical example.
[59] AN F¹cIII Morbihan 1, Amis de Liberté de Vannes, 15 floréal V (4 May 1797).

located in the departmental *chef-lieu*, who has been called a precursor of the Napoleonic prefect.[60] This bureaucratic innovation, enshrined in the Constitution of the Year III, has received far too little attention from historians, but there is evidence to suggest that some *commissaires* were given a role in elections as early as the Year IV. In the fifth *arrondissement* of Paris, for example, the *commissaire* felt it was essential 'to enlighten citizens regarding their choice of municipal councillors'.[61] Protesters retorted that the government had no right 'to rig the elections nor deprive the people of their choice', a response which possibly deterred the Directory from employing the gambit more widely the following year.

In the provinces, in the Year V, the *commissaires* do not appear to have acted as more than watchdogs, reporting upon the conduct of the elections and commenting upon the results. The notion of *esprit public* was born as these agents submitted analyses of the political situation and supplied personal details for second-degree electors, sometimes using printed pro-formas of the sort familiar to students of the First Empire.[62] This surprising degree of bureaucratic control and incipient centralisation is especially evident in the way that documentation on elections began to accumulate, not just in the localities but also in Paris. So far, however, the *commissaires* seemed content to track and document, but not to openly interfere with the electoral process.

This essentially passive role changed in the Year VI as *commissaires* were encouraged to adopt a much more interventionist approach, stand for election, canvass for votes and, if all else failed, foment schisms. In the Haute-Loire, for example, it has been suggested that the *commissaire central*, named Portal, effectively became a campaign manager for the Directory. He issued clear instructions to his colleagues in the cantons, who were told to 'work night and day on the elections ... it is essential that you collaborate with local administrators and that together you ensure the triumph of the republican cause over that of Blankenburg' (an allusion to the pretender Louis XVIII's headquarters in Germany, provided by the Duke of Brunswick).[63] *Commissaires* were encouraged to prepare for secessions in case of difficulties, though in the canton of Montfaucon the official was pleased to report: 'It has not been necessary to organise a schism; I have been nominated as a second-degree elector with a huge majority.'[64]

[60] Godechot, *Les institutions*, p. 471 and Reinhard, *Le département de la Sarthe*, p. 57.
[61] AN F^{1}cIII Seine 1, Commissaire du 5e arrondissement, 27 messidor IV (15 July 1796).
[62] M. Jusselin, *L'administration du département d'Eure-et-Loir pendant la Révolution* (Chartres, 1935), pp. 154–65.
[63] E. Delcambre, *La période du Directoire dans la Haute-Loire*, 3 vols. (Rodez, 1941–43), II, p. 254.   [64] *Ibid.*, II, p. 277.

In the Year VI large numbers of *commissaires* were elected to departmental colleges all over the country, including the capital. This could cause some embarrassment. Asked for comments on the electors, the official in one canton of the Seine confessed that he was numbered among them and added, 'it is not for me to judge myself'![65] Another *commissaire* in Paris expressed some qualms about his own nomination but salved his conscience by recalling that 'the Directory would be pleased to see its servants chosen as electors'.[66] Others relished their electoral role and exhibited an arrogant attitude, like the *commissaire* at Moncontour in the Côtes-du-Nord, who flatly refused to accept the results in one canton and warned the electors that he would never allow them to sit in the departmental assembly.[67]

In place of the declared candidates of the Year V the Directory had instituted 'official' candidates of its own, often chosen from the administration, in a manner which presaged practices more familiar in the nineteenth century. In 1798, as Suratteau suggests, the government attempted to organise the elections using public money.[68] Yet another striking innovation of the Year VI was the use of special electoral emissaries to help secure favourable returns. Merlin de Douai, who had recently become one of the five executive directors, was put in charge of this covert operation. A team of customs officials was sent out, ostensibly to establish toll-booths on some of the major highways, as a means of raising revenue for their improvement. The real purpose, however, was to disburse funds and supply intelligence on local electoral prospects in suitably cryptic language: political reliability was expressed by statements such as, 'all the roads in this department are in good repair'![69]

A further originality of the Year VI lay in the *fête* of the Sovereignty of the People, which was to be held on 30 ventôse (20 March 1798), the *décadi* or day of rest in the ten-day week which fell on the eve of polling. The Directory had already created a raft of such festivals, but this belated addition to the repertoire had immediate, practical aims.[70] Its intention was to raise civic consciousness and encourage a good electoral turnout on the part of responsible citizens. In the Var, as elsewhere, those who came to watch the processions of soldiers and school children were regaled with homilies from the government.[71] Only later did recreation

---

[65] AN AFIII 260, Commissaire de Pantin, 18 germinal VI (7 Apr. 1798).
[66] *Ibid.*, Commissaire du 1er arrondissement, 3 germinal VI (23 Mar. 1798).
[67] Pommeret, *L'esprit public dans le département des Côtes-du-Nord*, p. 435.
[68] Suratteau, *Les élections de l'an VI*, p. 108.
[69] *Ibid.*, pp. 182–92.
[70] M. Ozouf, *La fête révolutionnaire 1789–1799* (Paris, 1976), p. 194, though she has little to say about this particular example. [71] Poupé, *Le département du Var*, pp. 451–6.

replace pedagogy, as games were organised in the afternoon, followed by displays, fireworks and dancing in the evening. One cynical commentator suggested that citizens would be too tired to vote the next day; perhaps the elections should have been held on, rather than after the *fête*.

In the Year VI, those who survived the festivities and attended the primary assemblies were obliged to make a declaration of allegiance that had been dropped on the two previous occasions.[72] Loyalty to the Constitution of the Year III was demanded, along with an oath of hatred of royalism and anarchy. The Directory had commended this political *via media* in a trenchant proclamation of 9 ventôse (27 February 1798), which inveighed vehemently against both 'white cockades' and 'red bonnets', the terrible twins threatening the people with slavery or terror. Yet on the eve of these elections the government realised that it had committed a colossal tactical blunder. Transfixed by royalist success in the Year V it had expended too much ammunition in this direction. Repression of the Right since the *coup* of fructidor had facilitated, even encouraged a revival of the Left. In many places, certainly in South-West, Centre and South-East, it was the Jacobins who were to be feared most.

In a mood approaching panic the Directory hastily resorted to some old-fashioned repression.[73] Early in March 1798 newspapers and clubs associated with the Jacobins were closed. Suspect persons were arrested and cities like Marseille were placed under martial law, but it was too late. As soon as the polls opened reports from the departments predicted a massive triumph for radical opponents of the regime. 'What a contrast between germinal V and germinal VI', exclaimed a *commissaire* from the previously reactionary Eure-et-Loir.[74] Overall turnout seems to have been slightly down on the Year V, at just below 20 per cent, but its geographical distribution was substantially different. Departments and cantons sympathetic to the Republic polled more heavily in the Year VI, while refractory areas experienced a slump in attendance. Thus the Aude, Meurthe and Meuse doubled the level of participation recorded twelve months earlier. Conversely voting in the Norman departments of the Orne and Seine-Inférieure declined by almost half. In the West, *chouan*-dominated cantons of the Loire-Inférieure fell below the 10 per cent mark, showing far less propensity to participate than strongholds of republican sentiment.[75]

The re-imposition of an oath of allegiance may have taken a toll in reac-

---

[72] Aulard, *Histoire politique*, p. 584.   [73] Woloch, *Jacobin Legacy*, pp. 276–9.
[74] Jusselin, *L'administration du département d'Eure-et-Loir*, p. 179.
[75] Le Gall, *Les consultations générales*, II, pp. 841–2.

tionary areas. At Melrand, in the Morbihan, no one was prepared to swear it and the primary assembly dissolved without choosing any second-degree electors.[76] In the Sarthe priests and royalists seem to have organised an electoral boycott and it was frequently stated by *commissaires* that 'no aristocrats had appeared'.[77] In cases where republicans threatened to dominate the polls, royalists simply abandoned the field without a fight. When bitter enemies felt they were in too small a minority to stand any chance of success, it made more sense to abstain than to run the gauntlet of a hostile assembly. Something of this sort evidently occurred at Marseille in the Year VI. Twelve months earlier Jacobins had received little more than a handful of votes in many sections, but now the boot was on the other foot and they were obtaining thumping majorities while their opponents fared miserably.[78]

As always, levels of participation tended to be highest where rival parties were more evenly balanced and conflict most intense. In the Basses-Alpes, where royalists mounted some stiff resistance in the Year VI, turnout soared to a record 33 per cent. At Moulins, in the Allier, the *commissaire* reported that the primary assemblies were 'infinitely better attended than previous years', as reactionaries competed fiercely for electoral superiority.[79] Polling was also heavy in the Côte-d'Or, the scene of numerous schisms and deep enmity. At Dijon four sections out of six divided and both split at Semur, where the slogan 'Death to all Jacobins' was literally written on the wall of one assembly.[80] At the other the president was obliged to explain that he carried a cane because he was lame, not for use as an offensive weapon.

One *commissaire* in the capital suggested that Paris in the Year VI was divided between 'two well-defined parties' and that each possessed its particular social, as well as political characteristics. Walls in the capital were plastered with placards (the origins of an enduring French electoral tradition) and crowds were gathering outside the assemblies, molesting those who entered to vote.[81] As one disenchanted conservative in the Haute-Loire put it: 'It was preferable to withdraw gracefully than to rub shoulders with the hoi-polloi.'[82] Under the Directory it is rare to find *procès-verbaux* carrying lists of participants, still less names with occupational details appended. Where schisms occurred, however, more detail

---

[76] AD Morbihan L244, Procès-verbal d'élection, 1 germinal VI (21 Mar. 1798).
[77] Reinhard, *Le département de la Sarthe*, p. 324.
[78] AD Bouches-du-Rhône L270–1, Procès-verbaux d'élection, germinal V and VI (Mar. 1797 and 1798).
[79] AD Allier L140, Commissaire au ministre, 10 germinal VI (30 Mar. 1798).
[80] AD Côte-d'Or L245/7, Procès-verbaux d'élection, germinal VI (Mar. 1798).
[81] F.-A. Aulard, ed., *Paris pendant la réaction thermidorienne et sous le Directoire*, 5 vols. (Paris, 1898–1902), IV, p. 602.   [82] Delcambre, *La période du Directoire*, II, p. 368.

was sometimes supplied, permitting a glimpse of the socio-professional categories aligned on either side of the local political divide.

Evidence of this sort suggests that the Jacobins succeeded in mobilising a good deal of support among the popular classes. At Châlons-sur-Marne, for example, all four sections split in 1798 and in one of them republicans lambasted deliberate time-wasting by their 'Catholic and royalist' opponents. It was alleged that the proceedings were being spun out so as to deter the participation of craftsmen, for whom 'time is a most precious commodity . . . its theft is akin to stealing their food or clothing'.[83]

The high turnout of Jacobin forces, which produced a dilemma for the Directory, was a consequence of a determined campaign on the part of the *cercles constitutionnels*. These latter-day Jacobin clubs had begun to emerge in the wake of the fructidor *coup*. Many *chefs-lieux de département* were endowed with one in the autumn of 1797, but they spread especially rapidly into the smaller towns of departments in the South-West and Centre-West of France.[84] Their main aim was 'to ensure that the Republic triumphed in germinal', in other words to take a leaf out of their opponents' book and organise an effective electoral campaign for the following spring.

Clubs were technically permitted to operate under the Constitution, though on no account were they allowed to form networks, precisely what many *cercles* proceeded to do. The *commissaire* at Limoux in the Aude, for example, informed the ministry of police that the circle there had been in touch with similar organisations at both Carcassonne and Perpignan.[85] One of the best documented examples is the Sarthe, where a 'mobile' circle based in Le Mans, sallied forth to create new branches every *décadi*. On 15 ventôse VI (5 March 1798) a general meeting of affiliated circles was held in the departmental capital to formulate a plan of campaign for the primary assemblies.[86]

A similar ploy was utilised in the Allier, where a fraternal banquet was held a month before the polls opened. At Moulins, the *chef-lieu*, a manifesto declared that club-members should concentrate their choices upon the same persons: 'Yes, on the same names! Because if they disperse their votes they will lose the majority . . . We will indicate here those whom we are planning to name to the *bureaux*, as electors, as municipal administrators, as justices of the peace and their assistants.'[87] At Angoulême, in the Charente, the *commissaire central* complained that Jacobins at the local

---

[83] AD Marne 1L306, Procès-verbaux d'élection, germinal VI (Mar. 1798).
[84] Woloch, *Jacobin Legacy*, pp. 83–113 and *Atlas de la Révolution française*, VI, pp. 72–3.
[85] AN AFIII 216, Anon. au ministre, 15 germinal VI (4 Apr. 1798).
[86] Reinhard, *Le département de la Sarthe*, p. 319.
[87] AN AFIII 212, Commissaire au ministre, 7 germinal VI (27 Mar. 1798) and Woloch, *Jacobin Legacy*, pp. 268–71.

cercle were also establishing a list of 'candidates', having discussed the moral and political virtues of various individuals and 'then taken an oath to only elect those who had received the blessing of the club'.[88] At Villefranche-sur-Saône emissaries bearing lists of nominees were sent from the *cercle* into the town's workshops, allegedly promising reprisals against those who failed to toe the party line.[89]

Jacobin 'candidates' were thus challenging 'government candidates' and, in the absence of a huge turnout, a well-organised radical minority could expect to win the contest. This was the case at Paris where, despite the closure of clubs before the assemblies opened, long-laid plans were brought to fruition in March 1798.[90] The level of participation does not appear to have exceeded 30 per cent in any of the *arrondissements*, though this was not an especially poor performance for the capital's huge electorate. By pooling their resources, 'former members of the revolutionary committees, partisans of 1793 and acolytes of Babeuf', as the authorities put it, were able to gain the upper hand in many districts. 'The *cercle constitutionnel* sitting at (the church of) La Conception has just landed us with seven municipal administrators', wrote the *commissaire* of the first *arrondissement*, adding that the Jacobins had 'put to flight all those well-disposed towards the government and law and order'.

Faced with electoral disaster the government *commissaire* at Château-du-Loir in the Sarthe declared: 'What if the elections of theYearVI turn out to be as unsatisfactory as those of theYearV? Well, those who are chosen will simply provide some extra inhabitants for Madagascar and Guiana!'[91] On 9 germinal (29 March 1798), as the extent of the Jacobin triumph in the primaries became evident, the Directory issued a clear indication that it would not tolerate defeat. A rumour subsequently circulated in the Charente that 'a fresh 18 fructidor was being prepared against the terrorists'.[92] The proliferation of schisms, repeated at the departmental assemblies, provided a convenient pretext for the annulment of results via the *coup d'état* of 22 floréal (11 May 1798).[93] This purge of deputies to the Legislature was again accompanied by the wholesale replacement of locally elected Jacobins in the departmental and municipal administrations, as the wishes of many voters were repudiated for the second year in succession.

---

[88] AN AFIII 219, Rapport au département, no date but anVI (1798).
[89] B. Gainot, 'Espaces politiques, espaces publics, espaces civiques entre Saône et Loire sous le Directoire', in B.Benoit, ed., *Ville et Révolution française* (Lyon, 1994), p. 250.
[90] AN AFIII 260, Résumé des assemblées primaires, germinalVI (Mar. 1798) andWoloch, *Jacobin Legacy*, pp. 311–23. [91] Reinhard, *Le département de la Sarthe*, p. 315.
[92] AN AFIII 219, Commissaire de Cognac au ministre, 7 floréalVI (26 Apr. 1798).
[93] Suratteau, *Les élections de l'anVI*, pp. 311 ff.

An unrepentant Directory simply resolved to rig the elections more effectively in future. Historians have not always appreciated the extent of preparations made for the polls of the Year VII, but Bernard Gainot has convincingly demonstrated that the government's campaign was just as intensive in 1799 as a year earlier.[94] François de Neufchâteau, the famous agronomist then Minister of the Interior, was put in charge of operations. This fine administrator was well-versed in electoral matters. He continued to rely essentially upon the *commissaires*, informing them in the run-up to the assemblies, early in 1799: 'It is your job to stress to your fellow citizens the problems they will face if they allow themselves to be misled by the factions. Use all means at your disposal, exploit every one of your personal contacts.'[95]

The minister also resurrected the idea of electoral emissaries, to reinforce the network of officials. The *commissaire* in post at Brive, in the Corrèze, gave this particular game away when he stated on the eve of the elections: 'Whatever the choice of the people, the government will only accept those it has designated by means of a special agent despatched to the department.'[96] In the Year VII these men were posing as *commissaires sur les fleuves*, surveying rivers rather than roads! Their intelligence reports suggested that the main threat emanated from 'anarchists' who were refusing to lie down despite the harsh treatment they had endured.[97] Indeed, those who had been purged the previous year, the so-called *floréalisés*, formed a determined nucleus of Jacobin opponents, dedicated to repeating their electoral victory of the Year VI. In the Corrèze they were apparently up to their old tricks, seducing 'credulous country-folk with promises of tax cuts'.[98] Former members of the outlawed *cercles constitutionnels* were denounced in the Gironde too, though one local *commissaire* was rather disturbed by the absence of much overt campaigning: 'You would not think we were in the midst of elections; it seems to me that the various parties are adopting more insidious tactics this year than last.'[99]

A government address issued in ventôse, just before the polls opened, had raised the spectre of the throne as well as the guillotine, for in some departments it was royalists who were causing most concern. A *commissaire* in the Marne denounced reactionary efforts in rural areas, where the

---

[94] B. Gainot, Le mouvement néo-jacobin à la fin du Directoire. Structure et pratiques politiques, Thèse pour le Doctorat, 3 vols., Université de Paris I, 1993, I, pp. 20 ff. A. Meynier, *Les coups d'état du Directoire*, 3 vols. (Paris, 1927–29), II, p. 197, wrongly suggests that the employment of special agents was abandoned in the Year VII.

[95] Cited in Reinhard, *Le département de la Sarthe*, pp. 372–4.

[96] AN F¹cIII Corrèze 4, Commissaire au Directoire, 7 germinal VII (27 Mar. 1799).

[97] Poupé, *Le département du Var*, pp. 467–8.

[98] AN F¹cIII Corrèze 4, Agent au Directoire, 7 germinal VII (27 Mar. 1799).

[99] AN F¹cIII Gironde 1, Agent au ministre, 17 germinal VII (6 Apr. 1799).

peasants were being promised 'abolition of the ten-day week and the restoration of Sundays'.[100] One of his counterparts in the Morbihan, which would soon experience a renewed upsurge of *chouannerie*, was deeply dismayed by monarchist guerillas who 'assassinated republicans, fomented disorder and provoked divisions among patriots'.[101] In the South-West, which was also on the verge of a major counter-revolutionary uprising, similar preparations were being made: here royalists were promising 'the return of refractory priests and an end to conscription'.[102]

When the polls opened in germinal VII (late March 1799) there was a good deal of disorder in the Midi. At Saint-Lys, in the Haute-Garonne, 210 patriots managed to triumph but only after they had forced 199 *chouans* to quit after promising to make everyone sing the *Marseillaise* before they voted.[103] This closely fought contest produced a turnout in excess of 70 per cent and interest was keen wherever the parties were evenly balanced. There may have been fewer schisms in the primary assemblies than a year before, but separations remained commonplace, raising attendance in the process. Huge turnouts in excess of 50 per cent were recorded in the Doubs and the Saône-et-Loire, in cantons where splits occurred, though participation in undisturbed assemblies remained more modest and overall attendance was probably not much in excess of 11 per cent (see table 17).[104]

It is worth stressing examples of high turnout in the Year VII, since in many departments it fell to single percentage figures. The once enthusiastic electorates of the Marne and Meuse recorded an all-time low of little more than 7 per cent. At La Péruze, in the Charente, two sections merged into one 'on account of the paucity of citizens who appeared', and their second-degree electors were denied admission to the departmental assembly as a result.[105] Despite fears of a royalist resurgence in the Morbihan, a boycott seems to have occurred instead. Anti-republicans stayed at home in the Côtes-du-Nord and Sarthe too. The situation was calm, but it was the tranquillity of the graveyard. In rural areas, as one *commissaire* suggested, 'the civic spirit had been snuffed out', interest in politics was dead and some derisory attendances of only 1 or 2 per cent were recorded.[106] Elections at village level, held on 10 germinal (30 March), generally attracted a much bigger turnout, though in some com-

[100] AN F¹cIII Marne 1, Commissaire au ministre, 20 ventôse VII (10 Mar. 1799).
[101] B. Gainot, 'Les élections de 1799 dans le Morbihan. Les "réduits" républicains de l'Ouest', in A. Droguet, ed., *Les bleus de Bretagne de la Révolution à nos jours* (Saint-Brieuc, 1991), p. 178.
[102] Fournier, 'La participation électorale en Haute-Garonne', p. 69.   [103] *Ibid.*
[104] Gainot, Le mouvement néo-jacobin, I, pp. 310–18.
[105] AN AFIII 219, Commissaire au ministre, 26 germinal VII (15 Apr. 1799).
[106] Pommeret, *L'esprit public dans le département des Côtes-du-Nord*, pp. 472–3.

Table 17 *Turnout in primary elections of the Year VII (1799)*

Department	Ayant droit de voter	Participants	Percentage turnout
Doubs	19814	9087	45.9
Yonne	11946	3253	27.2
Hérault	44609	8164	18.3
Allier	15057	1923	12.8
Côtes-du-Nord	20716	2001	9.7
Aube	47481	4238	8.9
Charente-Inférieure	15040	841	5.6

Sources: AD Allier L142–5; Horn, Elections and Elites, p. 248; I am indebted to Bernard Gainot, who is working on the elections of the Year VII, for communicating the remainder of these figures to me.

munes of the Marne polling was abandoned because no one, apart from a few officials, had showed up to vote.[107]

Towns continued to poll more heavily than the countryside in the primary elections of 1799. In the Morbihan, for example, Vannes managed to attract 18 per cent of its electorate compared to just 3 per cent in the hinterland. As a *commissaire* in the canton of Muzillac put it: 'a republican in the countryside around here is a real rarity' and only republicans were showing any inclination to vote.[108] Yet even urban areas attracted fewer participants than they had in the past. At Marseille the *commissaire* deplored this pernicious trend: 'From the start supporters of the Constitution failed to attend the assemblies where, instead of the majestic and reassuring spectacle of the people meeting to exercise its sovereign rights, there were only small gatherings of smokers and drinkers, deliriously spouting revolutionary maxims.'[109]

One deputy had already predicted that repeated governmental interference with the electoral process would lead to disaffection and depoliticisation: 'Lacking confidence that their choices will be respected, the people will cease to take part in elections and they will fall into apathy, despondency and ultimately slavery.'[110] Yet the low turnout of the Year VII was not inherently terminal. Figures had fallen almost as low in the primary elections of the Year III, only to recover in the following round of

[107] AD Marne 1L307, Canton de Cormicy, 10–1 germinal VII (30–1 Mar. 1799).
[108] Gainot, 'Les élections de 1799', p.181.
[109] AN AFIII 217, Commissaire au ministre 2 germinal VII (22 Mar. 1799).
[110] BL FR 101, Lamarque, Discours, 11 floréal VI (30 Apr. 1798).

polls. Apart from the initial contests of 1790 – and sometimes not even then – the average level of participation had rarely topped 20 per cent. Even in the Year VII there were instances of considerable interest, despite government interference with two successive sets of electoral returns. The notion of a progressive and irreversible collapse is not, therefore, tenable. As Gueniffey has suggested: 'Political life under the Directory might appear humdrum, even mediocre; nonetheless it represented the initial stage of a democratic apprenticeship in the modern sense of the term.'[111]

[111] Gueniffey, *Le nombre et la raison*, p. 514.

7   An invisible aristocracy? The departmental assemblies and the emergence of a new political class

During the Revolution only municipal personnel and justices of the peace were directly elected to their posts. National deputies, like departmental officials and district administrators (until their suppression in 1795), were chosen at electoral colleges by second-degree electors who emanated from primary assemblies in the cantons. This indirect route to high office was a procedure retained from the *ancien régime*, exemplified by the successive stages of election to the Estates General in 1789. It was, above all, a means of vesting real power in the hands of a political elite which, even in the absence of a fiscal threshold in 1792, was drawn predominantly from wealthier elements of the broad electorate. The relatively small secondary assemblies in the departments were clearly the fulcrum of electoral authority in revolutionary France. Government officials and contenders for higher office alike were especially concerned to secure a favourable outcome at this level. Yet, despite the existence of a good deal of accessible documentation, these all-important departmental colleges have received surprisingly little attention from historians; much remains to be done, as this exploratory survey will suggest.[1]

Departmental assemblies were created on seven occasions during the revolutionary decade, in 1790, 1791, 1792, 1795, 1797, 1798 and 1799. They ranged in size from less than 200 to almost 1,000 members, reflecting the total of enfranchised citizens in each department: the Pyrénées-Orientales hosted the smallest, while the Seine (usually referred to as Paris) housed the largest assembly. In 1790 and 1791 one second-degree elector was awarded for every 100 *ayant droit de voter* residing in the canton, regardless of actual turnout. In 1792 the total of electors remained static, notwithstanding an extension of the franchise, because there was no time to compile new voter lists. Some primary assemblies,

---

[1] Since the *procès-verbaux* from the departmental assemblies were sent to Paris to serve as the national deputies' credentials, a virtually complete set for each election is conveniently located in AN *série* C and these documents have been used as the basic manuscript source for this chapter.

most notably in the sections of Paris, proceeded to nominate additional electors to match the estimated rise in numbers, but most of them were refused admission to the departmental assemblies.[2] Under the Directory, when only minimal restrictions were re-imposed upon the suffrage, the proportion of second-degree electors was reduced to one for every 200 enfranchised citizens so, after 1795, the size of the colleges dwindled.

The total of electors in France can be put at roughly 43,000 during the early years of the Revolution and perhaps 30,000 after 1795. As Jacques Godechot has suggested, this electoral elite was substantially smaller than the number of qualified voters under the Bourbon Restoration.[3] Yet his remark ignores the fact that during the 1790s a quasi-universal adult-male electorate was invited to share in the selection of second-degree electors. Moreover, these electors were drawn from a much larger pool of eligible citizens: as many as three million in 1790 and 1791; then five million in 1792; but only one million thereafter, when much more stringent criteria were applied.

Demands for abolition of the electoral colleges and the introduction of direct elections for national deputies was surprisingly slow to emerge. There was certainly criticism of the conservatism of second-degree electors chosen in 1790, accompanied by calls for their immediate replacement.[4] The weight of tradition, however, plus a reluctance to place important decisions directly in the hands of inexperienced voters doubtless explains their acceptance in principle. Only in the summer of 1792, with the fall of the monarchy, did a few radicals propose direct election to the forthcoming Convention. Robespierre was inevitably in the vanguard when he wrote advocating 'a simpler form of elections, more consonant with the rights of the people'. The issue was debated at the Jacobin Club of Paris on 12 August and a petition duly despatched to the Legislative Assembly demanding the abolition of the electoral colleges which, it was argued, had made such a poor choice of personnel in the past.[5]

In the event the two-tier system was retained, though at Paris there was some attempt to reduce its impact by remitting the names of deputies to the Convention to the primary assemblies for ratification.[6] The idea of direct election now became common currency and it was enshrined in the ill-fated Constitution of 1793. This acme of radicalism promised single-member constituencies of 39–41,000 inhabitants as a basis for future

[2] Charavay ed., *Assemblée électorale*, III, pp. vii–ix.
[3] Godechot, *Les institutions*, pp. 76–7.
[4] Kennedy, *The Jacobin Clubs*, I, pp. 218–19.
[5] Aulard, ed., *Recueil de documents*, IV, pp. 169–70.
[6] Aulard, *Histoire politique*, pp. 257–8 and Charavay, ed., *Assemblée électorale*, III, pp. 475–80.

national assemblies, though it retained departmental colleges for local elections in the districts and departments.[7] Since this scheme was never implemented the whole issue had to be re-examined two years later during debate on the Constitution of 1795. A large measure of support remained for the argument that second-degree electors were incapable of accurately reflecting the wishes of primary voters, but conservative Thermidorians eventually decided in favour of indirect elections and a departmental slate of deputies for the Legislature.[8] In practice electoral colleges were an enduring feature of the Revolution, perpetuating the *bailliage* and *sénéchaussée* assemblies to which they bore more than a passing resemblance.

During the early years of the Revolution, when the new régime was brought into being, electoral colleges met quite frequently. The electors of 1790, for example, initially gathered to choose departmental administrations in the late spring and summer months, before proceeding to select district officials separately. Then, early in 1791, they were recalled to elect bishops and *curés*. The electors of 1792 also met twice, first of all in September to select members of the Convention and then in November to elect an entirely new set of district and departmental administrators. Under the Directory, by contrast, second-degree electors, like the primary assemblies from which they emanated, were restricted to a solitary stint of strictly limited duration: 'The electoral assembly of each department will meet on 20 germinal (towards the end of March) each year and complete its business within a single session of ten days.'[9] After 1795 no extension or adjournment was permitted, doubtless to the relief of participants who had endured some marathon sessions in the past. In 1790 and 1791 most departmental colleges had met for at least a fortnight and some, like the Var, had continued in leisurely fashion for a whole month. Speed was obviously of the essence in the critical circumstances of summer 1792 and the Pyrénées-Orientales managed to elect its deputies to the Convention (there were only five of them) in a mere three days. Yet most departments still took a week and Paris needed eighteen days to choose its complement of twenty-four *conventionnels*.

The capital was exceptional in the demands it placed upon its overworked electors.[10] The first contingent had met for no less than 122 days between November 1790 and June 1791, while the new administrative system was being established (a little later than elsewhere due to its

---

[7] Godechot, ed., *Les constitutions*, pp. 84–5.
[8] BN Le³⁸ 1555, Opinion de J.P. Garran sur le mode des élections (Paris, an III), for example.   [9] Godechot, ed., *Les constitutions*, p. 108.
[10] Charavay, ed., *Assemblée électorale*, all 3 vols.

complexity). Members of the successor assembly were fortunate only to be summoned on eighty-four occasions over the next twelve months, unlike the third set of electors who broke the record by assembling 191 times between September 1792 and August 1793; on average there was a meeting one day in every two. No wonder the Parisian assembly set the maximum length of a sitting at five hours, periodically replacing president and secretaries who were obliged to remain in attendance throughout the day. Elsewhere it was not unusual for departmental colleges to begin work at 6.00am and continue until 9.00pm, albeit with a two-hour break for lunch.

Procedures at the departmental assemblies, like those in the primary assemblies whose organisation they generally followed, imposed a tremendous burden on participants. The preliminary election of officials to supervise the proceedings (unlike the assemblies of 1789 when personnel were appointed) was accompanied by verification of the electors' credentials. Deciding upon contentious cases, which were extremely numerous under the Directory when divided primaries frequently produced rival delegations, could consume an inordinate amount of time. In the Year V (1797) in the Loire-Inférieure, for example, six of the ten days allowed for the completion of business were taken up resolving this issue.[11] The electors' agony was prolonged by the employment of exhaustive ballots. Indeed, at this level the two or three rounds prescribed before a relative majority sufficed were rendered more onerous by the stipulation that each national deputy be chosen individually. In the acute situation of 1792 some assemblies elected *suppléants* (the 'reserve deputies' whose nomination avoided recourse to by-elections) on a single ballot, but the exacting electoral rules were scrupulously observed in general so as to avoid any possibility of disqualification.[12]

Yet this was by no means all that second-degree electors had to endure. Some of them could not understand or read French, so instructions had to be read out as well as displayed. There were speeches galore and tedious displays of rhetoric, from official addresses to votes of thanks. The assemblies were also wearied by deputations: municipal councils, popular societies and national guards all felt obliged to honour electors with a visit. There was equally the risk of involvement in local politics: in 1791 members of the electoral college of the Var were asked to settle a dispute between rival clubs at Toulon and the following year, after securing the release of a female food rioter from Calais jail, the electors of the Pas-de-

[11] Le Gall, Les consultations générales, II, p. 787.
[12] A. Patrick, *The Men of the First Republic*, pp. 143–4.

Calais were treated to a violent harangue from a local lady nicknamed *la mère Duchêne*.[13]

The assemblies of 1792 enjoyed, or perhaps endured a good deal of discussion; in the Seine-et-Oise, like the neighbouring Oise, demands for controls on bread prices were keenly debated.[14] The donning of caps of liberty during the election of deputies was obligatory elsewhere and other bizarre interruptions included the presentation of babies for baptism; in one case the unfortunate infant was blessed with the name Aluise Hyacinte Electeur![15] Small wonder that in the Charente-Inférieure it was decided to refuse admission to delegations of any kind, though there was no escaping two military detachments and the ladies of La Rochelle taking up patriotic collections.[16] In the Côtes-du-Nord all non-electoral business was restricted to the first hour of daily sessions and any items to be read out were broadcast during the counting of votes.[17]

Yet electors always found it difficult to resist engaging in debate, which the assembly mechanism facilitated, even encouraged, despite instructions to the contrary. The first electoral assembly of the Var in 1790, for instance, immediately confronted the vexed question of fixing a permanent *chef-lieu* for the department, though after a week of acrimonious discussion a decision was remitted to the National Assembly.[18] The electors of the Aveyron opened their proceedings the following year with a lengthy consideration of the activities of refractory priests, which had blighted the primary assemblies.[19] The Parisian assembly of the same year encountered plenty of distractions, waxing indignant over legal proceedings against members implicated in the Champ-de-Mars incident and also finding time to examine, only to reject, a machine for counting votes.[20]

In 1792, given the demise of the monarchical constitution and the consequent evaporation of executive authority, the electoral assemblies claimed still greater sovereignty over their own conduct. The admission of the public, hitherto denied entry, oral voting and the revival of mandates were adopted in numerous departments, but this crescendo of autonomous behaviour provoked a clarion call to order in the Constitution of 1795: 'The electoral assemblies may not concern them-

---

[13] AN C 178, Procès-verbal du Var, 20–7 Sept. 1791 and C 180, Procès-verbal du Pas-de-Calais, 8 Sept. 1792.
[14] Auvray, 'Les élections à la Convention', p. 254 and Baumont, 'Les assemblées primaires et électorale de l'Oise', p. 176.
[15] AN C 179, Procès-verbal de la Meurthe, 6 Sept. 1792 and C 180, Procès-verbal de l'Orne, 11 Sept. 1792.
[16] *Ibid*. C 178, Procès-verbal de la Charente-Inférieure, 6–7 Sept. 1792.
[17] Pommeret, *L'esprit public dans le département des Côtes-du-Nord*, p. 178.
[18] Poupé, *Le département du Var*, pp. 57–8.
[19] AN C 135, Procès-verbal de l'Aveyron, Sept. 1791.
[20] Charavay, ed., *Assemblée électorale*, II, p. 119.

selves with any matter other than the process of election; they must not send or receive any address, petition or delegation.'[21] Surprisingly enough several assemblies continued to admit the public throughout the directorial period; an attempt to close the gallery at Limoges in the Year VII actually caused disturbances in the town.[22] Future assemblies were certainly not lacking in dramatic incident, offering good spectator sport, but disruption was directly related to electoral matters, even if much of it was glossed over in the *procès-verbal*. Electors now conducted their business under the watchful eye of a *commissaire du directoire exécutif* who was obliged to scrutinise the record and report any irregularities to Paris.

Threatened with prosecution for the pursuit of any extraneous issues, as well as a fixed date for concluding the session, electors were obliged to become more businesslike after 1795. The most that an assembly could manage was a patriotic song or two. Republicans in the Eure-et-Loir in the Year VI concluded the session with a refrain they had composed that ended: 'Germinal has produced results to gladden the hearts of all good citizens.'[23] At Nancy in the Meurthe, in the Year VI (1798), republican triumph turned into an impromptu *fête* with the illumination of streets and houses and a celebration around the liberty tree, while electors in the Loire-Inférieure that same year were played into their meeting hall with an orchestral fanfare.[24] Under the Directory the nature of these festivities was entirely secular. The old-régime tradition of associating the electoral assemblies with a mass had been universally maintained in 1790, but by 1792 only twenty-two departments were keeping up this religious practice.[25] In the Year IV (1795) even pious electors like those of the Loire-Inférieure discontinued the custom.[26]

Before 1795 the protracted proceedings of the departmental assemblies had alienated a good many electors. As in the case of primary assemblies, the longer a session went on, the thinner attendance became. In 1790 the numbers voting for departmental administrators generally held up, but in the Côtes-du-Nord it was deemed politic to hold over the results for each district until all had cast their ballots.[27] The following year, when the election of deputies to the Legislative Assembly came first on the agenda,

[21] Godechot, ed., *Les constitutions*, p. 108.
[22] H. Labroue, *L'esprit public en Dordogne pendant la Révolution* (Paris, 1911), p. 121, A. Rochas, *Journal d'un bourgeois de Valence* (Grenoble, 1891), p. 334 and B. Gainot, 'Les troubles électoraux de l'an VII: dissolution du souverain ou vitalité de la democratie représentative?', *AhRF* LXVI (1994), pp. 49–51.
[23] Jusselin, *L'administration du département d'Eure-et-Loir*, p. 182.
[24] P. Clémendot, *Le département de la Meurthe à l'époque du Directoire* (Nancy, 1966), p. 274 and Le Gall, Les consultations générales, II, p. 850.
[25] Patrick, *The Men of the First Republic*, p. 166.
[26] Le Gall, Les consultations générales, II, p. 725.
[27] Pommeret, *L'esprit public dans le département des Côtes-du-Nord*, p. 103.

interest usually remained strong, though in the Charente only 356 electors took part in the choice of a sixth representative compared to 455 for the first.[28] By the time that *suppléants* were chosen, not to mention departmental administrators and judicial personnel, many participants were heading for home. The president of the assembly in the Haute-Saône pleaded with electors to remain in attendance for, 'having accepted the mission entrusted to you, you must endure the boredom, fatigue and expense that is involved'![29]

That same year, in September 1791, the president of the assembly in the Tarn appended a word of warning to the copy of the *procès-verbal* he was sending to Paris: 'You will see that the number of voters is falling every day. Should a third session of the electoral college become necessary this department will only be represented by a handful of electors.'[30] Some departmental assemblies had begun to meet at the end of June before being adjourned in the wake of Louis XVI's flight to Varennes and they had responded reluctantly to their recall at the end of August. Indeed, their predecessors, elected in 1790, had shown a disinclination to re-assemble when clergy were elected early in 1791, though in departments full of refractory clergy the decision not to attend was taken on principle rather than simply out of pique.[31]

Already, at the start of 1791, some Jacobin clubs were threatening recalcitrant electors with replacement and reprisals, sanctions which became widespread in September 1792. Ten assemblies followed the example of the Lot-et-Garonne where it was decreed that 'a list of those electors who fail to present themselves to vote will be drawn up and sent to the *chef-lieu* of their canton, so that their fellow citizens will be able to judge the conduct of their mandatories'.[32] In the nearby Haute-Garonne defaulters were declared ineligible for any public office and banned from becoming electors the following year. The Parisian sections of Quinze-Vingts and the Marais sought immediate action, claiming the right to recall any elector who absented himself from the departmental assembly for more than two days running.[33]

Like voters in the primary assemblies, second-degree electors were free to come and go more or less as they pleased. Bells or drums were used to summon them when the roll-call was about to be taken for a vote and

[28] AN C 135, Procès-verbal de la Charente, Sept. 1791.
[29] Girardot, *Le département de la Haute-Saône*, II, p. 102.
[30] AN C 138, Procès-verbal du Tarn, Sept. 1791.
[31] These ecclesiastical elections of 1791 deserve exploration for the insights they offer into reactions to the Civil Constitution of the Clergy. I intend to pursue the matter in the near future.   [32] AN C 179, Procès-verbal du Lot-et-Garonne, Sept. 1792.
[33] AN BI 14, Procès-verbaux des sections de Paris, Aug. 1792 and Gueniffey, *Le nombre et la raison*, p. 206.

sometimes thay were haled from their lodgings. Inevitably attendance fluctuated from one occasion to another and, in the absence of any nominative lists for each ballot, it is impossible to know which electors stayed the course best.[34] In order to determine the level of participation, there is a good case for retaining the highest recorded vote. This is what Gueniffy has done, but I have opted for a common point of reference: the first round of balloting for departmental administrators in 1790 and then for the national deputies who took precedence thereafter. Given a degree of uncertainty over exactly how many electors were entitled to attend the secondary assemblies, not to mention disputed credentials and exclusions, statistical precision is unattainable; as so often in this domain order of grandeur must suffice.

It is quite clear that absenteeism from the electoral colleges was always the exception rather than the rule; only a small minority of electors failed to put in any sort of appearance, exactly the reverse of the situation in the primary assemblies. Indeed, an initial surge of enthusiasm in the late spring and summer of 1790 produced attendances well in excess of 90 per cent. There was a fall everywhere a year later, in September 1791, when turnout dropped as low as 60 per cent in an increasingly disaffected Vendée. By contrast elections to the Convention, held in the late summer of 1792, witnessed a revival of enthusiasm, with attendance at the departmental assemblies once again averaging some 90 per cent. On this occasion even the Vendée approached 80 per cent, while a relatively poor attendance in the Ardennes, Meuse or Marne was caused by the threat of Prussian incursions into north-eastern France.

Under the Directory turnout by second-degree electors was generally high and attendance consistently held up better than during earlier years of the Revolution. The electoral assemblies of the Year IV (1795) did leave a good deal to be desired in this regard, but disaffection over the decree of the two-thirds, which drastically circumscribed the electors' choice of deputies, clearly contributed to abstention. Unrest was widespread and rebellious *chouan* strongholds such as eastern areas of the Côtes-du-Nord, or centres of White Terror such as western cantons of the Var, tended to withhold their delegations.[35] It was not an auspicious start, but thereafter an average of 80 per cent was regularly recorded at the electoral

---

[34] J.M. Thompson, *The French Revolution*, revised edn (Oxford, 1985), p. 227, has misled several historians by suggesting that only 200 electors out of almost 1,000 attended the Parisian electoral college of 1791. Similar claims were made in the National Assembly, to underline the need for reimbursement of electors' expenses: *AP* XXIX, p. 387, 12 Aug. 1791. Attendance was often poor during the final sessions, but not for any major elections.

[35] Poupé, *Le département du Var*, p. 413 and Pommeret, *L'esprit public dans le département des Côtes-du-Nord*, p. 326.

colleges, even in the Year VII when voting at the primary level collapsed. The widespread occurrence of schisms in the departmental assemblies, which invariably attracted rival electors from the same cantons, sometimes meant that overall attendance actually outstripped the maximum! This observation confirms the weakness of a purely statistical approach to the problem, yet it also illustrates the enduring commitment of the political elite to the secondary assemblies, despite the annulment of many of their electoral returns both in 1797 and 1798.

The shorter, annual sessions prescribed for departmental assemblies after 1795 evidently encouraged greater assiduity on the part of their members, but so did a commitment to meet their expenses. Most electors had consented to their nomination, for few were absent from the primary assemblies that selected them and refusals to serve were rare. Apologies for absence were occasionally submitted to the electoral colleges on the grounds of illness or occupational commitments, but some electors were undoubtedly deterred from attending, or obliged to depart prematurely, by the outlay involved. Meetings were held at the departmental *chef-lieu*, save for a brief experiment with district headquarters in 1792. Most electors were thus confronted with travel and subsistence costs of some significance. Their discomfort was sometimes deepened by local traders who sought to profit from their stay: members of the departmental assembly of the Morbihan complained in 1792 that 'honest defenders of the rights of man' were being bankrupted by 'the excessive price of lodgings and basic foodstuffs'.[36] Relaxation might prove equally ruinous: electors of the Year VII in the Côte-d'Or were said to have brought penury upon themselves by devoting their free time to drinking and gambling.[37]

No statutory provision was made for allowances in 1790 and, the following year, without any prospect of improvement, many electors decided to cut their losses. It was doubtless financial considerations as much as political disaffection that reduced participation at the secondary assemblies of 1791. When the National Assembly specifically ruled out any form of recompense it provoked a veritable storm of protest. The assembly of the Vosges responded by declaring that it was totally unreasonable to expect electors to pay for such patriotic endeavours out of their own pockets.[38] In the Var, where expenses had been paid the previous year, furious electors drafted an equally condemnatory address before proceeding to mandate their national deputies to seek redress at the Legislative Assembly.[39]

[36] AN C 179, Procès-verbal du Morbihan, Sept. 1792.
[37] AN F¹cIII Côte-d'Or 2, Journal de la Côte-d'Or, 30 germinal VII (19 Apr. 1799).
[38] AN C 138, Procès-verbal des Vosges, Sept. 1791.
[39] AN C 138, Procès-verbal du Var, Sept. 1791.

An invisible aristocracy?

The issue was eventually resolved in 1792, after the overthrow of the monarchy. In convoking the electoral assemblies for September, surviving deputies in the Legislature stipulated that electors should be allowed 1 *livre* per league in travel expenses and 3 *livres* a day to cover the cost of subsistence. This was less generous than the refunds awarded by some departments in 1790: the Var, for instance, had agreed 25 *sols* a league for displacement, while the Nord had granted no less than 7 *livres* per day for food and lodgings.[40] Nevertheless, the principle of reimbursement had been established and, when second-degree electors were eventually convened again in 1795, they were paid in kind to offset the ravages of inflation. The poor quality of bread and meat prompted angry outbursts in several assemblies; a monetary award was resumed in the Year V.[41]

Quite apart from its impact upon attendance, the issue of allowances raised the question of access to the electoral colleges. As petitioners from the Var pointed out, 'the right of participation is being restricted to the wealthy and denied to those who are virtuous but lack the requisite financial resources'.[42] Failure to pay expenses was tantamount to imposing an additional financial qualification upon electors and playing into the hands of those with time to spare. Robespierre was, as always, quick to raise the matter and argue that reimbursement was a means of democratising the secondary assemblies. Barnave, by contrast, contended that the absence of expenses was an excellent means of deterring less well-off electors, who would inevitably lack the independence to vote impartially.[43] When payment was promised in 1792, as a corollary to removing the tax threshold on electors, there was naturally great rejoicing among radicals. Another barrier to democracy had been torn down: 'Now that they are to be paid it will no longer be necessary to be rich, bourgeois, a priest or a former nobleman in order to accept the honour of becoming a second-degree elector.'[44]

Ironically this optimism was borne out to the greatest extent in Paris, where no allowances were awarded since urban delegates could claim neither travelling expenses nor subsistence costs. Members of the popular classes – clerks, small businessmen, shopkeepers, artisans and even a few unskilled workers – numerically outweighed the notables at the electoral assembly of the Seine in September 1792. True, as the table suggests, there had already been a shift in this direction a year earlier but, compared to the overwhelming preponderance of the metropolitan elite in 1790

[40] Gueniffey, *Le nombre et la raison*, pp. 207–8.
[41] L. Sciout, *Le Directoire*, 4 vols. (Paris, 1895–97), I, p. 398.
[42] AN C 138, Procès-verbal du Var, 18 Sept. 1791.
[43] *AP* XXIX, 11 Aug. 1791, pp. 366–8.   [44] Aulard, ed., *Recueil de documents*, IV, p. 233.

Table 18 *The occupational composition of second-degree electors from Paris, 1790–1792*

Occupational category	1790	1791	1792
		Percentages	
Military	1.3	1.8	0.1
Clergy	2.6	3.5	1.8
Rentiers	6.5	4.8	0.7
Officials	7.6	6.8	2.6
Liberal professions	32.2	19.4	14.0
Men of letters	4.4	4.8	5.3
Merchants	10.9	13.8	4.5
Retailers	13.2	9.9	9.3
Clerks	5.7	5.0	6.4
Artisans and shopkeepers	11.2	16.6	37.3
Unidentified	4.4	13.6	18.0
Numerical Total	781	829	849

Source: Charavay, ed., *Assemblée électorale*, I, pp. 1–80; II, pp. 1–69; and III, pp. 1–88

(and equally in 1789 in elections to the Estates General), a profound transformation had occurred. Members of the legal professions suffered especially badly in the process. In 1789 they had comprised over 40 per cent of 407 Parisian electors and the following year, in a body which more than doubled in size, they still took 30 per cent of the places. One discontented voter had written in protest in 1790: 'I do not have the honour of exercising a legal occupation and consequently I have not been allowed to speak or command attention'.[45] In 1792, by contrast, lawyers and notaries were marginalised, reduced to single percentage figures.

Outside the capital changes in the composition of the departmental assemblies seem to have been more limited. Bouloiseau declared that political inexperience 'led the sovereign people to abandon its electoral fortunes to the notables', though in truth there are precious few examples upon which to base any reliable generalisations.[46] Even in the case of Paris it is impossible to identify the occupation exercised by every single second-degree elector and in most departments the failure to record this basic information is still more problematic. Indeed, in many cases it is dif-

---

[45] Cited in Furet, 'Les élections de 1789 à Paris, le Tiers Etat et la naissance d'une classe dirigeante', in E. Hinrichs, E. Schmitt and R. Vierhaus, eds., *Vom Ancien Régime zur Französischen Revolution. Forschungen und Perspektiven* (Göttingen, 1978), p. 194.

[46] Bouloiseau, *La République jacobine*, pp. 54–5.

ficult to compile a complete set of names for consecutive years, let alone analyse the socio-professional composition of the lists. The process of classifying any data that are obtained poses a good many problems of its own, for professional titles are notoriously fluid; drawing the lines between diverse occupational categories is inevitably a rough and ready procedure. Above all, in the absence of any universally agreed schema, comparison between the findings presented by different historians is extremely difficult.

The Seine-et-Oise next door to Paris seems to offer an example of democratisation like the capital, for peasants and artisans made significant progress in 1792 at the expense of rentiers and farmers, who were blamed for the rise in the cost of foodstuffs and their refusal to support price controls.[47] Elsewhere no more than a slight shift in favour of the popular classes can be discerned. In the Eure-et-Loir in 1792 almost 10 per cent of second-degree electors were artisans, compared to just over 3 per cent in 1790.[48] Wealthy farmers (*laboureurs*) had suffered substantial reductions in their ranks since the election of the initial assembly, though these changes were more apparent than real due to the absence of occupational details for a fifth of the electors in 1791 and almost a third of them in 1792. By contrast members of the liberal professions appear to have suffered only small losses. At Chartres the *chef-lieu* of the department, as in other towns of the Eure-et-Loir, they remained in the driving seat throughout. Despite the legislative initiatives of 1792 few members of the *menu peuple* benefited. The urban and rural elites remained in charge of the departmental assembly during the early years of the Revolution, just as they had dominated the *bailliage* of Chartres in 1789.[49]

Evidence from the Finistère suggests a similar, limited evolution in the socio-professional composition of the electoral college.[50] Merchants (*négociants*) and artisans showed a substantial increase, at the expense of farmers, yet the preponderance of the rural and urban elites seems to have been eroded rather than overturned. This cautious conclusion is supported by three local studies worthy of confidence. In the Haute-Saône, according to Girardot, members of the liberal professions were almost as much in evidence in 1792 as they had been in previous years.[51] Edelstein concludes that in the Côte-d'Or 'the *classes populaires* remained for the most part excluded from the departmental assembly of

---

[47] Auvray, 'Les élections à la Convention', pp. 242–3.
[48] AN C 178, Procès-verbal de l'Eure-et-Loir, 1792.
[49] AN BIII 45, Procès-verbal du bailliage de Chartres, Apr. 1789.
[50] AD Finistère 10L79, Assemblées électorales, 1790–92.
[51] Girardot, *Le département de la Haute-Saône*, II, p. 183.

1792'.[52] Finally, in the Loire-Inférieure, Le Gall declares that very few previously ineligible citizens appeared at the electoral college of that same year. In a detailed analysis of the second-degree electors of Nantes he does, however, venture to suggest that while there was no 'real reversal' of the social profile in evidence on earlier occasions, 'popular elements did make some inroads into the domination of the urban notables'.[53]

This process of democratisation was more apparent in other urban centres. In Provence, at Marseille and Toulon alike, the fiscal criterion governing access to the electoral colleges was inoperable and from the outset of the Revolution all adult males could vote and become second-degree electors. In 1790 few members of the popular classes did either, allowing the entrenched mercantile and administrative elites to command the delegations from their cities to the departmental assemblies of Bouches-du-Rhône and Var respectively. The following year, however, a great transformation occurred when the notables were cast aside in many sections of both cities, as a result of concerted efforts on the part of Jacobins to unseat them.[54] Little information is available for the Marseillais electors of 1792, but artisans, sailors and dockyard workers continued to make political headway at Toulon where they virtually swept the board. In the Mediterranean naval port the popular classes predominated as electors to an even greater extent than they did at Paris, though the Toulonnais contingent was in a small minority at the departmental assembly of the Var, unlike Parisian counterparts who swamped the electoral college of the Seine.

The legislative changes of 1792 helped widen access to these assemblies, especially in departments with a powerful network of Jacobin clubs. Conversely, where the popular societies were weaker and political or social tensions less pronounced, the electoral ascendancy of the urban and rural elites was scarcely called into question. This was not only true of second-degree electors but also of municipal personnel, who had been subject to the same eligibility requirement of ten days' wages in taxation. In Marseille, Toulon and Paris, for example, well-heeled professional and mercantile elements were being edged out of office in 1791 and were completely routed in municipal elections at the end of 1792.[55] In many rural communes, by contrast, the democratic provisions of 1792 had rela-

[52] Edelstein, 'L'établissement de la République', p. 230.
[53] Le Gall, Les consultations générales, II, pp. 614–8.
[54] AN F^{1}cIII Bouches-du-Rhône 1 and AD Bouches-du-Rhône L1020, Procès-verbaux de Marseille, June 1790 and June 1791 and AD Var 1L218, 220 and 223, Procès-verbaux de Toulon, June 1790, June 1791 and Aug. 1792.
[55] Crook, 'Marseille, Aix et Toulon', pp. 201–15.

Table 19 *The occupational composition of second-degree electors from Toulon, 1790–1799*

Category	1790	1791	1792	1795	1797	1798	1799
				Percentages			
Clergy	5.3	3.6					
Military	14.0	1.8	1.8			3.1	
Officials	8.8	3.6		6.3	9.4		6.3
Rentiers	3.5	5.4	3.6	6.3		6.3	9.4
Liberal professions	40.4	21.4	5.5	9.4	18.7	15.6	6.3
Merchants	17.5	7.1		3.1	6.3		9.4
Retailers	7.0	16.1	12.4	6.3	6.3	6.3	6.3
Clerks	3.5	8.9	16.0	6.3	6.3	15.6	21.8
Artisans/shopkeepers		12.4	28.6	3.1	34.3	37.5	28.1
Dockyard workers		7.1	19.6				
Sailors		10.8	7.1		6.3		
Unskilled workers		1.8	5.4		12.4	3.1	9.4
Unidentified				59.2		12.5	3.1
Numerical total	57	56	56	32	32	32	32

Sources: AD Var 1L218/220/223/233

tively little impact and the same could also be said of a large city like Bordeaux.[56]

In less turbulent areas the plentiful evidence from 1790, when the electoral colleges were first created and many authorities printed full lists of participants, may be used as a reasonable guide to subsequent years. When due allowance has been made for the social physiognomy of the different regions – the tendency of rentiers and the liberal professions to represent the urbanised villages of the Midi, whereas farmers predominated in rural areas of northern France – the hegemony of the urban and rural notables emerges crystal clear.[57] Members of these elites were natural spokesmen for their communities. They enjoyed the wealth, leisure and education to engage in the task of creating the new district and departmental administrations; many had already drafted *cahiers* and elected deputies at secondary assemblies in 1789.[58]

---

[56] A. Forrest, *Society and Politics in Revolutionary Bordeaux* (Oxford, 1975), p. 61 and J.-P. Jessenne, 'Continuités et ruptures dans la détention des fonctions locales en Artois (1789–1800)', *La Révolution française et le monde rural* (Paris, 1989), pp. 402–5, for example.
[57] AN F¹cIII Bouches-du-Rhône 1, Listes des électeurs, 1790, AD Finistère 10L79, Assemblées électorales, 1790–2 and Bricaud, *L'administration du département d'Ille-et-Vilaine*, pp. 59 and 435, in addition to documents already cited.
[58] Crook, 'The Persistence of the Ancien Régime in France', p. 38.

It should be emphasised that in 1790 relatively few places at the electoral colleges were awarded to clergy and still less to nobles. The Breton departments were unusual in choosing over 5 per cent of their second-degree electors from the priesthood, while several historians have commented upon the conspicuous absence of aristocrats.[59] Yet a year earlier these so-called privileged classes had met in separate assemblies and were guaranteed a combined presence at *bailliage* and *sénéchaussée* level equal to that of the *tiers état*. The provincial assemblies of the late *ancien régime* had accorded them a similar proportion of seats, so in this sense even the oligarchical assemblies of 1790 represented an incipient bourgeois revolution.

To be sure, the second-degree electors of 1790 were bourgeois in the broad sense of the term, wealthy commoners in possession of considerable resources rather than agents of capitalism. An exceptional document emanating from the Landes, a far from prosperous department in the South-West, suggests that these electors were substantial property-owners, *la crème de la crème* of those eligible for this role in 1790.[60] The level of tax paid by members of this electoral college reveals that, on average, they paid ten times the eligibility requirement of 10 *livres*. Indeed, over two-thirds of them qualified as national deputies by paying a sum equivalent to the infamous *marc d'argent* of some 50 *livres* in taxation, a threshold crossed by only a very small minority of their fellow citizens. An interesting, if isolated comparison to the example of the Landes in 1790 is offered by the second-degree electors of Reims in 1791. By chance this contingent of fifty men has been listed with their tax returns, which show that less than a third of them were eligible to serve as national deputies.[61] The professions of these Rémois electors, like their wealth, reflect the shift in the balance of power that was occurring in some urban centres, though even in 1792 humbler individuals remained the exception rather than the rule in most departmental assemblies.

When the two-tier electoral system was put back to work in 1795, after the hiatus of the Terror, more stringent qualifications were imposed upon second-degree electors: only citizens who owned or rented property yielding an annual revenue of between 100 and 200 *livres per annum*, depending upon the size of their community, were now eligible to serve. The Constitution of 1795 also reduced the size of the electoral colleges to between 100 and 700 members, so fewer posts were available, but elec-

---

[59] P. Arches, 'Elections et participation électorale au début de la Révolution française, 1790-1791', *Bulletin de la Societé historique et scientifique des Deux-Sèvres*, XXI (1988), p. 380, for example.   [60] AD Landes 11L2, Tableau général, 1790.
[61] AD Marne 1L299, Liste des électeurs, 1791.

tors could not serve two years in succession. Did this legislation reverse the gradual progression of the popular classes and curtail their political apprenticeship at this level?

Information regarding the social composition of the electoral colleges in the late 1790s is scarce and rarely concentrated. As might be anticipated, in departmental terms the impression is one of a continuation, even a reinforcement of the notables' ascendancy. In the Allier, Basses-Alpes, Charente-Inférieure and Marne lists for various years contain little evidence that members of the popular classes made more than a token appearance.[62] On the other hand, in the Meurthe, Clémendot suggests that while rural proprietors, merchants and members of the liberal professions always held sway under the Directory, artisans and retailers did make a stronger showing in 1798, a year of Jacobin resurgence.[63]

In those towns where the popular classes had made substantial inroads into the electors' ranks in 1791 or 1792, there was something of a retreat after 1795, but it was far from total. At Toulon, for example, dockyard workers and sailors did not reappear on the lists of electors, but neither did many representatives of the old régime elite.[64] Naval clerks, artisans and small businessmen, like the shoemaker Thomas Blancard who was to participate in an abortive conspiracy against Bonaparte in 1812, maintained a strong presence at the elbows of Jacobin *nouveaux riches*. Whether the *sans-culotte* element was entitled to sit at the departmental assembly of the Var is another matter. In the year VII (1799), for instance, the directorial *commissaire* reported that the municipality of Toulon had failed to submit tax returns for its contingent of electors and he was doubtful that many of them qualified.[65]

Whatever the truth of the matter, which was always hard to determine since eligibility criteria were so complicated, members of the popular classes had not been completely excluded from the electoral colleges. As long as they enjoyed the support of complaisant local authorities and sympathetic officials at the primary assemblies it was impossible to keep them out. At Marseille, in the Year VII (1799), the *commissaire du directoire* wrote off much of the city's delegation to the departmental assembly of the Bouches-du-Rhône as 'the dregs of society', since better-off Jacobins had been elected the previous year and were not eligible to serve a second term in succession.[66] He claimed that in the sixth section of the city all

[62] AD Allier L141, Electeurs, an VI, AD Basses-Alpes L204, Asscmblée électorale, an VI, AN AFIII 246, Liste des électeurs de la Marne, an VI and M. Eschassériaux, *Assemblées électorales de la Charente-Inférieure* (Niort, 1868), pp. 218–33.
[63] Clémendot, *Le département de la Meurthe*, p. 268.
[64] AD Var 1L233, Assemblées électorales, ans IV-VII (1795–99).
[65] AN AFIII 265, Commissaire au ministre, 5 floréal VII (24 Apr. 1799).
[66] AN AFIII 217, Commissaire au ministre, 2 germinal VII (22 Mar. 1799).

four electors put together were unable to meet the individual property qualification!

Second-degree electors of a more conservative disposition such as those of the Year V (1797) were equally suspect in this regard: the patriots of Vannes urged the government to act against unqualified members of the reactionary Morbihan assembly in an effort to discredit its operations.[67] Yet the best-documented and most extensive evidence of persistent popular influence is to found at Paris, where more modest electors assumed an especially high profile.[68] Jacobins in the capital mounted a determined and successful campaign to keep the eligibility threshold as low as possible. This subsequently enabled them to roll back the professional and commercial bourgeoisie who bulked so large in the electoral colleges of the Years IV and V (1795 and 1797), when observers remarked upon the opulence of those attending. In the following two years the contribution of artisan and shopkeeping elements rose to roughly 40 per cent of those electors who have been occupationally identified (see table 20).

The departmental college in the capital had contained a large contingent from the popular classes in the past and its turnover of personnel had always been high. In 1792 less than 20 per cent of electors from Paris had sat during the two preceding years and only 7 per cent had appeared on all three occasions.[69] This degree of instability was actually exceeded at Toulon, where only 10 per cent of the town's electors possessed any previous experience in 1792 and not a single one had been ever-present. At a departmental level in the Var, however, much more personal continuity was generally in evidence.[70] True, in the Seine-et-Oise, adjacent to Paris, little more than 20 per cent of the second-degree electors of 1792 were old hands, but in the Basses-Alpes this proportion rose above 30 per cent.[71] Indeed, in the Eure-et-Loir and the Haute-Saône almost 40 per cent had served before and, in the latter, a quarter had been present in 1790, 1791 and 1792.[72]

After 1795 electors were prevented from sitting in consecutive electoral assemblies, yet there was a good deal of continuity especially with earlier years of the Revolution. In the Basses-Alpes, for instance, the proportion of men who had sat on previous occasions never fell below a third of the membership from the Year IV to the Year VII.[73] In the Loire-Inférieure

[67] AN F¹cIII Morbihan 1, Amis de la Liberté de Vannes, 15 floréal V (4 May 1797).
[68] Woloch, *Jacobin Legacy*, pp. 321–3.   [69] Charavay, ed., *Assemblée électorale*, III, pp. ix-xi.
[70] AD Var 1L 218, 220 and 223, Assemblées électorales, 1790–92.
[71] Gueniffey, *Le nombre et la raison*, p. 416.
[72] AN C 118, 136 and 178, Procès-verbaux de l'Eure-et-Loir, 1790–92 and Girardot, *Le département de la Haute-Saône*, II, pp. 182–3.
[73] Gueniffey, *Le nombre et la raison*, p. 416.

Table 20 *The occupational composition of second-degree electors from the Seine, Year IV to Year VII (1795–1799)*

Occupation	Year IV	Year V	Year VI	Year VII
		Percentages		
Military	1.1	0.4	2.0	1.1
Rentiers	6.5	7.8	6.7	9.1
Officials	29.5	23.8	29.6	35.3
Liberal professions	25.0	23.8	14.5	17.7
Men of letters	3.7	2.1	3.4	2.9
Merchants	11.8	10.6	4.4	4.0
Clerks	4.0	2.3	2.5	2.2
Artisans/shopkeepers	18.4	27.6	36.9	26.0
Farmers	1.6	1.7		1.6
Total identified	620	529	594	549

Source: Adapted from Woloch, *Jacobin Legacy*, p. 340

some 30 per cent of the electors of 1795 had participated before, though the comparable figure slipped to little more than 20 per cent in 1797, a year of royalist successes at the polls.[74] Prior experience as an elector could carry political significance in so far as individuals who had appeared in 1790 or 1791 tended to be associated with a more conservative outlook. In the Loire-Inférieure in 1797 fewer electors from 1792 were recalled than in 1798 and 1799 when the republicans were more firmly entrenched.[75] It was the same at Paris: in the Year IV a third of the members of the departmental college were experienced participants, though relatively few were of 1792 vintage.[76] In the Côte-d'Or, similar evidence points in the opposite direction: there the Thermidorean reaction of 1795 was moderated by the re-selection of just over a quarter of the electors of 1792 for the assembly of the Year IV.[77]

In the case of the Basses-Alpes and the Loire-Inférieure it has been calculated that roughly one third of all electors who sat during the revolutionary decade did so on more than one occasion, while a tenth of them served more than twice. Among the 'star-performers' of the Loire-Inférieure the professional classes predominated, presumably because

---

[74] Le Gall, Les consultations générales, ii, pp. 780 and 880.   [75] *Ibid.*
[76] E. Ducoudray, 'Les électeurs de l'an IV. Canton de Paris. Essai de prosopographie politique', *AhRf*, LIV (1982), pp. 857–60.
[77] M. Edelstein, 'De l'an I à l'an III: l'apprentissage de la démocratie en Côte-d'Or', forthcoming in S. Aberdam, ed., *L'an I et l'apprentissage de la démocratie*.

businessmen and farmers were deterred by the commitment involved.[78] Those who served regularly were seasoned individuals who had begun their political careers in 1790 or 1791, surviving the turmoil of the period and, one suspects, later forming the core of the Napoleonic notability. At Nantes Le Gall has highlighted the case of the architect, Alexis Marchais, who was a member of the electoral college from 1790 to 1792 and then again in the Years IV and VI; in the intervening years of the Directory he acted as president of his section in the city. Jean Merot, a procurator from Campbon, offers another splendid example of the 'professional politician' who sat as an elector for the maximum five times, was always an official at his primary assembly after 1791 and also served as a municipal officer and justice of the peace during this period.

Merot's career highlights the close not to say closed relationship between electors and administrators. Part of the difficulty in analysing the social composition of the departmental assemblies lies precisely in the fact that members were designated according to their posts as local administrators, rather than by professional denomination. Under the Directory some 40 per cent of electors in the Allier and Meurthe in 1798 were serving as municipal officers, justices of the peace and *commissaires du directoire exécutif*.[79] The figure rose as high as 60 per cent in the Basses-Alpes and reached a similar level in the Meurthe in 1799.[80] Municipal personnel had commanded a significant number of seats in the departmental assemblies from the outset. In the Haute-Garonne in 1790, for instance, one third of electors from the city of Toulouse were town councillors, while many villages in the surrounding district had included mayors in their delegations.[81] Local magistrates had already dominated the two-tiered elections to the Estates General a year earlier.[82] As Jessenne has put it, with reference to Artois: 'The function of second-degree electors seems to have been an extension of their municipal mandate, one of the tasks that their responsibility for the community involved.'[83]

The duplication between administrators and electors naturally increased with the development of a new local government apparatus. In Paris, in 1791, the assembly of the Seine contained seventy-eight officers in the National Guard, fifty-four members of the municipality, fifty-one *juges de paix* and fifteen departmental officials.[84] Even this large total may

---

[78] Le Gall, Les consultations générales, II, p. 917 ff.
[79] AD Allier L141, Liste des électeurs, an VI (1798) and Clémendot, *Le département de la Meurthe*, p. 268.
[80] AD Basses-Alpes L204, Assemblée électorale de l'an VI (1798) and Clémendot, *Le département de la Meurthe*, p. 314.
[81] AN DIVbis 37, Assemblée électorale de la Haute-Garonne, 1790.
[82] AN BIII 148, Sénéchaussée de Toulouse, Apr. 1789.
[83] Jessenne, 'De la citoyenneté', p. 835.   [84] Charavay, ed., *Assemblée électorale*, II, p. xviii.

underestimate the degree of interpenetration, since the detailed study of a sample of 409 Parisian electors for the same year suggests that over 80 per cent of them occupied administrative positions of one sort or another.[85] It has been estimated that by 1792 up to a third of the members of electoral colleges were office-holders of some description.[86] In the absence of openly organised party-politics and declared candidates such persons represented a perfectly logical choice as electors, since their names and status were familiar to voters. As the president of the municipal assembly at Epernay in the Marne had indicated, in 1790: 'Disaster will follow if you elect men without education or expertise; they alone possess the know-how necessary to run the administrative machinery.'[87]

It must be said that during the early years of the Revolution, if not later, there was a plethora of posts to fill, judicial as well as administrative. Gueniffey has suggested that over a million local offices were up for grabs in 1790.[88] He fails to explain exactly how he has arrived at this staggering total which, evenly shared, would provide one active citizen in four with a job, but there were more than 500,000 positions available in the 44,000 municipalities at the foot of the official hierarchy. The Constituent Assembly had set the full council for the smallest commune at ten officers and there were as many mayors as places for second-degree electors. In addition, each of the 6,000 cantons directly elected a justice of the peace and his four assistants (the *assesseurs*). No wonder so many of these officials appeared at the electoral colleges; willing workhorses must have been in short supply.

District, departmental and national personnel were of course chosen by the second-degree electors themselves, usually from within their own ranks. In 1790, in the Var, thirty-three out of thirty-six members of the new departmental council were members of the electoral college and so were virtually all those named for the nine districts.[89] In other words, almost 100 of the 500 electors who were present at the assembly were rewarded with a post. The following year all twenty-one replacements for the departmental administration were members of the assembly and even in 1792 only a handful were recruited outside the electoral college. Members of these assemblies thus automatically became candidates for higher office. An incestuous relationship emerged that was castigated by an anonymous correspondent from the section of Enfants-Rouges in Paris who wrote: 'Many citizens thrust themselves forward as second-degree electors, not with the objective of

---

[85] E. Ducoudray, 'Bourgeois parisiens en Révolution, 1790–1792', in M. Vovelle, ed., *Paris et la Révolution* (Paris, 1989), p. 77. [86] Gueniffey, *Le nombre et la raison*, p. 420.
[87] AN F¹cIII Marne 1, Procès-verbal d'Epernay, Jan. 1790.
[88] Gueniffey, *Le nombre et la raison*, p. 418. [89] Poupé, *Le département du Var*, pp. 527–36.

ensuring a good choice at the departmental assembly, but in the hope of being chosen themselves.'[90]

In 1791, when members of the National Constituent Assembly were denied the opportunity to sit in the Legislative Assembly they had created, and departments were instructed to choose residents as deputies, the electoral colleges naturally looked to the departmental administrators within their ranks. Such experienced individuals comprised some 40 per cent of the 749 legislators, of whom only 100 had failed to fulfil any function at the local level since 1789.[91] A splendid example of this *cursus honorum* is furnished by ambitious individuals from Montpellier who, despite pleas from the National Assembly that men remain in post until the expiry of their mandates, used their election to city council and electoral college of the Hérault as stepping-stones to higher office.[92] No less than five municipal officers selected in January 1790 decamped to the district and departmental administrations, while four subsequently became judges at local tribunals and another two were elected to the Legislative Assembly in 1791.

Even after 1792, when national deputies could be chosen from further afield, electors in the Loire-Inférieure continued to draw first and foremost upon their own colleagues.[93] Meanwhile, ex-deputies might move in the opposite direction and assume local responsibilities. The former marquis de Villette doubtless irked by his own failure to find a post, remarked bitterly in September 1791: 'If this sort of practice continues the judicial, administrative and municipal aristocracy, flitting from one place to another, will have discovered the means of perpetuating itself indefinitely in office.'[94] Villette coined the phrase 'invisible aristocracy' to describe the emerging political elite which the preceding pages have described. He also denounced the second-degree assemblies as 'electoral machines' and suggested either the introduction of direct elections, or a ban upon electors nominating men from their midst (a proposal that Mirabeau had put forward when the colleges were created in 1790).[95]

The charmed circle that Villette condemned did not remain completely intact during the years that followed, but the tradition of electoral colleges endured. The emergent political parties certainly focused their efforts upon them, despite the condemnation of both cabals and campaigns. Yet

[90] BN Lb³⁹ 10164, Projet d'instruction aux électeurs (Paris, 1791).
[91] A. Kuscinski, *Les députés à l'Assemblée législative de 1791* (Paris, 1900), pp. 31–107.
[92] J. Duval-Jouve, *Montpellier pendant la Révolution*, 2 vols. (Montpellier, 1879), I.
[93] Le Gall, Les consultations générales, II, p. 949.
[94] Cited in Charavay, ed., *Assemblée électorale*, II, p. xxxvi.
[95] Cited, in Le Gall, Les consultations générales, I, p. 258.

the complete absence of unofficial candidates and canvassing, could only produce chaos with no clear winners emerging, while misplaced votes could yield results just as unpopular as those secured by well-organised minorities. In the elections of 1791, almost half the deputies failed to gain a majority in the first two rounds of balloting. The following year over a third of *conventionnels* were still elected in a third round run-off, though the percentage of first-round winners did increase.[96] In a context of increasingly partisan conflicts, this trend seems to have continued thereafter and votes became more concentrated.

At the electoral colleges of 1790, with Jacobin clubs and revolutionary journalism scarcely out of the cradle, the main concern had been to ensure a share of the administrative spoils among different areas of the department. Tensions at this point were parochial rather than political. The National Assembly decreed that two councillors should be chosen from each district in the department, the remainder indiscriminately. A number of assemblies, however, decided otherwise and the authorities turned a blind eye. In the Eure-et-Loir, for example, it was decided to choose six administrators from each of six districts, with the electors of each district making a separate choice.[97] Though this arrangement was not repeated in subsequent years, a rough parity between districts was preserved. In the Landes, the districts of Dax and Tartes sought additional administrators in 1790, commensurate with their demographic preponderance, but the other two districts in the department insisted on equality and even threatened to withdraw in protest.[98]

A similar balance was often struck when it came to choosing national deputies. In the Loire-Inférieure eight out of nine districts supplied a legislator in 1791, while in the Var only three out of nine districts were bereft of their 'own' deputy.[99] As the Revolution progressed, however, localism became less pronounced and party-political influences welled up to the surface instead, creating broader loyalties in the process. Ever true to form, Paris had blazed a trail with the public discussion of 'candidates' in its first departmental elections at the end of 1790. A Society of Patriotic Electors was established to consider issues before they were debated at the assembly and to 'enlighten members concerning the vital choice of administrative personnel'.[100] To deflect the anticipated criticism of this device, it was stressed that no participant would be bound by any decisions taken in the Society.

[96] Gueniffey, 'Revolutionary Democracy', p. 94.
[97] Jusselin, *L'administration du département d'Eure-et-Loir*, pp. 25, 41 and 59.
[98] AN F1cIII Landes 1, Procès-verbal de l'assemblée électorale, Aug. 1790.
[99] Le Gall, Les consultations générales, II, p. 949 and Poupé, *Le département du Var*, p. 125.
[100] Charavay, ed., *Assemblée électorale*, II, p. xvii.

The following summer, when elections to the Legislative Assembly took place, activity intensified both inside and outside the departmental assembly of the Seine. Marat and Louvet cast aside journalistic coyness and began naming names as part of the explicit advice they were now offering regarding the choice of legislators. The electors themselves resumed the practice of meeting as a club to discuss business outside assembly hours.[101] It was indicative of growing political polarisation that they should separate into rival societies, one remaining at the Evêché (bishop's palace) where the electoral college was sitting, the other meeting at the church of La Sainte-Chapelle. Members of the latter seceded from the former in mid-September 1791, alleging that proceedings at the Evêché were Jacobin-dominated and excessively robust. As their numbers grew they moved from a private residence to La Sainte-Chapelle, where they mustered larger numbers than the body they had quit. Indeed, these so-called *chapelains* outdid their adversaries and managed to determine most places on the Parisian slate of deputies.

The radical journalist Brissot was only elected as twelfth deputy on a third ballot, while his colleague Condorcet scraped home in twenty-second place. Baulked in Paris, Jacobins fared poorly in many other departments too. Having enjoyed success in the primary assemblies of June 1791 they were looking forward to a good showing at the electoral colleges, only to suffer badly from the Feuillant secession in the meantime.[102] This split in the Jacobins' ranks, which followed republican demonstrations on the Champ de Mars in July, disconcerted the membership. Not all was lost: in the Cher, for instance, the Jacobin club of Bourges claimed that undesirables had been totally excluded from the departmental slate.[103] Yet only in vastly changed circumstances the following year, in unanticipated elections to the Convention, did the Jacobins really triumph.

In 1792 it was the Jacobins who were united and their rivals in disarray. Political choices at the electoral assemblies were facilitated both by the way in which recent events had laid bare allegiances and by the fact that deputies who remained at the depleted Legislative Assembly had effectively declared themselves candidates. On this occasion re-election was permitted and *conventionnels* could be chosen outside their department of residence. Several provincial clubs sought advice from the Jacobins at Paris, where leaders agreed to produce a *Tableau comparatif* containing

[101] *Ibid.*, II, pp. xx, xxx and 512 ff. and E. Ducoudray, 'De la presse aux groupes de pression: les clubs électoraux parisiens en 1791–1792', *Studies on Voltaire and the Eighteenth Century*, 297 (1991), pp. 293–307.   [102] Kennedy, *The Jacobin Clubs*, I, pp. 222–3.
[103] T. Lemas, *Etudes sur le Cher pendant la Révolution* (Paris, 1897), pp. 206–9.

the sort of roll-call analysis so dear to contemporary historians.[104] Besides publishing the results of seven key votes in the legislative Assembly this document also commended Pétion, Robespierre and 'forty immortals' from the earlier Constituent Assembly. The *Tableau* reached at least half the departments and more than 80 per cent of the deputies listed as 'serving the cause of liberty' were duly re-elected to the Convention.[105] Few with an unpatriotic voting record enjoyed the same honour.

The fact that the electoral assemblies were held in district *chefs-lieux* rather than in the departmental capitals (according to a principle of *alternance* subsequently abandoned), does not seem to have inhibited Jacobin endeavours. Many clubs had established powerful local networks, coordinated by *comités centraux*. Jacobins in the Gard, for example, simply moved their headquarters from Nîmes to Beaucaire for the duration of the secondary elections.[106] They met every day with sympathetic electors, proposing and discussing the names of potential deputies. The Jacobins of Bordeaux likewise kept in constant touch with the electoral college at Libourne, where two of their members, Boyer-Fonfrède and Marandon were serving as president and secretary. The societies of Coutances, Auray and Orthez, meanwhile, acted as social centres for electors from the Manche, Morbihan and Hautes-Pyrénées respectively. Alison Patrick's assertion that 'in 57 departments out of 83, there is no evidence of club activity during the elections', underestimates Jacobin pressure because it is based entirely upon the letter of the official *procès-verbaux*.[107] Kennedy suggests a more pervasive influence when he concludes that 'the overwhelming majority of Conventionnels, at the time of their election, were members of the Paris society or one of its affiliates'.[108]

Over one-third of departmental assemblies employed procedures in 1792 that had been proscribed beforehand and which seem to have assisted the Jacobin cause.[109] Strictly speaking such departures did not constitute irregularities since the rump of the Legislative Assembly was only able to 'invite' the electoral colleges to observe existing practice. Most did so, but a dozen adopted oral voting which, while it harked back to an old-régime tradition, was now recommended as a guarantee of political transparency. In the circumstances of 1792 it did save valuable time spent on counting written ballot papers and perhaps secured a greater likelihood of a result in the first round of voting. In ten depart-

---

[104] Kennedy, *The Jacobin Clubs*, II, pp. 288–91.
[105] Patrick, *The Men of the First Republic*, pp. 170–1.
[106] Rouvière, *Le mouvement électoral dans le Gard*, pp. 82–3.
[107] Patrick, *The Men of the First Republic*, p. 155.
[108] Kennedy, *The Jacobin Clubs*, II, p. 290.
[109] Patrick, *The Men of the First Republic*, pp. 162–5.

ments the public was admitted to the proceedings, though spectators were not always easily accommodated in cramped conditions. Barbaroux, in the Bouches-du-Rhône, even went so far as to propose their participation in the electoral business: 'Summon the People around us, so that as witnesses to these elections, they may indicate by their applause or by their disapproval whether we are performing well or badly.'[110]

Most departments invested their deputies with unlimited authority but some circumscribed their powers with mandates, another *ancien régime* practice which had re-surfaced as a weapon in the radicals' armoury. A number of *conventionnels* were threatened with recall if they failed to support a Republic, there was insistence upon a popular consultation for the new constitution to be drafted and the Dordogne informed its delegates: 'Your mandate will cease within eighteen months; at the end of this period you will take no further part in debate at the Convention . . . unless you are specifically empowered to do so by the citizens of this department.'[111]

Despite the upsurge of provincial radicalism, Paris preserved its prowess where unorthodoxy was concerned. Not only was the full set of political innovations utilised in the capital but, meeting at the Jacobin Club, the electoral assembly of the Seine adopted an especially partisan approach.[112] Action already taken by the insurrectionary Commune of Paris had prevented most conservatives from obtaining election to the departmental college, while others were subsequently removed from the assembly itself. The real division was between patriots, for Robespierre had vowed the destruction of Brissot and his friends, a conflict mirrored in the journalistic confrontation between Marat and Louvet. Allies of Robespierre were in the driving seat, electing him as first deputy and deciding nineteen of the twenty-four seats on the first ballot. Moderates did make a resolute effort to rally around Kersaint on 8 September, forcing Camille Desmoulins to a rare second ballot after no less than 936 out of 989 electors had voted in the initial round, but thereafter the Brissotins melted away.

Ousted from Paris, Brissot was able to secure election in his native Eure-et-Loir, besides two other departments. All told twenty-one *conventionnels* received multiple mandates.[113] The journalist Carra took the prize with eight nominations in 1792, as French electors inaugurated the nineteenth-century practice of 'plebisciting' deputies. The individuals so honoured were obliged to opt for one of the circumscriptions that had

---

[110] AN C 178, Procès-verbal des Bouches-du-Rhône, 3 Sept. 1792.
[111] Labroue, *L'esprit public en Dordogne*, p. 51.
[112] AN C 180, Procès-verbal de la Seine, Sept. 1792 and Charavay, ed., *Assemblée électorale*, III.   [113] Patrick, *The Men of the First Republic*, pp. 178–80.

favoured them, leaving a *suppléant* to step into the vacancy. In the event the electoral college of the Var was especially irked by the decision of Dubois-Crancé, a *militaire* on duty in the department, to sit instead for the Ardennes.[114] This adjutant-general had appeared at the assembly in Grasse and vowed to serve as a faithful 'adopted son', only to renege on his promise a few days later. It was to Dubois-Crancé's defection that *suppléant* Barras owed his entry to the Convention.

The departmental assemblies of 1792 had been subjected to much more political management than their predecessors. Yet many radicals continued to proclaim the virtues of free and unfettered electoral choices. A fellow military officer was in fact taken to task for the way he had 'caballed' on behalf of Dubois-Crancé in the Var.[115] His response, that the patriotic end justified the partisan means, far from satisfied the Jacobin editors of the *Journal des départements méridionaux* who had published the allegation. When elections resumed in 1795, after the interlude of the Terror (which, incidentally, put far more of the popular classes into administrative posts than the electoral assemblies), it was not long before party politics re-emerged with a vengeance. Under the Directory factions flourished, both divided and defined by the violent course the Revolution had taken in the recent past.

Little information has survived regarding compaigning at the electoral assemblies of the Year IV. Incidents like the circulation of a slate of names for election in the Marne, which was denounced to the local authorities, seem to have been relatively rare.[116] The infamous decree that two-thirds of deputies to the new Legislature must be chosen from members of the Convention had been bitterly resisted at the primary assemblies but, once that battle was lost, electoral options were severely restricted. In the Year V rather more was at stake and the date of the elections for a 'new third' of the Legislature was fixed far in advance, so plans could be carefully laid. Royalists in particular skilfully mobilised their resources in the hope of capturing the Legislative Councils, deploying the full range of electoral tactics that would become commonplace at departmental assemblies over the next few years.

In 1797, as the factions marshalled their supporters and drew up slates of names, the idea of declared candidatures briefly received official sanction. Since the start of the Revolution suggestions had been made for an initiative of this sort, both to avoid the fruitless scattering of votes and to deter the clandestine machinations of clienteles and clubs. The

[114] Poupé, *Le département du Var*, p. 195.
[115] *Journal des départements méridionaux*, II, p. 353, 15 Sept. 1792.
[116] AN C 481, Procès-verbal de la Marne, vendémiaire IV (Oct. 1795).

Constitution of 1795 finally made provision for candidatures, though the scheme did not come into effect until the Year V. Assuming all was in order, names submitted to the local authorities would be publicised and posted up in the electoral assemblies. Although few propositions were made for the primary elections of 1797, and voters could still nominate whomsoever they wished on their ballot papers, there was a reasonable response at departmental level.

In Paris the volume of propositions apparently exceeded 1,000, while the Gironde revealed rather less enthusiasm with a total of only ninety-two.[117] The departmental college of the Loire-Inférieure recorded over 200 nominations to various posts in the gift of its assembly, though most of the names were submitted from Nantes.[118] Members of the liberal professions bulked large in over 100 nominations for the Legislature, despite a plea for more commercial representation. Occupational considerations probably deterred businessmen from pursuing careers as national deputies since they were more numerous as candidates for the departmental administration. The list in the Loire-Inférieure, unlike its counterpart in the Gironde, proposed names from beyond the departmental boundaries which included the journalist Bonneville, former Minister Garat and, more fancifully, Bougainville 'the famous explorer', besides Bernardin de Saint-Pierre 'author of studies of nature'. Apart from General Pichegru, the names of both national and local royalists were lacking from this document, an indication that leading reactionaries preferred not to advertise their political ambitions in this way.[119]

Few of those listed as candidates in the Year V in either the Gironde or the Loire-Inférieure were actually elected to office, but this did not prevent republicans blaming the system for royalist success. More to the point, this was an innovation which sorely wounded contemporary sensibilities. The *savant* Quatremère de Quincy claimed that such lists would inevitably produce poor results. 'The real candidature', he argued 'emanates from public opinion . . . It should consist, not in a list of names subject to criticism, but in a reasoned set of principles upon which a proper judgement can be made. . .'. The worthy man is reluctant to proclaim his virtues; he prefers silent esteem, and shuns the limelight'.[120] Ironically Quatremère himself was nominated by several right-wing newspapers and duly elected at Paris, but it would clearly take a long time to erode such deeply rooted

---

[117] AN AFIII 261, Commissaire central au ministre, 27 germinal V (16 Apr. 1797) and AM Bordeaux K4, Liste des candidats, germinal V (Apr. 1797).

[118] AD Loire-Inférieure L173, Liste des citoyens désignés par les cantons, 23 pluviôse V (11 Feb. 1797).

[119] AD Loire-Inférieure L172, Liste des candidats and Le Gall, Les consultations générales, II, pp. 743–9.

[120] A.C. Quatremère de Quincy, *La véritable liste de candidats*, (Paris, an V), pp. 17–9.

prejudices against declared candidates. As it was, the disastrous outcome of the elections in 1797 damned the experiment in the eyes of the government. The following year the legislation on candidatures was repealed though, far from subsiding, factional struggle steadily increased.

The intensity of the electoral war waged by resurgent royalists and Jacobins, which left so little of the neutral ground that the Directory was anxious to cultivate, had begun to erupt in electoral schisms. The secession of disaffected minorities was a further drawback associated with the assembly method of voting. Yet it was only in the Year IV that schisms occurred within two departmental colleges, in the Doubs and the Lot. Both disputed elections took several months to resolve, though the latter was particularly problematic since dissenters seceded from the original assembly (*assemblée mère*) when it became clear that several cantons were grossly over-represented.[121] Having established their own independent assembly (*assemblée scissionnaire*) the protesters proceeded to conduct a separate election, *soi-disant* 'patriots of '89 saving the *patrie*'.

Deputies at the Legislature were horrified: 'The schism has produced what can be termed a monstrosity in the political order: a double-headed parliamentary deputation and a two-fold departmental administration.' The committee of inquiry recommended invalidating the work of both assemblies but, fearful of leaving the Lot without representation in the new legislative councils, it was decided that, here as in the Doubs, deputies chosen at the *assemblée mère*, should take their seats. As Paradis put it, in the Council of Elders: 'the minority must not be given the right to dictate to the majority'.[122]

Any hope that these schisms would remain an isolated aberration was scotched the following year when the electoral college of the Lot divided again. Despite some heated debate in the Legislature it was decided on this occasion to admit deputies from the breakaway assembly, which mustered a majority of electors who had been intimidated by Jacobin violence.[123] This verdict was understandable, but it appeared to endorse the practice of separation, albeit under particular circumstances. Though the councils quashed schisms which had occurred in two other departments in 1797, one in the Landes the other in the Deux-Nèthes (an annexed area of Belgium), the floodgates had been opened. Schisms assumed epidemic proportions at departmental as well as at primary level: there were twenty-seven divided electoral colleges in 1798 and twenty-six in 1799.[124]

---

[121] Sciout, *Le Directoire*, I, pp. 399–402 and Woloch, *The New Regime*, pp. 103–4.
[122] *Moniteur* XXVII, p. 360, 10 pluviôse IV (30 Jan. 1796).
[123] Sciout, *Le Directoire*, II, pp. 326–30. This decision was later reversed, and the election annulled, in the wake of the *fructidor* coup in September 1797.
[124] Suratteau, *Les élections de l'an VI*, pp. 231–7.

The electoral process was sometimes reduced to a complete shambles as a result.[125] In the Rhône in the Year VI there were actually three separate assemblies. Having failed to obtain the presidency, which was secured by reactionaries, Jacobin electors quit to set up shop on their own. A group of rural delegates meanwhile, decided to take refuge from both extremes and proceeded to meet on their own, though some of them subsequently returned to the *assemblée-mère* or joined the Jacobin gathering. Such toing and froing was not uncommon: one elector in the divided Marne voted for deputies in both *assemblée scissionnaire* and *assemblée-mère*. The schism-prone Landes also produced a double secession in 1798, though the two 'royalist' minorities arrived at similar results.[126] One small group met in prison after some second-degree electors had been arrested when they arrived in the *chef-lieu*, while the other fled Mont-de-Marsan and convened in the open air near Tartas.

The Directory itself encouraged secession as a means of securing satisfactory results when an undesirable outcome appeared likely. In a circular of the Year VI entitled *Avis aux vrais républicains*, schisms were declared permissible 'when the law had been violated' and moderate secessionists were virtually assured of endorsement.[127] Thus a veritable 'system of schisms' was conjured into existence. The government was conniving with its opponents at the subversion of the very electoral procedures it claimed to uphold.

In the year VI the Directory was not even prepared to wait for the report of a parliamentary inquiry into divided assemblies, which it hoped to use as a pretext for validating the more favourable returns. Instead, by means of the so-called *coup d'état* of 22 floréal VI (11 May 1798), it crudely exploited the chaos generated by the plague of schisms to conduct a purge of unwelcome deputies. The elections conducted by seceding minorities were endorsed in nine departments, even though in the case of the Puy-de-Dôme only thirty electors had taken part. Returns were also abrogated where no division had occurred, while selective annulments were imposed in other departments.[128]

The electors' choice had been severely circumscribed in the Year IV, extensively repudiated in the Year V and now blatantly distorted in the Year VI. On the first two occasions, when royalists triumphed, it might be argued that the existence of the Republic was at stake, but this alibi was rather less credible when confronted by Jacobin successes in 1798. The

---

[125] *Ibid.*, pp. 251–2.
[126] *Ibid.*, pp. 252–3 and AN AFIII 239, Commissaire au ministre and procès-verbaux, 21–30 germinal VI (10–19 Apr. 1798). [127] Sciout, *Le Directoire*, III, p. 445.
[128] Suratteau, *Les élections de l'an VI*, pp. 359 ff. and Woloch, *The Jacobin Revival*, pp. 299–310.

Directory was effectively determining the outcome of elections, totally reversing the non-interventionist stance adopted during earlier years of the Revolution. There were allegations that central agents had interfered with the Parisian elections of 1791 and the following year Roland, Minister of the Interior, did subsidise sympathetic journalists to write on behalf of his political allies; but that was about all.[129]

A lack of means, as much as principle or disinclination, explains the conspicuous absence of governmental involvement in elections down to 1792. The situation changed after 1795 with the establishment of centrally appointed *commissaires du directoire exécutif*, who were soon being denounced as 'government stooges', though the Directory was slow to recognise their potential as political agents. The electoral disaster of the Year V, however, galvanised the government into more resolute action. Careful preparations were made to organise the next annual round of elections with the *commissaires* playing a crucial role.

In the Year VI a determined and successful effort was made to secure their election to the departmental assemblies. Thirty-five or thirty-six *commissaires* were chosen in half the cantons of the Sarthe, for example, twenty-five in the Loire-Inférieure, thirty-five in the Côtes-du-Nord and forty in the Haute-Loire.[130] Though these totals represented only a tenth of the seats at the respective electoral colleges, it was hoped that *commissaires* would act in concert and use their influence to build majorities for official 'candidates' designated by the Directory. In the Landes, for instance, optimism regarding the electoral assembly 'resided in the presence of those whom the government has invested with authority', illustrating 'the perfect union of the people and the powers-that-be'.[131]

In the event this confidence proved misplaced. Fearing the worst the Directory issued a warning on 9 germinal (29 March 1798) that it would not stand idly by if the electoral outcome was again adverse. In fructidor Year V (September 1797) the Legislature had 'chased the traitors from its midst', and it was equally determined to 'exclude those anarchists whom some are now seeking to elect'.[132] Yet the government was subsequently obliged to implement its threat with another purge of deputies, because electors beholden to the resurgent Jacobin clubs, or Constitutional Circles, doggedly ignored its advice. *Commissaires* in the Haute-Garonne had been denounced as 'vile instruments of the government' and 'lackeys

---

[129] Charavay, ed., *Assemblée électorale*, II p. 517 and Gueniffey, *Le nombre et la raison*, pp. 433–4.

[130] Reinhard, *Le département de la Sarthe*, p. 333, Le Gall, Les consultations générales, II, p. 849, Pommeret, *L'esprit public dans le département des Côtes-du-Nord*, p. 436 and Delcambre, *La période du Directoire*, II, p. 281.

[131] AN AFIII 239, Bulletin de l'assemblée électorale, 23 germinal VI (12 Apr. 1798).

[132] Woloch, *Jacobin Legacy*, pp. 287–91.

of the Directory', while in the Bouches-du-Rhône *commissaire* Micoulin was reproached for his role as a *gouvernementiste* or *directorialiste*.[133]

In the circumstances the best that these agents could do was foment a schism, but many of their colleagues proved unreliable. In the Year VII, when the régime made renewed efforts to rig the elections and avoid the necessity for recourse to a purge, there was widespread evidence of disobedience. A weary *commissaire central* in the Sarthe, for instance, reported that only seven out of twenty-six cantonal *commissaires* had split from the Jacobin-dominated electoral assembly to join the officially sponsored *assemblée scissionnaire*.[134] There was similar disarray in the Landes, where some *commissaires de canton* had defected to a schism led by opponents of the government.[135] As always the problem lay in attracting sufficient 'enlightened and virtuous men who have always held aloof from party politics'. Such individuals had no wish to become involved or simply did not exist. As the *commissaire* at Marseille put it: 'When so much blood has been spilled . . . it is impossible to find good, impartial candidates . . . everyone wants people from their own faction to hold office.'[136]

In the Year VII the *commissaire central* of the Aveyron was pleased to inform the Minister of the Interior that, 'all three new members of the Legislature have been chosen from the list of suitable candidates you despatched to me'.[137] In most departments, however, it seems to have been disadvantageous to carry an official endorsement. It has been estimated that only sixty-six government nominees were elected out of almost 200.[138] One loyal newspaper confidently predicted that the executive would 'know how to put things right'.[139] Yet this time the Directory was not allowed to exploit the numerous schisms which had once more occurred in the departmental colleges, nor to manipulate the results in any way. The Legislative Councils forestalled any further intervention, seizing the initiative in prairial (June 1799) with a purge of the executive. This so-called parliamentary *coup d'état* was followed by a decision to validate the work of the *assemblées-meres* in almost every case where an electoral secession had taken place.[140] There were a number of difficult cases to resolve, but only the Bouches-du-Rhône was not decided in favour of the (extremely controversial) original assembly; enquiries were still continuing when the regime fell six months later.

---

[133] AN AFIII 230, Procès-verbal de l'assemblée scissionnaire de la Haute-Garonne, 30 germinal VII (19 Apr. 1799) and *ibid*. AFIII 217, Commissaire au ministre, 18 germinal VII (7 Apr. 1799).   [134] Reinhard, *Le département de la Sarthe*, p. 380.
[135] AN AFIII, Commissaire au ministre, 25 germinal VII (14 Apr. 1799).
[136] AN F¹bII Bouches-du-Rhône 17, Commissaire au ministre, 25 thermidor IV (12 Aug. 1796).   [137] AN AFIII 216, Commissaire au ministre, 1 floréal VII (20 Apr. 1799).
[138] Meynier, *Les coups d'état*, II, pp. 197–9.
[139] Cited in Woloch, *The New Regime*, p. 108.   [140] Meynier, *Les coups d'état*, II, p. 201.

In the meantime there were some encouraging indications of the parliamentarians' resolve to cleanse the Augean stables that elections had become. One deputy had already denounced a circular published by the *commissaire central* of the Sarthe, who urged his cantonal colleagues to use pressure and even threats to ensure favourable electoral returns. The response of the Directory to this excessive zeal was merely to suggest that 'enlightening the people' in this manner did 'not curtail the voters' liberty'.[141] Another member of the Legislature condemned schisms, which recalled 'the odious regime of local rebellion, enshrined in the *soi-disant* Constitution of 1793'; if they did not end, he concluded, the whole electoral system would collapse.[142]

During debate on the divided assemblies of the Year VII, in prairial (May), a report declared the word schism was 'a barbarism which offends the ear and the heart of every true republican'.[143] Once the Directory had been purged later that month the time had come to devise some remedies. In thermidor (August 1799), Français de Nantes promised deputies that they 'would shortly be presented with a draft bill to outlaw schisms, prevent the despatch of electoral agents into the departments and end all those manoeuvres that inhibit the voters' choice, which should be entirely free'. 'The decisions of all minority schisms will be declared null and void', he concluded.[144]

This project turned out to be the Legislative Councils' last will and testament where elections were concerned.[145] The proposals contained a number of flaws, not least the continuing reluctance to sanction party politics and overt electoral competition. Deputies were slow learners, still pursuing the utopia of untrammelled choices, clinging to the myth of a unanimous decision, arrived at without the pressures and partisanship that accompany a truly pluralistic political culture. It is difficult to be sanguine regarding the future of this fresh resolve to advance the revolutionary apprenticeship in democracy. In any case, it was hardly a propitious moment for further experiment given the magnitude of the internal and external crises that were threatening the First Republic. The *coup d'état* of brumaire which followed dealt a fatal blow to any lingering hopes of progress on the electoral front. The constitutional revisionists who came to power preferred an authoritarian solution to the unpredictability of the frequent polling that characterised the revolutionary decade.

---

[141] Sciout, *Le Directoire*, IV, pp. 322–5.
[142] Gaultier-Biauzat, *Appel aux principes contre les schismes* (Paris, no date).
[143] Sciout, *Le Directoire*, IV, p. 327.
[144] *Moniteur* XXIX, p. 719, 6 messidor VII (24 June 1799).
[145] BL FR 101, Duplantier, Code des droits politiques et des élections (Paris, an VII).

Conclusion

These days the electoral assemblies are very different to those of the Revolution. Then the people attached the greatest importance to voting and turned out *en masse*; as a result it was possible to discern the passions, opinions and even the most intimate thoughts of each class of citizen. Today, however, the people have come to realise that, on account of its expertise in assessing the contenders, the government alone should be entrusted with making the necessary choices. Indeed, there would be little objection if we revoked the articles in our Constitution which retain the practice of popular election.[1]

So wrote the acting sub-prefect of Toulon in 1813, in the wake of polls which attracted a mere 5 per cent of the electorate in the naval town. His impression of revolutionary elections was decidedly rose-tinted but, contrary to widely held belief, the Napoleonic régime did not entirely abolish elections; on the contrary, the Constitution of the Year VIII, which was hurriedly issued only a month after Bonaparte came to power, re-instated a broader suffrage.[2] Following revolutionary precedent, this constitutional document was immediately submitted to a referendum, but it was another twelve months before a further round of elections took place. Thereafter the electorate was consulted infrequently and, if the French apprenticeship in democracy and citizenship did not grind to a complete halt, it was severely dislocated under both Napoleon and his Bourbon successors.[3]

The turn of the nineteenth century is thus a good vantage point from which to survey the electoral endeavours of the preceding decade, weighing up what had been achieved against what was left to be desired. The latest rulers of republican France were anxious to demonstrate their popular credentials with a vote on the new Constitution which invited comparison with earlier referenda. This was why they felt obliged to manufacture a massive response when the actual number of participants

---

[1] AD Var 2M2–1, Sous-préfet de Toulon par intérim au ministre, 17 Sept. 1813.
[2] Godechot, ed., *Les constitutions*, p. 151.
[3] J.-Y. Coppolani, *Les élections en France à l'époque napoléonienne* (Paris, 1980), for a generally dim view of Napoleonic elections.

proved relatively low (though in the absence of any verification of the figures their gross deception has only recently come to light).[4] The poor turnout was hardly surprising given the difficult political and economic circumstances in which voting took place, in the depths of winter. No wonder only one in four adult males chose to record an opinion in nivôse VIII (December 1799–January 1800), despite being able to do so over several days in their own *commune*. The referendum dispensed with the assembly mechanism and, for the first time, offered an individual ballot, but not a secret one. Registers were opened at a variety of administrative *bureaux*, so there was no need to travel to vote on a particular day, though it took tremendous courage to openly enter a negative verdict.

Abstention was preferable to overt opposition (a mere 1,500 noes) and contemporaries were astonished when it was announced that 3,000,000 votes had been cast in favour of the constitution. In reality it was half that total, rather less than the vote of 1793 and not much more than 1795. Hence the decision to arbitrarily inflate the figures, in order to demonstrate that the Consulate was more popular than either the Jacobin régime or the Directory:

> The Constitution of the Year VIII has received over one million more votes than that of 1793 and almost two million more than that of 1795. The number of rejections is far smaller than in either previous instance. Yet earlier constitutions were presented to citizens at the primary assemblies . . . The Constitution of the Year VIII was submitted to dispassionate and individual reflection, in the greatest freedom and perfect security . . .[5]

This encomium concluded that not just the elite, but effectively the entire nation (those who could understand and judge for themselves out of some 6,000,000 *ayant droit de voter*, a revealing statement in itself) had approved the Constitution.

When fresh elections were held under this new system in the Year IX (1801), they were again conducted on an individual basis. This time citizens were asked to select one-tenth of their number to form a list of 'communal notables' from which local administrators would be chosen. These communal notables in turn nominated one tenth of their colleagues as 'departmental notables' and, last of all, the latter were invited to name another 10 per cent to produce a national list of just 60,000 persons.[6] This was indeed a simulacrum of democracy for, if indirect election for many posts had been a constant feature of the revolutionary decade, the choice of personnel did theoretically rest with the electoral assemblies,

---

[4] C. Langlois, 'Le plébiscite de l'an VIII ou le coup d'état du 18 pluviôse an VIII', *AhRf*, XLIV (1972), pp. 43–65, 231–46 and 390–415.
[5] *AP* (2ᵉ série) I, p. 177, Corps législatif, 21 pluviôse VIII (10 Feb. 1800).
[6] Coppolani, *Les élections*, p. 16.

not the government. In practice, however, the Directory had persistently interfered with the verdict of the electorate by purging and nominating on the convenient pretext of defending the Republic. So did the Consulate really destroy a healthy electoral organism, or merely breathe some artificial life into a moribund system?

It is worth accentuating the positive aspects of revolutionary elections to begin with, since its detractors have much too hastily concluded that the experiment was an arrant failure. Yet in terms of the basic suffrage the vast majority of adult males had enjoyed the right to vote throughout the decade. Even in 1790 and 1791, the notorious division between active and passive citizens had excluded no more than a minority of tax-paying heads of household. From the elections to the Estates General of 1789, to the final polls of the Directory ten years later, most if not all taxpayers were able to participate in the electoral assemblies. Nowhere else in the world was citizenship extended so far. Certainly not in backward Britain, which only enfranchised a comparable proportion of its adult males in 1884, nor even in the more progressive United States of America, where many states maintained suffrage restrictions, not to mention the institution of slavery.[7]

Of course, by no means all the *ayant droit de voter* in revolutionary France fulfilled the further requirements to vote (service in the National Guard or civic registration), nor actually participated in the elections. The relatively heavy turnout of 1790 was far from uniform and thereafter, as if subject to the law of diminishing returns, figures in excess of 50 per cent were rarely recorded in any instance. Yet in the case of Toulon, where it is possible to calculate how many different individuals made at least a fleeting appearance at the assemblies, it is evident that perhaps two-thirds of adult males had enjoyed some contact with the electoral process.[8]

The citizens of Toulon were not enthusiastic participants, but a crude extrapolation on this basis would suggest that over the country as a whole some 3 million citizens were at least occasionally involved in voting. This represents a far greater total than numbers enrolled in political clubs or encompassed by readership of the newspaper press. It should also be emphasised that the electoral apprenticeship under the Revolution was an extremely intensive one, especially for the minority (perhaps 500,000 Frenchmen) who attended regularly. The frequent elections (on average two or three *per annum* during the 1790s) and multiple ballots provided numerous opportunities for exercising the franchise. The assemblies themselves were schools for citizenship where, in the course of rhetoric

---

[7] Palmer, *The Age of the Democratic Revolution*, I, p. 527.
[8] Crook, 'The People at the Polls', p. 179.

and debate, local and national issues were raised. The potential for turning these assemblies into deliberative bodies, meeting outside of elections, only enhanced this educative role. In a society of limited literacy and poor communications these elections offered an unparalleled means of spreading information and generating political awareness.

The considerable time which the revolutionary leaders devoted to discussing and amending the franchise, on no less than five occasions, has distracted historians from investigating those aspects of the electoral system which were of far greater importance than a restricted suffrage. Yet lengthy procedures could offset the advantages to be derived from electoral assemblies by alienating participants. Even under the Directory when there was a single, annual, electoral cycle, held at a time when the weather was improving but agricultural activity remained relatively slack, much was still demanded. At Dijon in the Year V (1797) it was decided not to order a fresh ballot, despite inconsistencies in the preceding one, for 'on account of lassitude and loss of earnings it would be impossible to recall citizens who had already been assembled for six days'.[9] There was also an obverse to electoral sociability in terms of the hostility and even violence which marred many gatherings, whether this was a consequence of conflict between clienteles, rival parishes or warring political factions. In such cases the assemblies were hardly models for citizenship (Frenchmen did not always 'go to vote as calmly and then quietly return to work', as the Jacobins of Brest fondly liked to imagine), but instead reinforced a good deal of illiberal, atavistic behaviour.[10]

Abstention understandably resulted from the threats and pressures exerted by opposing factions, but it might also reflect a conscious decision to withdraw from the contest. Some boycotts stemmed from local wrangles over the location of cantonal *chef-lieux*, which prompted protestors to stay at home on polling day. Above all, when declarations of allegiance were required both to register and vote, participation could be construed as endorsing an unpalatable regime. In 1791 many Catholics refused to repeat an electoral oath that implied acceptance of the Civil Constitution of the Clergy. One pamphleteer attributed low turnout to such repugnance on the part of 'many honest and virtuous persons', who were following the example set by 'all the bishops and good priests in the kingdom'.[11]

Yet abstention might represent consensus, because the assembly method and the absence of declared candidates failed to allow for an unopposed return (as in eighteenth-century England). Traditional elec-

[9] AD Côte-d'Or L243, Procès-verbal d'élection, 6 germinal V (26 Mar. 1797).
[10] *Moniteur* XIII, p. 634, 8 Sept. 1792.
[11] AD Hérault L3884, Conversation entre un bon père et ses enfants (Montpellier, 1791).

toral practice did not necessarily require the presence of the whole community, simply a token number to authenticate the conduct of business. The choice of personnel might well be informally agreed beforehand, so the assembly itself was merely a ratification of the communal will. This collective rather than individualised approach to the selection of representatives was deeply entrenched in the popular consciousness and, like so many other aspects of electoral behaviour, it endured into the Revolution and even beyond. Where elections were concerned the persistence of established patterns of political culture certainly inhibited the emergence of 'modern' attitudes.

To assert that poor turnout was simply a consequence of indifference or a lack of civic awareness is therefore unfounded. What needs stressing, in view of the various obstacles that have been discussed, is the relatively high level of participation achieved in most years. What would be the consequences of employing a similar mechanism in our 'modern' society? Were it not for the current tendency of historians to gloss over the difficult circumstances of the period, such as war, civil disorder and severe economic disruption (all inimical to the experiment with electoral politics), there would be no need to underline just how difficult it must have been for many people to concentrate their minds upon voting. Inevitably it was the poor who participated least and, to this extent, the broader the franchise the lower the percentage turnout recorded.[12]

Modern psephology confirms that poverty remains a strong disincentive to electoral involvement, as well as the fact that voters are more inclined to participate when partisan allegiances are aroused. Throughout this study of the Revolution it has been evident that such rivalry stimulated higher turnout, even at a moment of apathy like the Year VII. Yet with the partial exception of the Year V, when declared candidatures were briefly introduced, there was a dogged refusal to acknowledge the open expression of electoral competition. Pluralism was not regarded as a sign of political health, rather the reverse; division was seen as an attack on the general will. All sides adhered to a vision of politics in which there were absolute choices to be made; party-political pressures would distort or destroy the voters' freedom. When Pons de Verdun spoke in favour of curtailing the experiment with declared candidatures, he commended 'the mysterious moral electricity' generated by gathering in assemblies as a much surer electoral guide than personal or partisan influences.[13]

Seasoned politicians were prisoners of a discourse that either con-

---

[12] Le Gall, *Les consultations générales*, II, p. 901.
[13] Pons de Verdun, *Rapport fait ... sur la suppression des listes de candidats* (Paris, an VI), p. 5.

demned the electorate to a vacuum or exposed them to undesirable pressures. In the one instance ballots were scattered in all directions and no clear winners emerged, while in the other voters were subject to illicit canvassing and campaigning that frequently overstepped the bounds of legitimate persuasion. The pursuit of unanimity meant that low turnout might be regarded as a sign of political purity which would compensate for the poor level of participation: 'What does it matter if the inhabitants have shown little interest, as long as the choice of the assembly is a good one', wrote the *commissaire* attached to the canton of Saint-Sébastien in the Loire-Inférieure, when only seventeen out of 334 *ayant droit de voter* appeared in the Year VI.[14] At Evans, in the Jura the same year, local Jacobins stated that: 'The only citizens in a Republic are the Democrats; consequently the right of citizenship for men or women has never belonged to aristocrats, royalists, papists or any of their associates.'[15]

Twentieth-century analyses also suggest that participation is encouraged by a voter feeling that his or her participation will have an influence upon the outcome, though this was something which was consistently denied under the Directory. Instead the electoral system tended to demand adherence to the orthodoxy of the day, to fabricate a false unity and to exclude any real form of opposition. Furet has consequently stated that elections did not bring about changes of régime in the same way as the various revolutionary *journées*.[16] This is to deny the importance of the polls in 1789 or 1792, not to mention many changes in local administration after 1789. However, when elections threatened to have an unwelcome effect in 1793 they were postponed indefinitely. After 1795 there was a constant succession of annulments: in the case of the municipality of Aix-en-Provence, for example, not once in four years was the voters' verdict allowed to stand.[17]

In this respect it was the elites who were to blame for shortcomings in the electoral experiment, just as it was their conscious decision to counterbalance the broad franchise with a two-tier procedure intended to filter out popular elements. This was the decisive barrier to democracy, above the municipal level, which an obsession with the basic suffrage has obscured. Moreover, it was a hurdle that remained in place even when the fiscal requirement for becoming a second-degree elector was abolished in 1792. This is where Gueniffey's distinction between 'number and reason' becomes fully apparent; save for the abortive Constitution of 1793, the parliamentarians were not prepared to let the people have a direct say in

[14] Le Gall, *Les consultations générales*, II, pp. 845–6.
[15] Cited in Woloch, *Jacobin Revival*, p. 253.
[16] In his preface to Gueniffey, *Le nombre et la raison*, p. i.
[17] Derobert-Ratel, *Institutions et vie municipale à Aix-en-Provence*, pp. 143–78.

whom they elected as their deputies. Leaving aside the two referenda of 1793 and 1795, there were no 'national' elections for the mass of the electorate, who were confined to a secondary role. Whether or not rural inhabitants in particular would have responded to the opportunity to play a leading part is debatable, for attitudes are far more difficult to alter than institutions, but they were never really given a chance to do so.

The 'invisible aristocracy' of the departmental assemblies points to the hidden agenda which elections were designed to serve: the legitimisation of a new political class. The emergence of the notables, the association of property and power, had been presaged under the *ancien régime* and was eventually consolidated under Napoleon. The 60,000 *plus imposés* of the First Empire, which re-integrated elements of the old nobility, should be compared to the 45,000 members of the electoral colleges in 1790 and the 50,000 third-estate *bailliage* deputies of 1789.[18] Those bourgeois who applied a radical solution to the political deadlock of 1789 had saddled themselves with a more thoroughgoing revolution than they intended. Even the imposition of more stringent criteria for eligibility as a second-degree elector during the Directory failed to provide a way out of the impasse. In turning to Bonaparte to save them from the vagaries of the electoral system they had created, they were obliged to surrender much of their political freedom, but their new-found status and power was secured. The study of elections suggests that the French Revolution was a social revolution after all.

[18] L. Bergeron and G. Chaussinand-Nogaret, *Les masses de granit. Cent mille notables du Premier Empire* (Paris, 1979) argue in favour of a somewhat broader elite, but only the 60,000 *plus imposés* could be selected to serve at national or departmental level.

Bibliography

MANUSCRIPT SOURCES

ARCHIVES NATIONALES

Série AF Papiers du gouvernement
AFIII 212–267 Rapports des commissaires du Directoire and pv. des assemblées électorales, ans VI et VII, a departmental series of fundamental importance
Série B Elections et Votes
BI Elections diverses, contains material on elections in Paris which is not otherwise available:
BI 1/2 Extraits des pv. des assemblées primaires, département de la Seine (Paris), 1790
BI 8 *Ibid.*, 1791
BI 14 *Ibid.*, 1792
BI 16 *Ibid.*, Elections municipales, thermidor IV (Aug. 1796)
BII Plébiscites, a departmental series:
BII 1–34 1793, Pv. des assemblées cantonales
BII 35–74 an III (1795), Pv. des assemblées cantonales
BII 75–471bis an VIII (1799), Registres des votes
BIII Elections aux Etats généraux de 1789
BIII 45 Pv. de l'assemblée de la sénéchaussée de Chartres
BIII 146 *Ibid.*, Toulon
BIII 148 *Ibid.*, Toulouse
Série C Assemblées nationales, a vital series containing petitions and addresses besides the record of proceedings at the Legislature but, above all, a virtually complete departmental series of pv. from the departmental electoral colleges:
C 118–21 Pv. des assemblées électorales, 1790
C 135–8 *Ibid.*, 1791
C 178–81 *Ibid.*, 1792
C 480–2 *Ibid.*, an IV (1795)
C 509–13 *Ibid.*, an V (1797)
C 530-6 *Ibid.*, an VI (1798)
C 571–84 *Ibid.*, an VII (1799)
DIV Comités des Assemblées
DIV Comité de Constitution, an interesting departmental series, containing questions and comments to the committee on a variety of electoral matters
DIVbis 37–53 Comité de Division, Contains tables and registers of voters and population from the departments, 1790–an II, but of a very uneven sort

Série F^1 Ministère de l'Intérieur: Administration générale

F^1bII Personnel, a departmental series with a mass of information relating to elected and nominated local bodies, little used here

F^1cIII Esprit public et élections, a departmental series of fundamental importance, though lists of voters, copies of pv. and masses of correspondence constitute something of a lottery. Cartons containing reports and addresses are useful as well as those specifically listed for elections

F^7 Police, can be dipped into with profit, mainly for the political activity accompanying the electoral process proper; e.g. reports from government agents in the Year VI on forthcoming elections

F^{20} 298–394 Statistique, a departmental series which contains material on population totals and, more importantly, tables of voters (*ayant droit de voter*) from 1793 to an VII; also includes preparations for the single-member constituencies proposed in the Constitution of 1793

ARCHIVES DEPARTEMENTALES

The main sources for primary elections, in the cantons, are to be found in the Archives départementales, which received (but have not always conserved) copies of the pv. brought by the second-degree electors as their *bona fides*. What remains is housed in *série* L, Révolution, often under the sub-heading Elections. However, as the following list suggests, some of the pv. have been gathered under the District sub-heading, rather than being grouped into cantons, at least until the suppression of the districts in 1795. So the inventories need to be examined carefully where electoral material is concerned, especially since lists of *ayant droit de voter* have sometimes been catalogued separately, under Population, for example. It proved extremely difficult to determine how profitable a visit to particular *archives départementales* might prove, purely on the basis of the *inventaire*; dossiers in local repositories are a lucky dip, like those in the Archives nationales, though different pieces of the jigsaw can be assembled from various sources to produce a more coherent picture.

ALLIER

Grouped by canton and by year, but little remains for either:
L132–45 Assemblées primaires, 1790–an VII
L146–7 Elections des juges de paix
L148 Assemblées électorales, 1790–an VII

ALPES-MARITIMES

Contains records emanating from eastern segments of the Var, which were appended to the Alpes-Maritimes in the nineteenth century. Material organised chronologically by canton, but nothing seems to have survived beyond 1793:
L542/7/50 Assemblées primaires, 1790–92
L543/4/8/9/50/1 Elections municipales, 1790–93

L545 Elections des juges de paix, 1791–93
Archives communales de Vence, IIIK 1, Elections 1790–an VII

AUDE

Organised according to district for the entire decade; almost a full complement of pv., only records from 1792 absent:
L356/65/75/9/81/5 Assemblées primaires du District de Carcassonne, 1790–an VII
L360/70/80/2/6 Assemblées primaires des Districts de Lagrasse et Limoux, 1790–an VII
L357–9 Elections municipales de Carcassonne, 1790

AVEYRON

Arranged according to district down to the Year III, then by canton; a pretty complete set of pv.:
1L576/90/620 Assemblées primaires du District de Mur-de-Barrès, 1790–an III
1L577/91/621 Assemblées primaires du District de Rodez, 1790–an III
1L578/92/622 Assemblées primaires du District de Saint-Affrique, 1790–an III
1L581/95/625 Assemblées primaires du District de Séverac, 1790–an III
1L599 Assemblées primaires, 1792
1L653–6 *Ibid.*, an V
1L683–7 *Ibid.*, an VII
1l600–43 Elections municipales
1L736–7 Listes des ayant droit de voter

BASSES-ALPES (ALPES DE HAUTE-PROVENCE)

Organised according to canton and virtually every set of pv. is available, but little ancillary material:
L199–203 Assemblées primaires, 1790–an VII
L204 Assemblées départementales, 1790–an VII

BOUCHES-DU-RHONE

Grouped under districts for 1790 and 1791, then by cantons for the following years; uneven quality:
L265–70 Assemblées primaires, 1792–an VII
L277–9 Assemblées électorales, 1790–an VII
L567–72 Assemblées primaires, District d'Aix, 1790–91
L1020 *Ibid.*, District de Marseille, 1791
L1964 Elections municipales, Marseille, 1793

CHARENTE

Organised by district down to 1792 and canton thereafter, but Years III and V are missing:

L126–7 Assemblées primaires, an VI–an VII
L532 Assemblées primaires du District d'Angoulême, 1790–92
L534 Elections municipales, 1790–92
L1007–8 Assemblées primaires du District de Cognac, 1790–92
L1010–2 Elections municipales, 1790–92
L1678–9 Assemblées primaires du District de Ruffec, 1790–92
L1681 Elections municipales, 1790–92

COTE-D'OR

The richest of all the departments explored, in terms of both breadth and depth of materials relating to primary and municipal elections, organised chronologically, by canton:
L194–209 Listes des ayant droit de voter
L210–221 Assemblées électorales, 1790–an VII
L222 Tableau des citoyens actifs, 1790
L224–50 Assemblées primaires, 1790–an VII
L251–78 Elections municipales
L497/506 Population

FINISTERE

Arranged by canton, but only 1791, an VI and an VII are complete:
10L74–6 Listes des ayant droit de voter
10L79 Assemblées électorales, 1790–an VII
10L81–94 Assemblées primaires, 1791–an VII
100J 336–42 Archives de Kernuz

HAUTE-GARONNE

Organised chronologically, by canton. Some years are thin, but there is plenty of interesting, supporting material:
L201–3 Listes de citoyens actifs, 1790
L234 Assemblées électorales, 1790–an VII
L237 Ayant droit de voter, 1790–91
L238–47 Assemblées primaires, 1790–an VII
L248–56 Elections municipales, 1790–an VII
L257 Listes des ayant droit de voter, an V-VII

LANDES

A very mixed bag, only an VI is complete:
11L1 Elections, 1790–92
11L2/7 Ayant droit de voter, 1790–an VI
11L5 Assemblées primaires, an VI
11L6 Elections municipales, an VII
11L8–9 Assemblées électorales, 1790–an VII

MARNE

An excellent department for the historian of elections, with plenty of supporting material, though no pv. remain for the Year V. Arranged by district down to the an III, then by cantons:

1L286 Listes des ayant droit de voter
1L296 Contestations électorales
1L297 Assemblées primaires, District de Châlons-sur-Marne, 1790–an III
1L298 *Ibid.*, Epernay
1L299–300 *Ibid.*, Reims
1L301 *Ibid.*, Sainte-Menehould
1L302 *Ibid.*, Sézanne
1L303–4 *Ibid.*, Vitry
1L305–11 Assemblées primaires, an VI-an VII
1L313 Formation des municipalités, 1790
1I385–7 Population
Supplément E5872 Archives municipales de Châlons-sur-Marne, K1–6 Elections, 1790–an VII

MEUSE

Pv. organised in chronological order by cantons, generally complete, though 1792 is poorly represented:
L341–52 Listes des ayant droit de voter
L353–60 Assemblées primaires, 1790–an VII
L364 Assemblées électorales, 1790–an VII
L409 Population
PL9295r Tableau des cantons, 1790

MORBIHAN

A reasonably full set of pv., organised chronologically, though not always easy to utilise due to changes in cantonal boundaries:
L233–46 Assemblées primaires, municipales et électorales, 1790–an VII
L354–5 Découpage des cantons

ORNE

A reasonably full complement of pv., arranged according to district down to 1792, then chronologically by canton thereafter:
L343/63/4/74 Assemblées primaires, District d'Alençon, 1790–92
L344/65/75 *Ibid.*, Argentan, 1790–92
L346/67/76 *Ibid.*, Domfront, 1790–92
L347/68/77 *Ibid.*, Laigle, 1790–92
L380 Assemblées électorales, 1790–an VII
L390–418 Assemblées primaires, an III-an VII

PYRENEES-ORIENTALES

A small department with a spotty set of pv., organised chronologically:
L428/30–3 Assemblées primaires, 1790–an VII
L429/35–8 Elections municipales, 1790–an VII
L434 Assemblées électorales, 1790–an VII
L469 Etats de population, 1790

VAR

Pv. very uneven for the early years of the Revolution and virtually non-existent after 1792; a mixture of municipal, cantonal and departmental records with an ostensibly chronological arrangement:
1L218–33 Assemblées primaires, municipales et électorales, 1790–an VII
1L1848 Elections des juges de paix, 1791–92

Visits were made to four other depots, but none of them yielded more than fragments. Few pv. remain at Archives départementales in the Bas-Rhin, Indre-et-Loire, Saône-et-Loire and Vendée.

ARCHIVES MUNICIPALES

Generally speaking only the larger towns have kept their own archives. Most *archives communales* have been deposited in the *Archives départementales*, where I have consulted a number of them in pursuit of information regarding local elections, but to little effect. Village polls are often recorded in their council minute books, rather than appearing separately, though it is rare to discover a good, solid series year to year save in rare cases, like that of Vence in the Var. Fortunately, the contemporary departmental authorities sometimes collected material relating to municipal elections and these data can be exploited with relative ease. By contrast, documentation on elections in the cities is usually very extensive and yields a good deal of information about the practicalites of the electoral process, including voter registration and the counting of votes, both for municipal and primary elections.

BORDEAUX

K3–10 Pv. des sections, 1790–an VII
K11–2 Listes des ayant droit de voter

BREST

1K7 2–19 Pv. des sections, 1790–an VII

DIJON

1D1/1–3 Délibérations du conseil municipal, 1790–93
Série K Elections, 1790 (no number)

Bibliography

MARSEILLE

K1 1–3 Tableaux des ayant droit de voter, an IV–an VII
K3–11 Elections municipales, 1790–an VII

MONTPELLIER

K1 3–4 Elections municipales, 1790–92

STRASBOURG

D1 Délibérations du conseil municipal, 1790–92

TOULON

L39 Elections aux Etats-généraux de 1789
L109 Pv. des assemblées primaires, 1790
L572–8 Pv. des élections municipales, 1790–an VII
L592–3 Elections des juges de paix, 1791–92

TOULOUSE

1K5–16 Tableaux des élections, 1790–an VII

PRINTED PRIMARY SOURCES

ARCHIVES NATIONALES

The series AD Imprimés contains a rich collection of reports and speeches, polemics, projects and pamphlets, which I did not consult to any great extent, since many are duplicated in the collections of the Bibliothèque nationale and British Library.

BIBLIOTHEQUE NATIONALE

It would be tedious to list the many pamphlets I consulted here, but an essential *instrument de travail* is: Tourneux, J.M., ed., *Bibliographie de l'histoire de Paris pendant la Révolution française*, 5 vols. (Paris, 1890–1913).

BRITISH LIBRARY AT THE BRITISH MUSEUM

The excellent sets of pamphlets in the Croker collections are extremely easy to use thanks to the manner in which they have been organised, according to subject matter. Of course, that is not to say that relevent material is not to be discovered under other headings, but the essential series are as follows:
F 292 Elections, discours et projets, 1789–99
F 1207–14 Elections primaires et assemblées départementales, 1788–99
FR 99–106 Elections diverses, 1789–1802
R 224 Elections parisiennes, 1789–1817

See the recently published guide, Fortescue, G.K. *French Revolutionary Collections in the British Library*, revised edn, A.C. Brodhurst (London, 1979).

NEWSPAPERS

These can be tracked down in Bibliothèque nationale, British Library and departmental archives. The national titles are also available at the John Rylands Library in Manchester which, for inhabitants of north-western England like myself, is also conveniently situated for the consultation of printed documentary collections like the *Archives parlementaires*.

Journal des départements méridionaux
Journal des hommes libres de tous les pays
L'Ami du Peuple
L'Anti-Terroriste (Toulouse)
La Sentinelle
Le Journal de la Côte-d'Or
Le Journal de Toulouse
Le Journal du département de la Marne
Le Patriote français
Mercure de France

MEMOIRS AND DOCUMENTS

Archives parlementaires. Recueil complet des débats législatifs et politiques des Chambres françaises. Première série 1787–99, ed. J. Mavidal and E. Laurent, 82 vols. (Paris, 1867–1913). Continuation by the Institut d'Histoire de la Révolution française, Paris, in progress since 1961. Deuxième série 1800–1815, 13 vols. (Paris, 1862–7)

Aulard, F.-A., ed., *Recueil de documents pour l'histoire du club des Jacobins de Paris*, 6 vols. (Paris, 1889–97)

Paris pendant la réaction thermidorienne et sous le Directoire, 5 vols. (Paris, 1898–1902)

Barnave, A., *De la Révolution et de la Constitution*, ed. P. Gueniffey (Grenoble, 1988)

Barras, P, *Mémoires*, ed. V. Duruy, 4 vols. (Paris, 1895–96)

Brette, A., ed., *Recueil de documents relatifs à la convocation des Etats généraux de 1789*, 4 vols. (Paris, 1894–1915)

Brissot, J.-P., *Mémoires 1754–1793*, ed. C. Perroud, 2 vols. (Paris, no date)

Buchez, B.-J., and Roux, J.-B., eds., *Histoire parlementaire de la Révolution française*, 40 vols. (Paris, 1834–38)

Charavay, E., ed., *Assemblée électorale de Paris*, 3 vols. (Paris, 1890–1905)

Chassin, C.-L., ed., *Les élections et les cahiers de Paris en 1789*, 4 vols. (Paris, 1888–89)

Combes de Patris, B., ed., *Procès-verbaux des séances de la société populaire de Rodez* (Rodez, 1912)

Condorcet, J., Marquis de, *Sur les élections et autres textes*, ed. O. de Bernon (Paris, 1986)

Donnadieu, J.-P., ed., *Etats généraux de 1789. Sénéchaussées de Béziers et Montpellier* (Montpellier, 1989)

Duplantier, J.P.F., *Code des droits politiques et des élections* (Paris, an VII)
Duvergier, J.-B., ed., *Collection complète des lois*, 24 vols. (Paris, 1825–28)
Gaultier-Biauzat, *Appel aux principes contre les schismes* (Paris, no date)
Godechot, J., ed., *Les constitutions de la France depuis 1789* (Paris, 1970)
Laplane, J.-L., *Journal d'un marseillais, 1789–1793*, eds. G. Fabre and V. Autheman (Marseille, 1989)
Louvet, J.-B., *La Sentinelle*, rep. (Paris, 1981)
Malouet, P.-V., *Mémoires*, 2 vols. (Paris, 1874)
Montesquieu, *The Spirit of the Laws*, ed. F. Neumann (New York, 1949)
Pfister, C., ed., *Les assemblées électorales dans le département de la Meurthe, le district, les cantons et la ville de Nancy. Procès-verbaux originaux* (Nancy, 1912)
Quatremère de Quincy, A.C., *La véritable liste de candidats* (Paris, an V)
Réimpression de l'ancien Moniteur, 32 vols. (Paris, 1858–63)
Robespierre, M., *Oeuvres Complètes*, eds. M. Bouloiseau, G. Lefebvre and A. Soboul, 10 vols. (Paris, 1910–67)
Rochas, A., *Journal d'un bourgeois de Valence* (Grenoble, 1891)
Rousseau, J.-J., *Oeuvres complètes*, Bibliothèque de la Pléiade (Paris, 1964)
Sieyès, E.-J., *Ecrits politiques*, ed. R. Zapperi (Paris, 1985)
Thibaudeau, A.-C., *Mémoires sur la Convention et le Directoire* (Paris, 1824)
Vaughan, C.E., ed., *The Political Writings of Jean-Jacques Rousseau*, 2 vols. (Cambridge, 1915)
Walzer, M., ed., *Regicide and Revolution. Speeches at the Trial of Louis XVI* (Cambridge, 1974)
Wickham-Legg, L.G., ed., *Select Documents Illustrative of the History of the French Revolution*, 2 vols. (Oxford, 1905)

SECONDARY SOURCES

Aimond, C., *Histoire de Bar-le-Duc*, new edn (Bar-le-Duc, 1982)
Alonso, H., Elections et personnel politique en Aveyron pendant la Révolution française, 1789–1799, Mémoire pour la Maîtrise, Université de Toulouse-Le Mirail, 1990
Arches, P., 'Elections et participation électorale au début de la Révolution française, 1790–1791', *Bulletin de la Société historique et scientifique des Deux-Sèvres*, 21 (1988), pp. 323–86
Arnaud, G., *Histoire de la Révolution dans le département de l'Ariège (1789–1795)* (Toulouse, 1904)
Atlas de la Révolution française, various eds., 7 vols. (Paris, 1987–93)
Audevart, O., Les élections en Haute-Vienne pendant la Révolution (1789–99), Mémoire pour la Maîtrise, Université de Limoges, 1988
Aulard, F.-A., *Histoire politique de la Révolution française. Origines et développement de la démocratie et de la République (1789–1804)*, fourth edn (Paris, 1909)
Auvray, M.E., 'Les élections à la Convention nationale dans le département de la Seine-et-Oise (26 août-2 septembre 1792)', *Actes 78e con. nat.* (1953), pp. 239–56
Baczko, B., *Comment sortir de la Terreur. Thermidor et la Révolution* (Paris, 1989)
Badinter, E. and R., *Condorcet. Un intellectuel en politique* (Paris, 1988)
Baker, K.M., *Condorcet. From Natural Philosophy to Social Mathematics* (Chicago, 1975)

Inventing the French Revolution (Cambridge, 1990)
with Furet, F., and Lucas, C., eds., *The French Revolution and the Creation of Modern Political Culture*, 4 vols. (Oxford, 1987–94)
Barrey, P., 'Les élections à la Convention dans la Seine-Inférieure', *Rf*, 64 (1913), pp. 135–48
Baticle, R., 'Le plébiscite sur la Constitution de 1793', *Rf*, 57 (1909), pp. 496–524 and 58 (1910), pp. 5–30, 117–55, 193–237, 327–41 and 385–410
Baumont, H., 'Les assemblées primaires et électorale de l'Oise en 1792 (août-septembre)', *Rf*, 47 (1904), pp. 135–78
Bergeron, L., and Chaussinand-Nogaret, G., *Les masses de granit. Cent mille notables du Premier Empire* (Paris, 1979)
Biernawski, L., *Un département sous la Révolution française, l'Allier* (Moulins, 1909)
Blayo, Y., and Henry, L., 'La population de la France de 1740 à 1860', *Population*, 30 (1975), pp. 71–122
Bloch, C., 'Le recrutement du personnel municipal en l'an IV', *Rf*, 46 (1904), pp. 153–67
Bois, P. *Paysans de l'Ouest. Des structures économiques et sociales aux options politiques depuis l'époque révolutionnaire dans la Sarthe* (Le Mans, 1960)
Bordes, M., *L'administration provinciale et municipale en France au XVIIIe siècle* (Paris, 1972)
'L'administration des communautés d'habitants en Provence et dans le comté de Nice à la fin de l'ancien régime. Traits communs et diversité', *Ann. Midi*, 84 (1972), pp. 369–96
Bossenga, G., *The Politics of Privilege. Old Regime and Revolution in Lille* (Cambridge, 1991)
Bouloiseau, M., 'Elections de 1789 et communautés rurales en Haute-Normandie', *AhRf*, XXVIII (1956), pp. 29–47
'Notables ruraux et élections municipales dans la région rouennaise en 1787', *Comm. hist. éc. soc. Mémoires et documents*, XIII (1958), pp. 7–36
Cahiers de doléances du tiers état du bailliage de Rouen pour les Etats généraux de 1789, 2 vols. (Paris, 1957–60)
'La campagne électorale pour les Etats-généraux de 1789. L'exemple d'Orléans', *Actes 88e con. nat.* (1963)
La République jacobine 10 août 1792–9 thermidor an II (Paris, 1972)
and Buchoux, A., 'Les municipalités tourangelles de 1787', *Comm. hist. éc. soc. Mémoires et documents*, XXIII (1969)
Bourdin, I., *Les sociétés populaires à Paris pendant la Révolution* (Paris, 1937)
Bourdin, P., 'Les paysans et le pouvoir directorial dans le Puy-de-Dôme', *AhRf*, LIX (1987), pp. 314–37
Bourdon, J., 'Les élections de la Côte-d'Or en 1792 et en 1795', *Annales de Bourgogne* (1955–56), pp. 189–94
Boutier, J., and Boutry, P., 'La diffusion des sociétés politiques en France (1789–an III). Une enquête nationale', *AhRf*, LVIII (1986), pp. 365–98
'Les sociétés politiques en France de 1789 à l'an III: "une machine"?', *Rhmc*, 36 (1989), pp. 29–67
Boutier, J., Cassan, M., d'Hollander, P., and Pommaret, B., eds., *Limousin en Révolution* (Treignac, 1989)
Brelot, C., *Besançon révolutionnaire* (Paris, 1966)

Brelot, J., *La vie politique en Côte-d'Or sous le Directoire* (Dijon, 1932)
Bricaud, J., *L'administration du département d'Ille-et-Vilaine au début de la Révolution 1790–1791* (Rennes, 1965)
Bruneau, M., *Les débuts de la Révolution dans les départements du Cher et de l'Indre, 1789–1791* (Paris, 1902)
• Brunel, F., 'Partis politiques en Révolution', *La Pensée* (1985), pp. 113–23
Brunet, M., *Le Roussillon face à la Révolution française* (Perpignan, 1989)
Cadart, J., *Le régime électoral des Etats-généraux de 1789 et ses origines, 1302–1614* (Paris, 1952)
Cassagnau, G., *L'esprit public et les élections dans le département des Basses-Pyrénées de 1789 à 1804* (Paris, 1906)
Castellan, G., *Une cité provençale dans la Révolution. Chronique de la ville de Vence en 1790* (Paris, 1978)
Cazanave, J., 'Le personnel municipal de Belpech de 1790 à 1800', *Ann. Midi*, 97 (1985), pp. 301–16
Chartier, R., 'La convocation aux Etats de 1614: note sur les formes politiques', in R. Chartier and D. Richet, eds., *Représentation et vouloir politiques. Autour des Etats-généraux de 1614* (Paris, 1982), pp. 53–61
Chomel, V., ed., *Les débuts de la Révolution française en Dauphiné* (Grenoble, 1988)
Clémendot, P., *Le département de la Meurthe à l'époque du Directoire* (Nancy, 1966)
Cochin, A., *L'esprit du jacobinisme*, ed. J. Baechler (Paris, 1979)
• Cole, A. and Campbell, P., *French Electoral Systems and Elections since 1789*, third edn (Aldershot, 1989)
Collins, I., *Napoleon and his Parliaments, 1800–1815* (London, 1979)
Comité régional d'histoire de la Révolution, *La Révolution en Haute-Normandie, 1789–1802* (Rouen, 1989)
Connelly, O., ed., *Historical Dictionary of Napoleonic France, 1799–1815* (Westport, 1985)
Coppolani, J.-Y., *Les élections en France à l'époque napoléonienne* (Paris, 1980)
Corgne, E., *Pontivy et son district pendant la Révolution, 1789–germinal an V* (Rennes, 1938)
Crook, M., 'Les français devant le vote: participation et pratique électorale à l'époque de la Révolution', in Centre d'histoire contemporaine du Languedoc méditerranéen et du Roussillon, *Les pratiques politiques en province à l'époque de la Révolution* (Montpellier, 1988), pp. 27–37
Toulon in War and Revolution. From the Ancien Régime to the Restoration, 1750–1820 (Manchester, 1991)
'"Aux Urnes Citoyens!" Rural and Urban Electoral Behaviour during the French Revolution, 1789–1799', in A. Forrest and P.M. Jones, eds., *Reshaping France. Town, Country and Region in the French Revolution* (Manchester, 1991), pp. 152–67
'The People at the Polls: Electoral Behaviour in Revolutionary Toulon, 1789–1799', *French History*, 5 (1991), pp. 164–79
'The Persistence of the Ancien Régime in France: the Estates General of 1789 and the Origins of the Revolutionary Electoral System', *Parliaments, Estates and Representation*, 13 (1993), pp. 29–40
'French Elections, 1789–1848', *History Today*, 43 (1993), pp. 41–6
'Les élections à la Convention nationale en 1792', in P. Barlet, ed., *1792, Naissance de la République dans le Centre-Ouest* (Tours, 1993), pp. 211–21

'Marseille, Aix et Toulon: vicissitudes du personnel municipal de trois grandes villes provençales à l'époque de la Révolution', in B. Benoit, ed., *Ville et Révolution française* (Lyon, 1994), pp. 200–15

'Le fédéralisme et le vote sur la Constitution de 1793', in M. Cubells, ed., *Les fédéralismes: réalités et représentations, 1789–1874* (Aix-en-Provence, 1995), pp. 239–50

Crossouard, R., *La Révolution dans le District de Vitré, 1789–1795* (Rennes, 1989)

Cubells, M., *Les horizons de la liberté. Naissance de la Révolution en Provence (1787–1789)* (Aix-en-Provence, 1987)

Delcambre, E., *La période du Directoire dans la Haute-Loire*, 3 vols. (Rodez, 1941–43)

Derlange, M., 'En Provence au XVIIIe siècle: la représentation des habitants aux conseils généraux des communautés', *Ann. Midi*, 86 (1974), pp. 45–67

Derobert-Ratel, C., *Institutions et vie municipale à Aix-en-Provence sous la Révolution, 1789–an VIII* (Millau, 1981)

Dinkin, R.J., *Voting in Revolutionary America. A Study of Elections in the Original Thirteen States, 1776–1789* (Westport, 1982)

Doucet, R., *L'esprit public dans le département de la Vienne pendant la Révolution* (Paris, 1910)

Doyle, W., *Origins of the French Revolution* (Oxford, 1980)

The Oxford History of the French Revolution (Oxford, 1989)

Du Châtelier, A., 'Essai de monographie électorale pour les années 1790–91 et 92', *Bulletin de la Société académique de Brest* (1882), pp. 1–46

Ducoudray, E., 'Les électeurs de l'an IV. Canton de Paris. Essai de prosopographie politique', *AhRf*, LIV (1982), pp. 654–60

'Bourgeois parisiens en Révolution, 1790–1792', in M. Vovelle, ed., *Paris et la Révolution* (Paris, 1989), pp. 71–88

'De la presse aux groupes de pression: les clubs électoraux parisiens en 1791–1792', *Studies on Voltaire and the Eighteenth Century*, 297 (1991), pp. 293–307

Dupeux, G., 'The Orientations of Electoral Sociology in France', *British Journal of Sociology*, 6 (1955), pp. 328–34

Dupuy, R., *De la Révolution à la chouannerie. Paysans en Bretagne 1788–1794* (Paris, 1988)

and Lebrun, F., eds., *Les résistances à la Révolution* (Paris, 1986)

Durand, Y., 'Les Etats généraux de 1614 et de 1789: vie et mort de la monarchie absolue', *XVIIe Siècle*, 41 (1989), pp. 131–44

Duval-Jouve, J., *Montpellier pendant la Révolution*, 2 vols. (Montpellier, 1879)

Edelstein, M., 'Vers une "sociologie électorale" de la Révolution française: la participation des citadins et campagnards (1789–1793)', *Rhmc*, 22 (1975), pp. 508–29

'La place de la Révolution française dans la politisation des paysans', *AhRf*, LXI (1989), pp. 135–49

'L'apprentissage de la citoyenneté: participation électorale des campagnards et citadins (1789–1793)', in M. Vovelle, ed., *L'image de la Révolution française*, 4 vols. (Oxford, 1989–90), I, pp. 15–25

'Integrating the French Peasants into the Nation-State: the Transformation of Electoral Participation (1789–1870)', *History of European Ideas*, 15 (1992), pp. 319–26

'La participation électorale des français (1789–1870)', *Rhmc*, 40 (1993), pp. 629–42

'Electoral Behaviour during the Constitutional Monarchy (1790–1791): a "Community" Interpretation', in Waldinger, R., Dawson, P., and Woloch, I., eds., *The French Revolution and the Meaning of Citizenship* (Westport, 1993), pp. 105–22

'L'établissement de la République en Côte-d'Or: étude électorale et politique' in M. Vovelle, ed., *Révolution et République: l'exception française* (Paris, 1994), pp. 226–36

'De l'an I à l'an III: l'apprentissage de la démocratie en Côte-d'Or', forthcoming in S. Aberdam, ed., *L'an I et l'apprentissage de la démocratie*

Egret, J., *La pré-révolution française (1787–1788)* (Paris, 1962)

Eschassériaux, M., *Assemblées électorales de la Charente-Inférieure* (Niort, 1868)

Faye, H., *La Révolution au jour le jour en Touraine (1789–1800)* (Angers, 1903)

Fehér, F., ed., *The French Revolution and the Birth of Modernity* (Berkeley, 1990)

Fitzsimmons, M.P., *The Remaking of France. The National Assembly and the Constitution of 1791* (Cambridge, 1994)

Flickinger, R.S. and Studlar, D.T., 'The Disappearing Voters? Exploring Declining Turnout in Western European Elections', *West European Politics*, 15 (1992), pp. 1–16

Forrest, A., *Society and Politics in Revolutionary Bordeaux* (Oxford, 1975)

and Jones, P.M., eds., *Reshaping France. Town, Country and Region during the French Revolution* (Manchester, 1991)

Forsyth, M., *Reason and Revolution. The Political Thought of the Abbé Sieyès* (Leicester, 1987)

Fortunet, F., Fossier, M., Kozlowski, N., and Vienne, S., *Pouvoir municipal et communauté rurale à l'époque révolutionnaire en Côte-d'Or, 1789–an IV* (Dijon, 1981)

Fournier, G., 'Sur l'administration municipale de quelques communautés languedociennes de 1750 à 1789', *Ann. Midi*, 84 (1972), pp. 459–82

'Structures sociales et révolution dans quelques villes languedociennes', *Ann. Midi*, 96 (1984), pp. 401–32

'Les incidents électoraux dans la Haute-Garonne, l'Aude, l'Hérault, pendant la Révolution', in Centre d'histoire contemporaine du Languedoc méditerranéen et du Roussillon, *Les pratiques politiques en province à l'époque de la Révolution française* (Montpellier, 1988), pp. 63–76

'La participation électorale en Haute-Garonne pendant la Révolution', *Ann. Midi*, 101 (1989), pp. 47–71

Démocratie et vie municipale en Languedoc du milieu du XVIIIe siècle au début du XIXe siècle, Thèse pour le Doctorat, Université de Toulouse-Le Mirail, 1991

and Péronnet, M., *La Révolution dans le département de l'Aude, 1789–1799* (Le Coteau, 1989)

Fridieff, M., *Les origines du referendum dans la Constitution de 1793* (Paris, 1932)

Fryer, W.R., *Republic or Restoration in France? 1794–1797* (Manchester, 1965)

Furet, F., 'Les Etats-généraux de 1789. Deux bailliages élisent leurs députés', in *Conjoncture économique, structures sociales. Hommage à Ernest Labrousse* (Paris-The Hague, 1974), pp. 433–48

Penser la Révolution française (Paris, 1978)

'Les élections de 1789 à Paris, le Tiers Etat et la naissance d'une classe dirigeante', in E. Hinrichs, E. Schmitt and R. Vierhaus, eds., *Vom Ancien Régime zur Französischen Revolution. Forschungen und Perspektiven* (Göttingen, 1978), pp. 188–206

'La monarchie et le règlement électoral de 1789', in Baker *et al.*, eds., *The French Revolution*, I, pp. 375–86

La Révolution française. De Turgot à Jules Ferry, 1770–1880 (Paris, 1988)

and Ozouf, M., eds., *A Critical Dictionary of the French Revolution*, trans. (Cambridge, Mass., 1989)

Gainot, B., 'Le département de Saône-et-Loire à la fin du Directoire', *Actes 113/114ᵉ con. nat.* (1988–89), pp. 373–80

'Les élections de 1799 dans le Morbihan. Les "réduits" républicains de l'Ouest', in A. Droguet, ed., *Les bleus de Bretagne de la Révolution à nos jours* (Saint-Brieuc, 1991), pp. 177–87

Le mouvement néo-jacobin à la fin du Directoire. Structure et pratiques politiques. Thèse pour le Doctorat, 3 vols., Université de Paris I, 1993

'Espaces politiques, espaces publics, espaces civiques entre Saône et Loire sous le Directoire', in B. Benoit, ed., *Ville et Révolution française* (Lyon, 1994), pp. 245–55

'Les troubles électoraux de l'an VII: dissolution du souverain ou vitalité de la démocratie représentative?', *AhRf*, LXVI (1994), pp. 447–62

Garrioch, D., 'The Revolution in Local Politics in Paris', in R. Aldrich, ed., *France: Politics, Society, Culture and International Relations* (Sydney, 1990), pp. 13–24

Gaxie, D., ed., *L'explication du vote. Un bilan des études électorales en France* (Paris, 1985)

• Genty, M., *Paris 1789–1795. L'apprentissage de la citoyenneté* (Paris, 1987)

'Les élections parisiennes de 1789 à 1792. Etude socio-professionnelle des élus locaux', in M. Vovelle, ed., *Paris et la Révolution* (Paris, 1989), pp. 59–70

Girardot, J., *Le département de la Haute-Saône pendant la Révolution*, 3 vols. (Vesoul, 1972–74)

Godechot, J., *La contre-révolution, 1789–1804. Doctrine et action* (Paris, 1961)

Les institutions de la France sous la Révolution et l'Empire, second edn (Paris, 1968)

'Aux origines du régime représentatif en France: des conseils politiques languedociens aux conseils municipaux de l'époque révolutionnaire', in E. Hinrichs, E. Schmitt and R. Vierhaus, eds., *Vom Ancien Régime zur Französischen Revolution. Forschungen und Perspektiven* (Göttingen, 1978), pp. 11–23

Gough, H., 'The Provincial Jacobin Club Press during the French Revolution', *European History Quarterly*, 16 (1986), pp. 47–76

The Newspaper Press in the French Revolution (London, 1988)

'National Politics and the Provincial Jacobin Press during the Directory', *History of European Ideas*, 10 (1989), pp. 443–54

Gouyou, J., and Moreau, R., 'Formation des municipalités dans l'élection de Montreuil-Bellay en 1787', *Actes 87ᵉ con. nat.* (1962), pp. 193–231

Grandadam, C., and Hours, H., 'Les élections municipales du début de l'année 1790 dans le Jura', *Travaux de la Société d'Emulation du Jura* (1990), pp. 203–25

Gruder, V., 'The Society of Orders at its Demise: the Vision of the Elite at the end of the Ancien Régime', *French History*, 1 (1987), pp. 210–37

Gueniffey, P., La Révolution française et les élections. Suffrage, participation et élections pendant la période constitutionnelle (1790–1792), Thèse pour le Doctorat, Ecole des Hautes Etudes en Sciences Sociales, Paris, 1989

Le nombre et la raison. La Révolution française et les élections (Paris, 1993)

'Revolutionary Democracy and the Elections', in Waldinger, R., Dawson, P., and Woloch, I., eds., *The French Revolution and the Meaning of Citizenship* (Westport, 1993), pp. 89–103

Halévi, R., *Les loges maçonniques dans la France d'Ancien Régime. Aux origines de la sociabilité démocratique* (Paris, 1984)

'La monarchie et les élections: position des problèmes', in Baker *et al.*, eds., *The French Revolution*, I, pp. 387–402

Hampson, N., *Saint-Just* (Oxford, 1991)

Hanson, P., 'The Federalist Revolt: An Affirmation or a Denial of Popular Sovereignty?', *French History*, 6 (1992), pp. 335–355

Harris, R.D. *Necker and the Revolution of 1789* (Lanham, 1986)

Hayden, M., *France and the Estates General of 1614* (Cambridge, 1974)

Heater, D., *Citizenship: The Civic Ideal in World History, Politics and Education* (London, 1990)

Henwood, P., and Monange, E., *Brest. Un port en Révolution 1789–1799* (Rennes, 1989)

Holt, M.P., 'Popular Political Culture and Mayoral Elections in Sixteenth-Century Dijon', in M.P. Holt, ed., *Society and Institutions in Early-Modern France* (Athens, Ga., 1991), pp. 98–116

Homan, G.D., *Jean-François Reubell* (The Hague, 1971)

Horn, J., Elections and Elites: The Development of Local Political Power in Southern Champagne, 1765–1812, PhD Thesis, University of Pennsylvania, 1993

Huard, R., *Le suffrage universel en France, 1848–1946* (Paris, 1991)

Hufton, O.H. *Bayeux in the Late Eighteenth Century. A Social Study* (Oxford, 1967)

Women and the Limits of Citizenship in the French Revolution (Toronto, 1992)

Hunt, L., *Revolution and Urban Politics in Provincial France: Troyes and Reims, 1786–1790* (Stanford, 1978)

Politics, Culture and Class in the French Revolution (Berkeley, 1984)

'The Political Geography of Revolutionary France', *Journal of Interdisciplinary History*, 14 (1984), pp. 535–59

Jaurès, J., *Histoire socialiste de la Révolution française*, 7 vols., Editions sociales (Paris, 1968–73)

Jessenne, J.-P., *Pouvoir au village et Révolution. Artois, 1760–1848* (Lille, 1987)

'Continuités et ruptures dans la détention des fonctions locales en Artois (1789–1800)', in *La Révolution française et le monde rural* (Paris, 1989), pp. 397–412

'De la citoyenneté proclamée à la citoyenneté appliquée: l'exercice du droit de vote dans le District d'Arras en 1790', *Revue du Nord*, 72 (1990), pp. 789–839

Jones, C., *The Longman Companion to the French Revolution* (London, 1988)

Jones, P.M., 'La République au Village in the Southern Massif Central, 1789–1799', *The Historical Journal*, 23 (1980), pp. 793–812

'Political Commitment and Rural Society in the Southern Massif Central', *European Studies Review*, 10 (1980), pp. 337–56

Politics and Rural Society. The Southern Massif Central c.1750–1880 (Cambridge, 1985)

The Peasantry in the French Revolution (Cambridge, 1988)

'Reforming Absolutism and the Ending of the Old Regime in France', *Australian Journal of French Studies*, XXIX (1992), pp. 220–9

Jordan, D.P., *The King's Trial. Louis XVI vs. the French Revolution* (Berkeley, 1979)

Jouany, D., *La formation du département du Morbihan* (Vannes, 1920)

Jusselin, M., *L'administration du département d'Eure-et-Loir pendant la Révolution* (Chartres, 1935)

Kaplow, J., *Elbeuf during the Revolutionary Period: History and Social Structure* (Baltimore, 1964)

Kates, G., 'Jews into Frenchmen: Nationality and Representation in Revolutionary France', in F. Fehér, ed., *The French Revolution and the Birth of Modernity* (Berkeley, 1990)

Kennedy, M., *The Jacobin Clubs in the French Revolution*, 2 vols. (Princeton, 1982–88)

Kozlowski, N., 'La mise en place des municipalités révolutionnaires dans les communes rurales. L'exemple du canton de Saint-Jean de Losne (1789–an IV) Côte-d'Or', *Comm. hist. éc. soc. Bulletin* (1982–83), pp. 69–85

Kuscinski, A., *Les députés à l'Assemblée législative de 1791* (Paris, 1900)

Les députés au Corps législatif, Conseil des Cinq-Cents, Conseil des Anciens, de l'an IV à l'an VIII (Paris, 1905)

Labrouc, H., *L'esprit public en Dordogne pendant la Révolution* (Paris, 1911)

Lacroix, S., 'L'élection du maire de Paris en 1792', *Rf*, 38 (1900), pp. 500–22

Lajusan, A., 'Le plébiscite de l'an III', *Rf*, 60 (1911), pp. 5–37, 106–32 and 237–63

Lallié, A.-F., *Les assemblées primaires de la Loire-Inférieure en 1790, 1791 et 1792* (Vannes, 1902)

Lamarre, C., 'Les élections de 1790 et la révolution municipale en Côte-d'Or', in B. Benoit, ed., *Ville et Révolution française* (Lyon, 1994), pp. 183–99

Lancelot, A., *L'abstentionnisme électoral en France* (Paris, 1968)

Landes, J.B. *Women and the Public Sphere in the Age of the French Revolution* (Ithaca, 1988)

Langlois, C., 'Le plébiscite de l'an VIII ou le coup d'état du 18 pluviôse an VIII', *AhRf*, XLIV (1972), pp. 43–65, 231–46 and 391–415

'Napoléon Bonaparte plébiscité?', in L. Hamon and G. Lobrichon, eds., *L'élection du chef de l'état en France de Hugues Capet à nos jours* (Paris, 1988)

Larguier, G., *Cahiers de doléances audois* (Carcassonne, 1989)

Laurent, G., *Les assemblées primaires et l'élection des députés du départment de la Marne à la Convention nationale (26 août-6 septembre 1792)* (Reims, 1902)

Le Cour Grandmaison, O., 'La citoyenneté à l'époque de la Constituante', *AhRf*, LIX (1987), pp. 248–65

Les citoyennetés en Révolution (1789–1794) (Paris, 1992)

Le Gall, Y., Les consultations générales en Loire-Inférieure 1789–an VII, Thèse pour le Doctorat en Droit, 2 vols., Université de Nantes, 1976

Le Goff, T., *Vannes and its Region: a Study of Town and Country in Eighteenth-Century France* (Oxford, 1981)

Lefebvre, G., *La Révolution française* (Paris, 1951)
  La France sous le Directoire, 1795–1799 (Paris, 1977)
Lemarchand, G., *La fin du féodalisme dans le pays de Caux* (Paris, 1989)
Lemas, T., *Etudes sur le Cher pendant la Révolution* (Paris, 1897)
Lemay, E.H., 'La composition de l'Assemblée nationale constituante: les hommes de la continuité?', *Rhmc*, 24 (1977), pp. 341–63
  ed., *Dictionnaire des Constituants 1789–1791*, 2 vols. (Paris, 1991)
Lesage, G., ed., *Episodes de la Révolution à Caen racontés par un bourgeois et un homme du peuple* (Paris, 1926)
Levot, P., *Histoire de la ville et du port de Brest*, 4 vols. (Brest, 1864–70)
Lewis, G., *The French Revolution. Rethinking the Debate* (London, 1993)
  and Lucas, C., eds., *Beyond the Terror. Essays in French Regional and Social History, 1794–1815* (Cambridge, 1983)
Ligou, D., *Montauban à la fin de l'ancien régime et aux débuts de la Révolution, 1787–1794* (Paris, 1958)
  'Population, citoyens actifs et électeurs à Dijon aux débuts de la Révolution française, 1790–1791', *Actes 88ᵉ con. nat.* (1963), pp. 243–75
Lough, J., *The Philosophes and Post-Revolutionary France* (Oxford, 1982)
Lucas, C., 'The First Directory and the Rule of Law', *FHS*, 10 (1977), pp. 231–60
  'The Rules of the Game in Local Politics under the Directory', *FHS*, 16 (1989), pp. 345–71
Lyons, M., *France under the Directory* (Cambridge, 1975)
  Napoleon Bonaparte and the Legacy of the French Revolution (Basingstoke, 1994)
Major, J.R., *The Estates General of 1560* (Princeton, 1951)
  The Deputies to the Estates General in Renaissance France (Madison, 1960)
Margadant, T.W., *Urban Rivalries in the French Revolution* (Princeton, 1992)
Marx, R., *Recherches sur la vie politique de l'Alsace prérévolutionnaire et révolutionnaire* (Strasbourg, 1966)
Mathiez, A., *La Révolution française*, 3 vols., Editions Denoël (Paris, 1985)
Mattei, G.-J., Marseille: une cité face à la Révolution (1788–1792), Thèse pour le Doctorat en Droit, 2 vols., Université d'Aix-Marseille, 1978
Mazars, L., *La Révolution en Rouergue. District d'Aubin, 1789–1795*, 2 vols. (Villefranche-de-Rouergue, 1976–78)
Mazauric, C., 'Voies nouvelles d'histoire politique', *AhRf*, XLVII (1975), pp. 134–73
McPhee, P., 'Electoral Democracy and Direct Democracy in France, 1789–1851', *European History Quarterly*, 16 (1986), pp. 77–96
  Collioure 1780–1815. The French Revolution in a Mediterranean Community (Melbourne, 1989)
  A Social History of France, 1780–1880 (London, 1992)
Médard, J., *La région de Montlhéry dans la Révolution* (Le Mée-sur-Seine, 1989)
Meynier, A., *Les coups d'état du Directoire*, 3 vols. (Paris, 1927–29)
Mitchell, H., *The Underground War against Revolutionary France. The Missions of William Wickham 1794–1800* (Oxford, 1965)
Moulin, L., 'Les origines religieuses des techniques électorales et délibératives modernes', *Revue internationale d'histoire politique et constitutionnelle*, Nouvelle série, 3–4 (1953–54), pp. 106–48

Naudin, M., 'Les élections aux Etats-généraux pour la ville de Nîmes', *AhRf*, LVI (1984), pp. 495–513

Structures et doléances du tiers état de Moulins en 1789 (Paris, 1987)

Nicolas, R., *L'esprit public et les élections dans le département de la Marne de 1790 à l'anVIII* (Châlons-sur-Marne, 1909)

La municipalité cantonale deVertus (1795–1799) (Châlons-sur-Marne, 1912)

Nicolle, P., *Histoire deVire pendant la Révolution* (Vire, 1923)

O'Gorman, F., *Voters, Patrons and Parties: The Unreformed Electorate of Hanoverian England, 1734–1832* (Oxford, 1989)

Offerlé, M., *Un homme, une voix? Histoire du suffrage universel* (Paris, 1993)

Onou, A., 'La comparution des paroisses en 1789', *Rf*, 32 (1897), pp. 193–224 and 316–47

Ormières, J.-L., 'Politique et religion dans l'Ouest', *Annales ESC*, 40 (1985), pp. 1041–66

'Les scrutins de 1790 et 1791 et le soulèvement de 1793: interprétation du comportement électoral', in R. Dupuy and F. Lebrun, eds., *Les résistances à la Révolution* (Paris, 1986), pp. 82–6

Ozouf, M., *La fête révolutionnaire 1789–1799* (Paris, 1976)

Palmer, R.R., *The Age of the Democratic Revolution*, 2 vols. (Princeton, 1959–64)

Patrick, A., *The Men of the First Republic. Political Alignments in the National Convention of 1792* (Baltimore, 1972)

Petitfrère, C., *L'oeil du maître. Maîtres et serviteurs de l'époque classique au romantisme* (Paris, 1986)

Pfister, C., *Les préliminaires de la Révolution à Nancy. Les élections aux Etats généraux et le cahier de la ville de Nancy* (Nancy, 1910)

Poitrineau, A., 'Les assemblées primaires du bailliage de Salers en 1789', *Rhmc*, 25 (1978), pp. 419–41

Pommeret, H., *L'esprit public dans le département des Côtes-du-Nord pendant la Révolution, 1789–1799* (Saint-Brieuc, 1921)

Popkin, J.D., *The Right-Wing Press in France, 1792–1800* (Chapel Hill, 1980)

'The Directory and the Republican Press: the Case of the *Amis des Lois*', *History of European Ideas*, 10 (1989), pp. 429–42

Revolutionary News: The Press in France 1789–1799 (Durham, 1990)

'The Provincial Newspaper Press and Revolutionary Politics', *FHS*, 18 (1993), pp. 434–56

Poupé, E., *Le département duVar 1790–anVIII* (Cannes, 1933)

Ramet, H., *Histoire de Toulouse*, new edn (Marseille, 1977)

Reinhard, M., *Le département de la Sarthe sous le régime directorial* (Saint-Brieuc, 1935)

Nouvelle histoire de Paris, 2 La Révolution, 1788–1799 (Paris, 1971)

Renouvin, P., *Les assemblées provinciales de 1787. Origines, développement, résultats* (Paris, 1921)

Revillaud, E., *Histoire politique et parlementaire de la Charente et de la Charente-Inférieure de 1789 à 1830* (Saint-Jean d'Angély, 1911)

Reynolds, S., 'Marianne's Citizens? Women, the Republic and Universal Suffrage in France', in S. Reynolds, ed., *Women, State and Revolution. Essays on Power and Gender in Europe since 1789* (Brighton, 1986), pp. 102–22

Rioufol, M., *La Révolution de 1789 dans leVelay* (Le Puy, 1904)

Robin, R., *La société française en 1789: Semur-en-Auxois* (Paris, 1970)

Root, H.L., *Peasants and King in Burgundy. Agrarian Foundations of French Absolutism* (Berkeley, 1987)

Roquette, A., *J.-J. Roquette ou la Révolution à Saint-Amans-des-Cots 1789–1795* (no place, no date)

Rosanvallon, P., *Le moment Guizot* (Paris, 1985)

Le sacre du citoyen. Histoire du suffrage universel en France (Paris, 1992)

Rose, R.B., *The Making of the Sans-Culottes. Democratic Ideas and Institutions in Paris, 1789–1792* (Manchester, 1983)

Rougeron, G., *Les consultations politiques dans le département de l'Allier* (Moulins, 1963)

Rouvière, F., *Le mouvement électoral dans le Gard en 1792* (Nîmes, 1884)

Histoire de la Révolution française dans le département du Gard, 4 vols. (Nîmes, 1887–89)

Sciout, L., *Le Directoire*, 4 vols. (Paris, 1895–97)

Scott, S.F. and Rothaus, B., eds., *Historical Dictionary of the French Revolution, 1789–1799*, 2 vols. (Westport, 1985)

Sentou, J., 'Impôts et citoyens actifs à Toulouse au début de la Révolution', *Ann. Midi*, 61 (1948), pp. 159–79

Sewell, W.H. jnr, 'Le citoyen/la citoyenne: Activity, Passivity, and the Revolutionary Concept of Citizenship', in Baker et al., eds., *The French Revolution*, II, pp. 105–23

Sheppard, T.F., *Lourmarin in the Eighteenth Century. A Study of a French Village* (Baltimore, 1971)

Signor, A., *La Révolution à Pont-l'Abbé* (Paris, 1969)

Slavin, M., *The French Revolution in Miniature. Section Droits-de-l'Homme, 1789–1795* (Princeton, 1984)

Soboul, A., *The Parisian Sans-Culottes and the French Revolution, 1793–4*, trans. (Oxford, 1964)

La Révolution française (Paris, 1965)

The French Revolution, trans., 2 vols. (London, 1974)

ed., *Dictionnaire historique de la Révolution française* (Paris, 1989)

Stone, B., *The Parlement of Paris, 1774–1789* (Chapel Hill, 1981)

Subileau, F., *Les chemins de l'abstention* (Paris, 1992)

Suratteau, J.-R., 'Les élections de l'an IV', *AhRf*, XXIII (1951), pp. 374–93 and XXIV (1952), pp. 32–62

'Les opérations de l'assemblée électorale de France', *AhRf*, XXVII (1955), pp. 228–50

'Les élections de l'an V aux Conseils du Directoire', *AhRf*, XXX (1958), pp. 21–63

Le département du Mont-Terrible sous le Directoire (Paris, 1965)

'Heurs et malheurs de la sociologie électorale pour l'époque de la Révolution française', *Annales ESC*, 23 (1968), pp.556–80

Les élections de l'an VI et le coup d'état du 22 floréal (11 mai 1798) (Paris, 1971)

'Le Directoire, comme modèle de régime ou mode de gouvernement?', in *Colloque Albert Mathiez-Georges Lefebvre. Voies nouvelles pour l'histoire de la Révolution française* (Paris, 1978), pp. 381–99

Sutherland, D., *The Chouans. The Social Origins of Popular Counter-Revolution in Upper Brittany, 1770–1796* (Oxford, 1982)

France, 1789–1815: Revolution and Counter-Revolution (London, 1985)

Sydenham, M., *The First French Republic 1792–1804* (London, 1974)
Tackett, T., *Religion, Revolution and Regional Culture in Eighteenth-Century France. The Ecclesiastical Oath of 1791* (Princeton, 1986)
Temple, N., 'Municipal Elections and Municipal Oligarchies in Eighteenth-Century France', in J.F. Bosher, ed., *French Government and Society 1500–1850* (London, 1973), pp. 70–91
Thompson, E., *Popular Sovereignty and the French Constituent Assembly, 1789–1791* (Manchester, 1952)
Thompson, J.M., *The French Revolution*, rev. edn (Oxford, 1985)
Todd, E., *The Making of Modern France. Politics, Ideology and Culture*, trans. (Oxford, 1991)
Troux, A., *La vie politique dans le département de la Meurthe d' août 1792 à octobre 1795*, 2 vols. (Nancy, 1936)
Vaillandet, P., 'Le plébiscite de l'an III en Vaucluse', *AhRf*, IV (1932), pp. 501–16
Vidal, P., *La Révolution dans les Pyrénées-Orientales, 1789–1800*, 3 vols. (Perpignan, 1885–89)
Vovelle, M., *La chute de la monarchie 1787–1792* (Paris, 1972)
La découverte de la politique. Géopolitique de la Révolution française (Paris, 1993)
Waldinger, R., Dawson, P., and Woloch, I., eds., *The French Revolution and the Meaning of Citizenship* (Westport, 1993)
Weber, E., *Peasants into Frenchmen: The Modernization of Rural France 1870–1914* (Stanford, 1976)
Williamson, C., *American Suffrage from Property to Democracy 1760–1860* (Princeton, 1960)
Windsor, J., 'Chouans and Sans-Culottes. Actions and Reactions in a Provençal Community in the Years V and VI of the Revolution', in D. Williams, ed., *1789: The Long and the Short of It* (Sheffield, 1991), pp. 73–98
Woloch, I., *Jacobin Legacy. The Democratic Movement under the Directory* (Princeton, 1970)
The New Regime. Transformations of the French Civic Order, 1789–1820s (New York, 1994)
Woronoff, D., *La République bourgeoise de thermidor à brumaire 1794–1799* (Paris, 1972)
Zivy, H., *Le 13 vendémiaire an IV* (Paris, 1898)

Index

abstention 51–3, 67–78, 92–5, 98–100, 108–9, 113, 124, 133, 156–7, 163–6, 193–4
acclamation 19, 69, 81, 88, 110
active citizens 14, 30–5, 38–44, 80, 117, 192
age of voting 11, 34, 80, 103, 106, 112
Ain 81
Aix-en-Provence 22, 46, 195
Allier 67, 94–5, 97, 151, 152, 173, 176
Alpes-Maritimes 106, 138
Amboise 22
Angoulême 152–3
Ardèche 95
Ardennes 105, 165
Arles 10
Arras 41, 45, 63, 76
Artois 16, 23, 41, 176
assembly *en permanence* 90, 97, 128–9
assemblées scissionnaires 22, 55, 57, 145–7, 151–2, 153, 155, 166, 185–6, 188–9
Assembly of Notables 1788 10–11
Aube 129
Aude 57, 75, 126, 133, 135, 150, 152
Aveyron 61, 69, 72–3, 92, 93, 125, 126, 133, 162
ayant droit de voter see voter registration

bailliages 10–11, 23–6, 160, 172, 196
Bar-le-Duc 48
Barbaroux, Charles Jean Marie 4, 182
Barère, Bertrand 34, 46, 104, 115
Barnave, Antoine Pierre 34–6, 43, 167
Barras, Jean Nicolas François 183
Bas-Rhin 128, 144
Basses-Alpes (Alpes de Haute-Provence) 105, 114, 133, 144, 146–7, 151, 173, 174–6
Basses-Pyrénées (Pyrénées-Atlantiques) 39
Bayeux 42
Béziers 16, 17, 22
Boissy d'Anglas, François Antoine 116

Bonaparte, *see* Napoleon
Bordeaux 133, 136, 171, 181
Bouches-du-Rhône 4, 6, 109, 111, 182, 188
Brest 41, 104, 110, 114, 134, 136, 193
Brienne, Loménie de 9, 10, 14
Brissot, Jacques Pierre 52, 87, 96, 180, 182
Britain 7, 44, 52, 69–70, 142, 192, 193
Brittany 10, 16, 27
bureau (in assemblies) 18–19, 55, 57, 87, 146
Burgundy 14, 16, 21, 27
Buzot, François Nicolas Léonard 52

Caen 97
cahiers de doléances 8, 18, 20, 96–7, 113, 171
Calvados 113, 114, 128
candidatures 26–8, 69–70, 76, 91, 144, 149, 153, 177, 179–80, 183–5, 194–5
Cantal 107
Carcassonne 108, 152
Carra, Jean-Louis 182
Cazalès, Jacques Antoine-Marie de 37
cens électoral, see tax requirement
Cercles constitutionnels 152–4, 187
Châlons-sur-Marne 108, 121, 125, 134, 152
Champ de Mars incident, 1791 162, 180
Charente 59, 61, 70, 71, 92, 107, 152, 153, 155, 164
Charente-Inférieure (Charente-Maritime) 162, 173
Chartres 25, 169
Cher 75, 180
chouans 150, 155, 165
Civil Constitution of the Clergy 72–3, 113, 193
clergy 10–11, 28, 32, 50, 72–3, 74, 91, 94–5, 113, 122, 140, 142–3, 151, 160, 164, 167, 172, 193
Colmar 17

217

218   Index

commissaires du directoire exécutif 147–9, 153, 154–5, 163, 187–9
Commission des Six (1793) 105–6
Comité de Constitution 30–1, 36, 38, 42, 47, 50–3, 70
Comité de Division 106
Comité des Contributions Publiques 38–9
Condorcet, Jean Antoine Nicolas 26, 33, 35, 103, 180
Constitution of 1791 38, 47–9, 79, 82, 103, 118–19, 124
Constitution of 1793 79, 81, 83, 102–4, 108, 112–13, 115, 120, 124, 159–60, 189, 195
Constitution of 1795 (Year III) 48, 102, 115–20, 123–5, 126, 131–2, 135–6, 138, 148, 160, 162–3, 172–3, 184
Constitution of 1799 (Year VIII) 190–1
Consulate 191–2
contribution patriotique 50
Cordeliers club 33
Corrèze 107, 154
Corsica 108
Côtes-du-Nord (Côtes-d'Armor) 114, 126, 149, 155, 162, 163, 165, 187
Côte-d'Or 6, 21, 42, 45, 62, 68, 79–80, 82, 83, 88, 108, 124, 127–8, 140, 151, 166, 169–70, 175
coup d'état of 18 brumaire VIII 189
coup d'état of 22 floréal VI 153, 186
coup d'état of 18 fructidor 147
Courrier de Provence 32, 37

D'André, Antoine Balthazar Joseph 142
Danton, Georges Jacques 92
Dauphiné 9, 10
Declaration of the Rights of Man 33–4, 104, 112–13, 124
Defermon, deputy 33
Delacroix, Charles 115
Démeunier, Jean-Nicolas 32, 53, 70
decree of the two-thirds 126–30, 183
departmental assemblies; general description 158–60; business 160–3; participation 163–6; attendance allowances 166–7; social composition 167–75; turnover of personnel 174–6; career patterns 176–8; procedures 178–89
Desmoulins, Camille 32, 91, 182
deputies at Estates General 28–9
Deux-Nèthes 185
Dijon 14, 27, 42, 46, 50, 108, 129, 134, 136, 151, 193
direct democracy 19–21, 30, 96–7, 101, 102–3, 120, 124–5

Directory 4, 6, 48, 116, 130, 131, 147–50, 153–4, 160, 183, 186–9, 191–2, 193, 195–6
Dordogne 182
Doubs 44, 95, 128, 155, 185
Drôme 114
Dubois-Crancé, Edmond Louis 31, 43, 183
Dupont de Nemours 33, 36, 38, 117

elections of the Year IX (1801) 191
electoral colleges, *see* departmental assemblies
eligibility for office 14, 44–51, 76–7, 118–19, 167, 170, 173
émigrés 140–1
Estates General of 1614 9, 10, 11, 28, 87
Estates General of 1789 2, 6, 8–10, 13, 18–21, 28–9, 30–1, 35, 41, 53, 95, 118, 158, 168, 176
Eure 88
Eure-et-Loir 94, 123, 150, 163, 169, 174, 179

'federalism' 113–15, 129
female franchise 35, 80
fête of the Sovereignty of the People 149–50
Finistère 46, 61, 71, 76, 109, 112–13, 141, 169
First Empire 148, 196
Foix 43
Français de Nantes 189
franchise, old regime 14; 1789 11–14; 1790 30–5; 1792 79–84; 1793 103–4, 106; 1795 116–18, 120, 124, 133; 1795–99 140–1; 1799 190; and taxes 11–14, 39–44, 49–52, 79–81, 112, 116–18, 192, 193
François de Neufchâteau 154
free masonry 28

Garat, Joseph-Dominique 46
Gard 51, 73, 85, 90
Gascony 14
Gironde 105, 154, 184
Girondins 103
Gohier, Louis Jérôme 93
Grégoire, Henri, abbé 33, 49
Guadet, Marguerite Elie 80
Guizot, François 32

Haute-Garonne 50, 57, 63, 70, 74, 78, 83, 111, 114, 143, 146–7, 155, 164, 176, 187–8
Haute-Loire 148, 151, 187

Index

Hautes-Pyrénées 112
Haute-Saône 44, 85–86, 164, 169, 174
Haute-Vienne 62, 67, 100
Hérault 57, 178
Hérault de Séchelles 103
Holbach, baron d' 31

Ille-et-Vilaine 62, 68
Indre-et-Loire 50
Instituts philanthropiques 142

Jacobin club of Paris 33, 47, 89, 159, 180–1, 182
Jacobin clubs in provinces 77–8, 89–91, 150–3, 164, 170–1, 179–80
Jacobins 3, 94, 124, 140, 145, 150–3, 154, 170, 173–4, 180–1, 185–6
Jews 35
Jura 62, 103, 128, 195
justices of the peace 45, 67, 100, 135, 177

Kersaint, Armand Gui Simon 182

L'Ami du Peuple 92
La Rochelle 109
La Sentinelle 91–2
Landes 60, 74, 77, 112, 140, 141, 147, 172, 179, 185–6, 187–8
Languedoc 11, 14, 16
Lanjuinais, Jean-Denis 116–17
Lanthenas, François-Xavier 92, 116
Lasource, Marie-David 103
Le Mans 152
Le Patriote français 94
Le Puy-en-Velay (Haute-Loire) 27
Legislative Assembly 48, 79–82, 87, 93–4, 159, 163–4, 166–7, 178, 180–1
Legislative Councils (under Directory) 119, 183, 187–9
Les Invalides 5
Les Révolutions de France et de Brabant 32, 37
Les Révolutions de Paris 37
Lille 42
Limoges 124, 163
literacy 16, 18, 61, 69, 88, 117, 193
local officials 177
Loir-et-Cher 55
Loire-Inférieure (Atlantique) 39, 43, 45, 50–1, 59, 68, 73, 76–7, 82, 86, 87, 93, 109, 114, 128, 144, 146–7, 150, 161, 163, 170, 174–6, 178, 179, 184, 187, 195
Loiret 135
Lorraine 22
Lot 185

Lot-et-Garonne 164
Louis XVI 21, 37, 47, 79, 94, 97, 103, 164
Louis XVIII 142, 148
Loustalot, Elysée 37
Louvet, Jean-Baptiste 91–2, 96, 180, 182
Lyon 22, 107, 136

Maine-et-Loire 95
Mallet du Pan, Jacques 74
Malouet, Pierre Victor 102
Manche 110–11
mandates 19–21, 27, 96–7, 120, 128–9, 162, 182
Manuel, Pierre Louis 103
Marant, deputy 81
Marat, Jean-Paul 91, 96, 180, 182
marc d'argent 36–8, 46–9, 119, 172
Marne 44–6, 59, 62, 93, 94–5, 108, 133, 154–6, 165, 173, 177, 183, 186
Marseille 11, 12, 18, 41, 91, 108, 127, 136–8, 150–1, 156, 170, 173–4
mass 72–3, 111, 163
Merlin de Douai 117, 149
Meurthe 133, 143, 150, 173, 176
Meuse 48, 75, 133, 143, 150, 155, 165
Mirabeau, Gabriel Honoré Riqueti 32, 34, 178
Mont-Blanc 106
Montagnards 103–4, 114
Montauban 17
Montesquieu, baron de 30, 36
Montpellier 17, 20, 70, 178
Morbihan 45, 58–9, 70, 72–3, 95, 122, 125, 147, 150, 155, 156, 166
Moulins 18, 23, 151, 152
municipal elections, 1788 14; 1790 62–6; 1791 65–6; 1792 99–100, 170–1
  under the Directory 135–8
municipal reform, 1787 14, 16, 18, 22

Nancy 141, 163
Nantes 14, 42, 86, 88, 109, 115, 121, 128, 134, 141, 144, 147, 170, 176
Napoleon 53, 111, 173, 190, 196
National (Constituent) Assembly 18, 19, 21, 29, 30, 41, 43, 52, 92, 102, 126, 162, 166, 178, 179
National Convention 2, 79, 87, 90, 93, 101, 115, 125, 126–9, 159, 160
National Guard 49–50, 84, 141, 176
Necker, Jacques 10, 11, 12, 28
Nîmes 18, 90, 181
nobility 10–11, 27–8, 50, 74, 91, 140–1, 167, 172, 196
Nord 167

220   Index

Normandy 15, 16, 17
notables 28, 76, 168–73, 196

Oise 69, 86, 88, 94, 162
Orléans 23, 24, 27
Orne 44, 82, 142, 150

Paine, Tom 116
Paradis, deputy 185
Paris, elections of 1789 10, 13, 17, 25; Commune 92, 97–8, 182; districts 37; franchise 45–6; sections 49, 51–2, 69, 82, 84, 88, 97, 98, 100, 103; politics 47; municipal elections 62, 100; elections of 1792 92–4, 96–7; referendum of 1793 104, 108–9, 110–11, 112; referendum of 1795 121–2, 124–5; two-thirds decree 127–9; elections under Directory 136–8, 148–9, 151, 153; departmental assembly 160–1, 162, 164, 167–8, 174–5, 176–8, 179–80, 182, 184
Parlement of Paris 9
participation, *see* turnout
Pas-de-Calais 39, 41, 49, 59, 62, 161–2
passive citizens 14, 30–1, 33–4, 80, 82, 86, 117, 192
pays d'états 9–10
peasant voting 61–5
Perpignan 44, 134, 152
Pétion, Jérôme 36, 49, 100, 102, 181
plebiscites, *see* referenda
plus imposés 196
Poland 20
political culture 3, 5, 18, 29, 91, 189, 193
Pons de Verdun 194
poor 12, 124
poverty 42–4, 76–8, 117, 194
press 91–2, 96, 142, 144–5, 180
priests, *see* clergy
Protestants 34, 73
Provence 9, 11, 12, 14, 16, 23, 26, 93
Puy-de-Dôme 186
Pyrénées-Orientales 73–4, 108, 121, 126, 133, 158, 160

Quatremère de Quincy 184

referenda 54, 101, 102–5, 195; referendum of 1793 104–15; referendum of 1795 120–5; referendum of Year VIII 190–1
Reims 93, 172
représentants en mission 101, 114–15, 136
Rhône 186

Robespierre, Maximilien 33–4, 41, 47, 77, 92, 96, 103, 159, 167, 181–2
Roland, Jean-Marie 92
Rouen 15, 107
Rouergue 16
Rousseau, Jean-Jacques 19, 21, 31, 35, 95
royalists 95, 124, 129, 140, 141–3, 151, 154–5, 175, 183–6
rural-urban contrast 16–18, 45–6, 65, 74–5, 88, 108, 121–2, 128, 134–6, 151, 156

Saint-Just, Louis Antoine de 49
sans-culottes 115, 117, 173–4
Saône-et-Loire 155
Sarthe 43, 61–2, 68, 142, 151, 152, 155, 187–9
second-degree electors 21–5, 35–8, 44–9, 54–5, 76, 96–7, 124, 148, 158–9, 167, 177, 195
Seine (department) 124–5, 158
Seine-Inférieure (Maritime) 88, 107, 127, 142, 150
Seine-et-Oise 48–50, 86, 88, 124–5, 162, 174
Semur-en-Auxois (Côte-d'Or) 16, 23, 24, 27, 151
sénéchaussées, *see* bailliages
serment civique 49, 72, 93, 111, 150
servants 34, 80, 100, 112, 117
Sieyès, Emmanuel-Joseph, abbé 14, 30–1, 34–6, 38
Souhait, deputy 116
Strasbourg 17, 36, 92, 144
suffrage, *see* franchise
suppléants 70, 161, 164, 183

Tableau comparatif, 1792 180–1
Target, Guy Jean-Baptiste 13, 34, 46
Tarn 164
tax requirement 11–14, 31–4, 39–44, 79–81, 117–18
Terror 101, 115, 116, 120, 143, 172, 183
Thermidorean reaction 48, 101, 102, 115, 160
Thibaudeau, Antoine-Claire 116
Thouret, Jacques Guillaume 31, 47–8
tiers état 10–14, 27–8, 172
Toulon 6, 12, 24, 25, 26, 42, 45, 50, 56, 59, 67, 68, 70, 71, 75, 76, 77–8, 84, 86, 90–1, 94, 99–100, 108, 136, 143, 170–1, 173, 174, 190, 191
Toulouse 46, 48, 73, 82, 94, 136, 143, 145, 146
Tours 36, 94
Troyes, *bailliage* 17, 23; town 24, 42

turnout in primary elections, 1789 15–18; 1790 59–66, 76–8; 1791 54–9; 1792 84–8; 1793 (referendum) 105–9; 1795 (referendum) 120–4; 1795 131–4; 1795–1799 138–9; 1797 141–3; 1798 150–1; 1799 155–6; 1799 (referendum) 191

United States 7, 44, 192

Vannes 108, 121, 156, 174
Var 39, 41, 61, 67, 68, 73, 74, 78, 82, 100, 108, 109, 121, 138–9, 145, 149–50, 160, 161, 162, 165, 166–7, 173, 174, 177, 179, 183
Varennes, Flight to 47, 58, 164
Vaucluse 121, 129–30
Vendée 5, 6, 109, 112, 165
vendémiaire rebellion (1795) 129

Vergniaud, Pierre Victurnien 103
Versailles 46, 94
Villefranche-sur-Saône 153
Villette, marquis de 178
Vitré 16
Vosges 166
voter registration 11, 49–52, 55, 82–4, 106, 118–19, 120, 133, 138–41, 191, 192
voting mechanism 18–19, 52–3, 55–7, 67–9, 76, 81–2, 87–8, 110–11, 125, 142, 161, 191, 193
voting out loud 19, 21, 81–2, 88, 95–6, 100, 110, 162, 181

White Terror 122, 165
women voters 35, 49, 80, 111–12

Yonne 44, 112

THE UNIVERSITY OF MICHIGAN

DATE DUE